SHOLEM ALEICHEM'S
WANDERING STAR
AND OTHER PLAYS
OF JEWISH LIFE

OTHER WORKS BY DAVID S. LIFSON:

Familiar Pattern (a play) (1944)
Mummers and Men (a play) (1962)
The Yiddish Theatre in America (1965)
Le Poseur (a play) (1974)
Epic and Folk Plays of the Yiddish Theatre (1975)
How to Rob a Bank (a play) (1977)
Headless Victory (a novel) (1978)

To Dorothy
for her faith and patience

Then we shall still have *Playes!* and though we may
Not them in their full Glories yet display;
Yet we may please our selves by reading them,
Till a more Noble Act this Act condemne.

—Aston Cokaine, *A Praeludium to Mr. Richard Bromes Plays*, 1653

CONTENTS

INTRODUCTION

Is there any other people on the globe, is there any other nation in history that has had so dramatic a life as the Jews? The Jewish story, rich in history, oversubscribed in sorrow, cannot be matched. A people in diaspora weaves patterns in which each member's experience, a thread of its own, can be extricated from the big tapestry and presented as a spectacle on its own. These biographies are embodied in Torah accounts, in popular song, in folk legend, in novels and non-fiction and, most vividly, in theater.

The playwright who draws his themes from Jewish life need never want for a format into which he can insert his own perspective. Whether in Yiddish, English, Hebrew, Spanish, or whatever, the playwright or, for that matter, any writer at all, finds heroes and villains who have leaped from crisis to crisis. Sometimes the characters are those he has heard about. Again, they may be relatives or even the writer himself.

The reason for this particular source of drama is the eternal tremors that have shaken the Jews during the 5,000 years of their existence. The ancient homeland was cut from beneath their feet, to be resurrected several millennia later. In the meantime, they became part of new homelands that created illusions of security only to spit them out in the most revolting manner. Jews learned, most of them, to keep a mental bag packed in the recesses of their minds, a carrying case that could be whisked along with them when the inevitable moment of departure arrived.

Departures were not only physical migrations. There were spiritual departures that took them to variations on the old faith, to breaks with the traditional belief that brought them to new creeds and ideologies, some of which they themselves created. They were at both ends of the human outlook, limitless universality and fraternal parochialism. Both proclaimed that they were guarantors of security, and Jews were prominent at the extremes and in combinations. Catastrophe bred despair, despair that was not so complete that it did not come with a tinge of hope just behind it. Small wonder that the dramatist is never at a loss for themes that are cosmic even when they are small.

David S. Lifson is such a writer. A scholar with a poetic license, he is familiar with the paths that the Jews have followed in their time and he has placed them in a format that takes them to the stage. In these six plays, together, the reader realizes that although Mr. Lifson's palette bears a riot of colors, he is wise enough to give us not murals but portraits. Even when the scope is broad, as in *Appointment in Minsk,* which spans a period from World War I until the establishment of Israel, the story is personified by the experiences of the individuals in it. One tastes the flavor of the times without having the feeling of being professorially tutored in it. It is a play ostensibly about actors, but through their stories we relive the scattering and the division of a people in the worst of times.

At a more introspective, microscopic terminal of perception, Mr. Lifson, in *A Shtetl in the Bronx,* introduces us to the crises of faith that erupt in a small Bronx shul at Simchat Torah. It is more than a mere vignette; it is a short story that, with admirable conciseness, examines clashes of culture and character.

Jewish tradition did not die with the emigration from Eastern Europe to America and Mr. Lifson shrewdly notes the acculturation in *The Flatbush Football Golem.* In this slice of Brooklyn life, Orthodox meets secular, football invades the Yeshiva, and a golem, a real golem, wins one, wins many for the school. It is a musical, lively and full of laughter, but, with true reflection on the Jewish fact that things are never purely comic, it is also thoughtful and provocative in its premises.

David Lifson loves Yiddish theater, and that may be an understatement. He has put together anthologies of Yiddish plays, has done critiques of Yiddish theater and, as we now learn, he has written theater pieces about Yiddish theater.

Wandering Star is a comedy adapted from Sholem Aleichem's timeless *Blondzhedeh Shtern,* the saga of Yiddish actors in Europe, in England, in America. Mr. Lifson has been able to trap in English the Yiddish insights of Sholem Aleichem, who understood acting, theater, and audiences.

Four of the plays, as we see, are about Yiddish-based Ashkenazic life. That is why the fifth, *The Queen's Physician,* comes as a mild surprise. But surprise it should not be. Mr. Lifson is also a reader and a teacher interested in all aspects of the Jewish story. This is a historical drama about Roderigo Lopez, a doctor of Sephardic background, who attended Queen Elizabeth I and who was hung, drawn, and quartered in 1594 on trumped-up charges. How many playwrights could find a graceful and meaningful way to have Shakespeare as a character in the cast of a Jewish play? Mr. Lifson, who speculates that Shylock may have been modeled on the unfortunate real doctor, gives us a play in which we may learn about the so-little-known part played by Jewish refugees from Iberia in the diplomatic life of their times.

Usually, it takes some special aptitude to appreciate a play in script. Plays are written to be fleshed out onstage. But these particular plays make easy reading. The language is clear and they are not cluttered with directorial minutiae. What is more, the topics are interesting and the presentation is lively and lucid. What more could one ask? Perhaps only for a production of them to come to the neighborhood.

Richard F. Shepard
New York Times

SHOLEM ALEICHEM'S
WANDERING STAR
AND OTHER PLAYS
OF JEWISH LIFE

WANDERING STAR
from Sholem Aleichem's *Blondzhedeh Shtern*

When the brilliant writer, lyricist, and composer of *Fiddler on the Roof* embarked on their project, the travail of Sholem Aleichem's Tevye was far from their minds. In a published interview with them by the Dramatists Guild *Quarterly,* they said they originally were intent upon a musical derived from Sholem Aleichem's eternally popular novel, *Blondzhedeh Shtern,* which had been made into a play by the legendary Maurice Schwartz almost a half century ago. Apparently the sprawling scope of the novel seemed impractical, even though it contains the sure-fire ingredients of laughter and tears that had been the hallmark of successful Yiddish theater. So, they decided to oblige the audience to identify with the beloved character of Tevye. The rest is theatrical history.

David Lifson was contracted by a Broadway producer to pick up this novel and adapt it as the book for a Broadway musical. With its roots in Jewish tradition, in Jewish folklore, this play with music is the happy outcome. As the second generation of the immigrant Ashkenazic Jews from the Czar's Russian-Polish Pale, together with his lifetime association with theatre, both Yiddish and American, Lifson has written a play that does justice to the immortal Sholem Aleichem.

In this comedy, we find the aspirations, dreams, triumphs, and frustrations of the itinerant Yiddish actors parallel, and become identical with the millions of Jews who fled a proscribed, tyrannical life to this golden land.

The characters in this comedy are recognizable to devotees of Yiddish theater as well as being known as flesh-and-blood Jews. I cannot say where Sholem Aleichem stops and Lifson carries on, but I am delighted by Lifson's interpolation of a balcony scene, à la Romeo and Juliet, and that staple in a Yiddish comedy—a wedding scene. This is a most felicitous adaptation.

Ran Avni
Artistic Director
Jewish Repertory Theatre, New York City

WANDERING STAR

A Comedy in Two Acts
Adapted from Sholem Aleichem's *Blondzhedeh Shtern*

by *David S. Lifson*

CHARACTERS

ALBERT SHUPAK, theatrical director
SHOLEM MEYER, theatrical promoter and advance man
BEN RAPALOVICH, richest man in Holeneshti
LEIBELE, his son; later the actor LEON RAPALESCO
BREINDELE KOSSAK, an actress, also MME. CHERNIAK (her real name)
BERNARD HOLTZMAN, director and actor, known for his role as HUTZMACH; also
    called Berele by his sister
A PRIMA DONNA (the name for a leading lady)
AN ELDERLY ACTOR
A TALL YOUNG MAN
YISROEL THE CANTOR
LEAH, his wife
REIZELE, their daughter
A WOMAN
A TEAMSTER
ISAAC SCHWALB, an actor-manager
HENRIETTA SCHWALB, his sister, a Prima Donna
SARAH BRUCHE, HOLTZMAN's mother
ZLATKA, HOLTZMAN's sister
DR. LEVITT

16

MEYER STELMACH, a rich man and concert manager
NISSEL SCHWALB, brother of ISAAC and HENRIETTA
MR. KLAMMER, an English patron of the theater
GRISHA STELMACH, MEYER STELMACH'S son, a violin prodigy
THE LOMZER CANTOR
THE BEADLE
PIANO ACCOMPANIST
ACTORS, DOCTOR, BELLHOP, WOMEN, CHILDREN

Music for a production of this play may be selected from *Music Is Mayn Lid,* by Maurice Rauch (New York: The Jewish Music Alliance), 1986; and from *Great Songs of the Yiddish Theater,* by Warembud and Mlotek (New York: Quadrangle/N.Y. Times), 1975.

ACT I

SCENE 1

In the shtetl (village) of Holeneshti in Bessarabia, outside Ben Rapalovich's barn. SHOLEM MEYER MURAVICH, *a flashy theatrical promoter, wearing a derby, drooping moustache that he ineffectually primps, and loud clothes, enters with* ALBERT SHUPAK, *the managing director of the traveling troupe of Yiddish actors.* SHUPAK *is grandly cloaked, wears a battered top hat, carries a walking stick, and his fingers shine with brilliant rings.* SHUPAK *disdainfully assesses the surroundings.*

SHUPAK. When God created the world in six days, maybe *he* could have spent a half hour to provide a Yiddish theater. Now we're stuck with this rotten barn.
SHOLEM. Wait, you'll see. Everyone for miles around will come to the theater. . . .
SHUPAK. The shtetl is as big as a yawn, and most of the audience is already

lying in the cemetery . . . but maybe a half dozen starving cows.
SHOLEM. I know these people. They're Jews who are starved for good theater.
SHUPAK. Starved for a good meal like me. All they eat is marmaliga—this cornmeal mush. And they guzzle wine like water.
SHOLEM. We'll make plenty money here and we'll have enough to go to London and Bucharest. We'll travel the world!
SHUPAK. And if not, we'll cut our throats. We'd better make some money. My first wife writes that unless I send her money, she'll have me arrested the minute I set foot in Romania. And my second wife. . .
SHOLEM. You worry too much. As long as we have our health and play theater. . .
(Song: *"The Broder Singers."* SHUPAK *and* SHOLEM *are joined by the arriv-*

ing actors who sing and dance with them. At conclusion of the song and dance, ACTORS *go into the barn. Enter* BEN RAPALOVICH, *the richest man in the shtetl; he is extremely fat. He owns the barn.*)

RAPALOVICH. Did you see my son Leibele? He's always hanging around with your actor Hutzmach instead of going to Hebrew school.

SHOLEM. No.

RAPALOVICH. Wait'll I catch him! Food and cigarettes are missing from my house and store. I think he's feeding your actors out of my pocket. I rented you my barn, but it doesn't include feeding your vagabonds.

SHUPAK. About your own son you talk like that, call him a thief? Maybe there are thieves in Holeneshti.

RAPALOVICH. This is a good shtetl. We have no thieves.

SHUPAK. This is some shtetl! It's not like my home shtetl. (*Song:* SHUPAK *sings "Beltz" or "Slutzk." At the end of song, a youth tries to sneak into the barn.* SHOLEM *douses him with water out of a pail.*)

YOUNG MAN. I just wanted to see Hutzmach before I buy a ticket. (*He runs away.*)

SHOLEM. I know his kind. They all try to sneak in for free.

RAPALOVICH. (*To* SHUPAK.) Your bargain here, your Mr. Sholem Meyer, promised me free tickets for my family.

SHUPAK. They should live and be well, how many are in your family?

RAPALOVICH. There's my brothers with their wives and children, my sons and daughters, my three helpers—all together, maybe forty-five only.

SHUPAK. Only! Gevald!

RAPALOVICH. We all love the theater. Every Purim we have the purimshpilers put on a play right here in the barn. My poor horses have to stand out in the cold and rain . . .

SHUPAK. All right. We'll reserve the tickets for your family—but for only tonight's performance. We're playing only this week. Saturday night after the performance, we leave for Bucharest, Paris, and London. (RAPALOVICH *exits.*)

SHOLEM. Good riddance. Why was I born to be in the theater? Why not a carpenter, a tailor, or a shoemaker?

SHUPAK. Yes, you would have been a good shoemaker. (*Voices and music from the barn.* SHUPAK *and* SHOLEM *exit into the barn.* HUTZMACH *enters en route to the barn. He is an actor, the company's comic, around fifty years old, and constantly coughs.* LEIBELE RAPALOVICH, *a handsome youth, about sixteen, dressed as a young Hassidic student, furtively accosts* HUTZMACH.)

LEIBELE. Hutzmach!

HUTZMACH. I've been looking for you. I'm starved. (*From his pockets and from hiding inside his coat,* LEIBELE *takes out food and hands it to* HUTZMACH.) I'm late for rehearsal. How can I rehearse on an empty stomach? We have no money, and my landlady, she should burn on a slow flame—she has no heart. (*He eagerly grabs the food and starts biting into a chicken leg.*) Did you bring cigarettes?

LIEBELE. Yes. And here's some of my father's favorite wine. (*He hands cigarettes and a bottle of wine to*

HUTZMACH. *(They draw aside in order not to be seen.)* Go ahead, eat. I'll watch if anyone comes.

HUTZMACH. *(He eats and talks.)* I like you, my Liebele. You have the looks and your voice is as clear as a bell. I'll train you to be the world's greatest actor. You can do it. You'll play in the great tragedies, the classics from Schiller, Lessing, Shakespeare. You'll be the toast of Paris, London, Buenos Aires. Here, drink some wine. A toast to your triumph, your success. *(They each drink from the wine bottle.)*

LEIBELE. Will your director take me with him?

HUTZMACH. Yes. But once we leave here, we won't need him. I'll form my own company and train you to be its star. I'll keep my promise—you'll come with me. *(He coughs violently.)* When I became a comedian . . . *(Coughs.)* With this cough I should be a tragedian. I told Shupak, but no, he said, the public loves only comics. Because I was an orphan without a father, it fits I should be a comic. He was right, because when I play Shmendrik or Kuni Leml, I stop the show. Especially when I sing. . . *(Song:* HUTZMACH *sings "Romania, Romania.")*

LEIBELE. Saturday night? For sure?

HUTZMACH. Yes. And you come with us. *(He craftily eyes* LEIBELE.*)* Don't forget to bring money, plenty of it. Only the paper kind. Like I explained to you. . .

LIEBELE. Only if . . . my father . . . I think maybe . . . But it will be stealing.

HUTZMACH. I, too, ran away from home to go on the stage. I left my poor mother, long may she live, and my little sister Zlatka. They lived on the few pennies I earned. It broke my heart to leave them. And I starved— like you see. So don't be foolish and starve. We'll need the money. After 120 years, your father's money will come to you. Why not now? For the greater glory of the Yiddish Theater! Don't let your father exploit you or hold you down.

LEIBELE. The way he beats me! I feel like I want to die.

HUTZMACH. His hands should wither.

LEIBELE. And my mother? How will she survive without me?

HUTZMACH. Then hide under your mother's apron. If you want to be a great Yiddish actor, you mustn't let a mother, a bride, or even a wife stand in your way. Not even a sweetheart.

LEIBELE. For my father I don't care. But to leave my mother. . .

HUTZMACH. You don't fool me. It's the Cantor's daughter. She's the one Sholem Meyer is always leering at. Soooo, for a mother and a Cantor's daughter you'll destroy yourself and all my hopes for your great career. Ah, an actor cannot belong to himself, he belongs to the world.

LIEBELE. That's how I feel when I play in the purimshpil. When I come before Pharoah and I call out to him, "I am Moishe ben Amris, and I want you to release the Jews from Egypt. How long will you punish them? And for what? Why do you torture them? Why do you kill their children and bathe in their blood? You monster! Do you know with whom you are dealing!"

HUTZMACH. Foolish boy, you're a genius! Such talent! You're a treasure for the Yiddish Theater. Shupak can go to the devil. When you are world famous, your father will realize you did the right thing. Once you walk out on the stage, you'll feel like me. We forget our troubles, they float away like smoke. I see no one, only lights and loving people's eyes. Maybe bald heads shining from the stage lights. Then applause like thunder. Right then, who is equal to me! Your father maybe, with his stuffed pockets? What a magnet the stage is, it draws you into its flame and you burn like an eternal torch, it reaches out to you, chases you, you find no rest— damn it all! (RAPALOVICH *enters, carrying a whip. He espies* LEIBELE *and* HUTZMACH.)

RAPALOVICH. Soooo, that's how you go to Hebrew school! And there's a bottle of my best wine. You thief, my own son steals from his father! (HUTZMACH *quickly dashes into the barn.*) I'll teach you a lesson you won't forget! (RAPALOVICH *mercilessly whips a stunned* LEIBELE *as the lights dim.*)

SCENE 2

When the lights go on, the barn walls will have risen to reveal the interior of the barn. It has an improvised stage with unfinished scenery, a tattered and patched curtain. Some actors are eating chunks of bread, an apple, an orange. Much turmoil. Only perhaps two rows of benches are visible with suggestion of more behind them. A few children sneak in and try to hide under the benches. SHOLEM *discovers them and hurls water at them as they run out.* SHUPAK *tests the sturdiness of the benches.*

SHOLEM. They're strong enough. But they could use padding.

BREINDELE. (BREINDELE KOSSAK *enters. Her real name is* MME. CHERNIAK, *but she is known by her established role in Goldfado's play* Breindele Kossak. *She is extremely stout.*) What's all the noise about? I must have quiet before the performance. (To SHUPAK.) Just look at this costume! You call these costumes? They're rags! You're some director— where did they dig you up? All you can do is pick on us poor actors and drive us crazy. (*She turns to* SHOLEM.) For eight years I've slaved for him and I haven't earned enough for my shroud. And where is the contract you promised to sign with us actors?

SHUPAK. Tonight for sure, we'll all sign black on white right after the show.

BREINDELE. You better not fool us this time.

SHUPAK. (*To* SHOLEM.) Have the contracts ready. And remember: straight shares after expenses. And no percentages—I don't need more partners. And let me take care of Hutzmach's contract. I'll make sure he can't steal away the actors and start his own company.

SHOLEM. We better get them to sign tonight. That Breindele could make trouble. She threatens to go to the authorities and tell them we're playing Yiddish theater. We could all be arrested.

SHUPAK. Rapalovich has it fixed with the police. He'll warn us if they come so we can switch to a Chinese spectacle. (SHOLEM *espies another interloper; He grabs a pail of water and chases after him. Voice of actor offstage: "Hutzmach, where are my sandals?", etc.*) I should have thrown that Breindele Kossak out of my troupe long ago. What a curse she is! She should burn like a fire! Ten choleras aren't enough for her. (*Voice offstage: "Hutzmach, you call this a coat?", etc.*)

PRIMA DONNA. My braids have been stolen. I won't be able to perform.

SHUPAK. If you took care of your things instead of Hutzmach, no one would steal from you.

PRIMA DONNA. Help yourself. Get another prima donna. If not for Hutzmach you'd starve to death. I need my braids. . . .

SHOLEM. (*Calling to actors offstage.*) Take it easy. What's all the noise about!

HUTZMACH. (*Enters. He's dressed as a dandy.*) You're now a fireman, Sholem Meyer? The people won't come to the theater—they'll be afraid you'll drown them.) (SHOLEM *takes pail of water offstage and returns.*)

SHUPAK. Where in this black year have you been, Hutzmach? We're all hoarse from shouting for you.

ACTOR. Where are my sandals, Hutzmach?

BREINDELE. Hutzmach, get me the costumer.

HUTZMACH. So where is the costumer, that yellow cow?

PRIMA DONNA. (*She is charming and coquettish to* HUTZMACH.) Hutzmach, before my entrance, I'd like a pitcher of cold milk.

HUTZMACH. Yes, my precious soul, my pet, my darling Shulamith. For you I'd go through flame and put out the fire with sour milk.

SHUPAK. The cholera should take them both!

SHOLEM. They're only trying to spite you. Keep quiet, you have no choice.

ACTOR. (*To* HUTZMACH.) Hutzmach, you should burn in hell, who stole my false nose?

HUTZMACH. You can all go to hell and fall into a deep grave. I'm carrying all of you on my back. The public comes to the theater only to see me, and don't you forget it! They won't let me off the stage. They love *me*—so you know what all of you can do! (*He stares at* SHUPAK *and* SHOLEM.) I mean you, too. (*He mimics them.*) "Hutzmach, get busy. Do what they want. Get their costumes. Take care of the curtain. Arrange the scenery. Make sure the horses and wagons are ready when we leave." You don't care if I die ten times a day—just do the job and keep quiet! Hutzmach here, Hutzmach there—I'm sick of it!

SHUPAK. This is the thanks I get from the poor orphan whom I made into an actor. My name shouldn't be Albert Shupak if I don't have a reckoning with you—after all I did for you!

HUTZMACH. I really owe you my thanks—for what? For the mess I'm in with my cough, half starved? For taking me from a loving mother and dear little sister who may be starving for all I know? All for your promises that you'd make me a world-famous star! (*Actors again take up a cry for* HUTZMACH *to get them props, rouge, etc.*) What am I? A pack horse? (*Actors continue their clamor.*) You can all go to the devil! All right, I'm coming. You should all get cholera and disappear from my life.

SHUPAK. And what did I take you from? From being a miserable helper for a Hebrew teacher where you wiped the noses of the students. (*He consults his flashy watch.*) Sholem Meyer, it's time to let in the audience. The musicians aren't ready yet. Where are they? Places, everyone. Places!

SHOLEM. They're hungry. They'll eat the scenery.

SHUPAK. After the performance they'll eat. That's my order. (*Voices: "Where's Hutzmach, where's the prima donna?" Sound of orchestra tuning up. Lights dim.*)

SCENE 3

The same scene a little later. Seats are filled. RAPALOVICH *and his family occupy the front seats. One woman is breast-feeding a baby. Children on ladders leading to the hayloft. Some people are seated at edge of the hayloft with their feet dangling down. Orchestra plays the Overture from* Shulamith. *Curtain is closed.* SHOLEM *steps out in front of the curtain.*

SHOLEM. Dear public, ladies and gentlemen. The famous Albert Shupak, director of our internationally known Yiddish–German Theater, in behalf of our troupe of actors, welcomes you. The great number of you, maybe half of the shtetl, who broke the windows and crashed down the doors to get in without paying, shows that you are hungry for our artistic theater . . . (*Applause.*) Very well, if you haven't paid today, you will have to pay tomorrow because we will have two strong guards and our director watching. Today we present *Shulamith* . . .

VOICES. (*From audience.*) You're supposed to play *The Witch.* We want Bube Yachne and Hutzmach. Hutzmach! Hutzmach!

SHOLEM. I beg you good people to be dumb—QUIET! (*He reaches behind curtain for the pail of water.*) Even though many of you are here without tickets—that's the fate of the Yiddish Theater—everyone wants a Yiddish Theater but no one wants to pay for the tickets.

VOICES. Hutzmach! Hutzmach!

RAPALOVICH. (*Rises and glowers at the audience.*) Stop braying like horses! Let the man speak. Quiet, you animals!

VOICE. Who is that fat idiot insulting! Go talk to your horses. . .

RAPALOVICH. (*To two of his sons.*) Throw that troublemaker out of my theater. (*The two sons carry out the troublemaker.*)

SHOLEM. Easy there. Don't hurt him. Jews of Holeneshti, honored public, you are about to see and hear our distinguished Albert Shupak in the role of Shulamith. He also plays Absolom. Tomorrow we don't play because it is the eve of Shavuoth. Anyone who will invite an actor to his home for the holiday dinner, leave your name at the box office. Director Shupak and myself have invited ourselves to the home of your esteemed

Cantor Yisroel for his wife's delicious blintzes. Now, we present *Shulamith.*

VOICES. We want Bube Yachne. Don't let them cheat us. This is Holeneshti—we'll break your bones. We'll show you. We're not liars.

SHOLEM. Dear friends of Holeneshti. . . *(Cries drown out his voice.)*

RAPALOVICH. *(Rising.)* Open the curtain. To hell with these loudmouths. *(Music louder amidst the turmoil.* HATZMACH, *as stage manager, drags open the curtain. Characters on stage are in ragtail costumes. Catchall scenery is supposed to be a desert. The* PRIMA DONNA *starts to sing her opening song from* SHULAMITH, *while the chorus stumbles around the stage.*

Voices from audience continue to cry, "liars," "cheats," "You can't fool us in Holeneshti." LEIBELE *and* REIZELE, *the beautiful daughter of the Cantor, quietly try to enter unobserved, and find seats near* RAPALOVICH. *He sees them.)* So, where were you?

LEIBELE. The Cantor's wife wouldn't let Reizele come, so we waited till she fell asleep.

RAPALOVICH. You meant you went against the Hazenteh? The lesson I taught you is only a sample. Just wait. . .

SHOLEM. *(Reappearing.)* The director Albert Shupak is about to make his entrance. Once you hear him, you won't let him leave Holeneshti. Quiet!

VOICES. Shulamith is Shulamith and Bube Yachne is Bube Yachne! You can't cheat us. *(Continued uproar while* SHUPAK *and* PRIMA DONNA *attempt to sing.)* Sha, sha. . .

Hutzmach! We'll beat you up. . . *(*BREINDELE *rushes out on stage.)*

BREINDELE. Who will beat us up? Who are you to threaten us? *(To* SHUPAK *and* PRIMA DONNA.*)* Dumbbells, why are you playing to these mujiks, these peasants! Let's pack up and get out of this mudhole, tonight! You're trying to give them honey, but they're used to vinegar. We're doing *Shulamith* because it's a play that even animals like you can understand. Bube Yachne needs an audience with brains. . .

VOICES. We have more brains than you. We're more educated than you gypsies. We know what's good. Enough of your tricks. Give us Bube Yachne.

BREINDELE. A sickness we'll play for you.

SHUPAK. My friends, let us finish singing, then we'll give you your Bube Yachne. *(Music starts again.* SHUPAK *signs in comic style. Audience relaxes.)*

VOICES. Our Cantor sings better than that. We know that at least. *(Audience continues clamor.)*

VOICE. I'll show you what kind of people we have in Holeneshti. I'll give fifty if you'll play Bube Yachne. Who else will chip in?

RAPALOVICH. I'll give ten.

A WOMAN. I'll give three pennies.

A GIRL. I'll give a pair of galoshes. *(*SHUPAK *and* SHOLEM *consult and quickly agree.)*

SHUPAK. How can we go against the will of the people? It's like God's law to us. Yes, we'll give you Bube Yachne. *(He walks off stage as audience cheers.* SHOLEM *passes his hat among the audience.)*

SHOLEM. While your generous donations are collected, our famous comedian, Bernard Holtzman, known throughout the world as Hutzmach, will now sing "A Chussidl" followed by "Nukh und Noukh." While he entertains you, we will set the stage for Goldfadn's *The Witch*, with its Bube Yachne. The first scene of *Shulamith* was supposed to be a desert. We are now changing it for Bube Yachne's scene in a flower garden. And now, I have the honor to present our great Bernard Holtzman as Hutzmach. (HUTZMACH *enters while the music strikes up "Hassidl."*)

HUTZMACH. *(To musicians.)* Play together, please, and not like rabbits running in all directions. *(He sings, dances, and does a few comic turns. While he goes through his routine,* the boisterous audience demonstrates its joy: they clap hands in beating time. A half dozen men from the audience join HUTZMACH on stage and, with HUTZMACH leading, they perform an Hassidic dance. People in audience stand on their seats; some crush forward. A woman shrieks, "You're crushing my baby." End of dance, SHOLEM reenters.)

SHOLEM. Dear public, we now present for the first time in Holeneshti, *The Witch* by Abraham Goldfadn, with Bube Yachne. The first act is in the flower garden of Rabbi Abrumchin. *(Applause. The curtain opens to the same scene as the previous one for* Shulamith. *Blackout.)*

SCENE 4

Outside the home of CANTOR YISROEL. *The house is constructed so that there is a kitchen wing with its roof providing a small balcony outside* REIZLE's *bedroom. At rise,* REIZLE *is at a window on the street level. She is sewing and sings at her work. The song is "Rozhinkes mit Mandlin." It is the following early evening. Unseen by her,* SHUPAK *and* SHOLEM *enter and stop, enraptured, to listen to her sing. At the conclusion of her song,* SHOLEM *approaches her.*

SHOLEM. Bravo, Bravo! (REIZLE *is startled, draws her shawl around her previously exposed shoulders.*) I've seen **you** before. Yes, at the theater. You **were** sitting on the same bench with Rapolovich's son last night.

SHUPAK. Your voice is as beautiful as your luminous eyes. *(She rises as though to withdraw.)* No, please don't go. This is the house of the golden voiced Cantor Yisroel, yes?

REIZLE. Yes.

SHUPAK. You must be his talented daughter . . . *(She shyly nods.)* Well, if the Cantor and your dear mother are home, we'd like to come in and share her delicious Shavuoth blintzes. (REIZELE *leaves the window.* SHOLEM *conspires with* SHUPAK.)

SHOLEM. If we could get her to join our company, she'll be sensational. (RE-IZELE *has opened the front door for them to enter.*)

SHUPAK. Leave it to me. *(To* REIZELE.) If I live to be a hundred and twenty years, I don't think I've ever seen an actress as pretty as you. Beautiful, or my name isn't Albert Shupak.

REIZELE. Come in. (SHUPAK *and* SHOLEM *enter. The wall rises. They are inside the combined kitchen-dining room of the cottage. Furniture is rudimentary but comfortable. Candles in brass candlesticks are aglow. The* CANTOR *sits at the table.)*

CANTOR. Goot Yontif. Come in. This is my wife Leah and my daughter Reizele. (REIZELE *sits on the sofa.)*

LEAH. Sit down. *(She places two chairs at the table.)* I made plenty blintzes.

SHOLEM. A blessing on your food. Eat it with good appetite.

SHUPAK. Don't fuss for us. We're simple people like yourself. But your blintzes! We've heard nothing but praise, or my name isn't Albert Shupak.

LEAH. Who ever heard of such a thing!

SHOLEM. You can believe him. He is the famous Albert Shupak, the director of our Yiddish–German Theater, and I am his chief assistant Sholem Meyer. Let's drink to this happy meeting . . . if you have a bottle . . . if not . . . well . . . the blintzes. . .

SHUPAK. The best way to celebrate our fortunate meeting is for the esteemed Cantor to sing. I was once a choir boy myself. Ah yes, music is my life, especially our Yiddish folk music. When I was still young, I used to sing at weddings, circumcisions, all kinds of celebrations. My own compositions, too.

SHOLEM. Before we came to Bessarabia, we already heard about the golden voice of Yisroel, the esteemed Cantor of Holeneshti. We came for your wife's delicious blintzes, too. But we'd rather starve than not hear you sing. (LEAH *serves blintzes;* SHUPAK *and* SHOLEM *pitch in.)*

CANTOR. I sing in the synagogue and teach Hebrew to the children.

LEAH. So sing already. Did you ever hear of such a thing. (*The* CANTOR

overcomes his diffidence and sings a short cantorial song.)

SHUPAK. So sweet! Did you ever hear such singing, Sholem? Not even I, Albert Shupak. . .

SHOLEM. Now for a dessert.

CANTOR. *(Eager to sing again.)* What kind of dessert? I can sing a. . .

SHUPAK. A song from your sweet daughter, long may she live and be healthy. We've heard that her voice is like a nightingale's.

LEAH. Who told you such a thing?

SHOLEM. Your husband has a wonderful voice. So, my dear madame. . .

LEAH. Just like that? For no reason a pious girl should start singing in front of strangers? Did you ever hear of such a thing . . .

SHUPAK. We are no longer strangers. My name shouldn't be Albert Shupak if your lovely daughter shouldn't bloom like a beautiful flower. Her voice is better than Patti or Melba . . .

SHOLEM. That's what we heard.

SHUPAK. So why shouldn't the world share this treasure? Why should she be hidden away in this pigsty and mud puddle of a shtetl with its corn meal mush marmaliga and sleep with goats! Such a beauty, such a diamond with her gypsy eyes. My name shouldn't be Albert Shupak if I don't make her world famous.

SHOLEM. Albert . . . Albert. . .*(fearful that* SHUPAK *is coming on too strong.)*

LEAH. What are you talking about! What do you think we are? We aren't shoemakers or tailors! Do you think we'll let our flower shlepp around with vagabonds, hooligan actors, commedians—a cholera should grab them! Did you ever hear of such a thing!

SHUPAK. My dear woman, you make the most delicious blintzes I ever tasted, but don't forget you're talking to Albert Shupak, director of the Yiddish–German Theatrical Troupe.

CANTOR. My wife didn't really mean anything personal, God forbid. . .

SHUPAK. My actors, my comedians, yes—even my tragedians won't take this abuse from a fishwife, even the great Cantor's wife. (*While* SHUPAK *and* LEAH *and the* CANTOR, *argue,* SHOLEM *edges over to* REIZELE *and whispers to her.*)

CANTOR. (*To* LEAH.) You needed this? Why must you always come out with your curses?

SHOLEM. (*Turning to the others.*) Sha, sha. You can get more with honey than with vinegar. My dear madame, you're a devoted mother and mean well, but you're maybe a little too crude. Our director meant well. Bless you, Cantor Yisroel, and you, too, madame. (*He nudges* SHUPAK *to leave.*)

SHUPAK. Thank you for your blintzes—and your welcome.

SHOLEM. (*Whispers to Shupak.*) Leave it to me. When we leave Holeneshti, that singing gypsy will be with us. (*They ad lib their exit.*)

LEAH. They should go deep into hell. And you, my darling daughter, no more Yiddish theater with that Rapalovich boy. Never again, as long as I'm alive. After Shavuoth, I'll fix you yet. After all my hard work feeding them, they pay me back by trying to trick me out of my daughter. Did you ever hear of such a thing.

CANTOR. So wait already till after the holiday. (*Noise offstage as a red glow*

mounts. A WOMAN *runs by and shouts to them.*)

WOMAN. Gevald! Save yourselves—fire—the street is on fire! (NEIGHBOR *runs off.*)

LEAH. (*Looking out.*) Woe is me! Yisroel, Reizele, quick, let's save what we can. Don't stand there! Who started it? I know—those miserable actors, they should burn in hell. (*Packs things into a tablecloth; She douses the candles and packs the brass candlesticks. The room darkens. The red glow mounts. Shouts and turmoil from direction of the blaze.*)

CANTOR. What am I standing for . . . I'm the fire chief of the Holeneshti volunteers. No one can fight a fire like me.

REIZELE. (*Looking out the window—She's excited.*) Papa, the fire is spreading. It's near the synagogue.

LEAH. You'll be a Cantor without a synagogue, because of those barefoot actors. They should burn in hell.

CANTOR. No synagogue! Where will I sing? I'll put out the fire if I fight it with my bare hands. (*Church bells ring clamorously.*)

REIZELE. The church bells are ringing. They'll send the regular firemen from the city.

CANTOR. Who needs them . . . Where's the pail?

REIZELE. The roof of another house is starting to burn.

LEAH. Where are you running with your pails? The city firemen will be here soon. Stay with us here in the house. While you're helping others we could burn to death.

CANTOR. I have to go. How will we live without the synagogue? I'll save it.

LEAH. (*To* REIZELE.) Don't you dare

leave the house. I'm going to help bring the water. If the fire comes closer, run to tell us. (LEAH *runs, carrying a pail, after* YISROEL. REIZELE *hurries back to the window where* SHOLEM *suddenly appears.* REIZELE *is frightened.*)

SHOLEM. Don't be frightened. The shtetl is on fire. I said the shtetl can burn, but I must save our beautiful canary—even if I have to kidnap her.

REIZELE. Kidnap?

SHOLEM. Yes, even by force. Let your father and mother play with fires, but you listen to me. I have a fire in my own heart. I mean only the best for you. Your fanatical mother must not keep your great talent from the world. When you'll stand on the stage and sing "Shulamith," wearing a short skirt and shining shoes . . .

REIZELE. I'm frightened. Please . . . my mother may come back. . .

SHOLEM. Come see me at the theater by Rapalovich. We'll talk more. (SHOLEM *hurries away.* REIZELE *leaves the window.* LEIBELE *appears. He calls out "Reizele." She soon appears at the window of her bedroom on the upper floor.*)

LEIBELE. Reizele.

REIZELE. I'm up here.

LEIBELE. There's a fire. Do you know there's a fire? Let's go and help put out the fire. Come down.

REIZELE. I can't. I have to watch the house if the fire comes closer. Come up here, Leibele.

LEIBELE. (*While climbing.*) I was almost in bed already when I heard all the noise about the fire. I ran here right away.

REIZELE. Why here?

LEIBELE. I don't know why. Even if the fire wasn't on God's Street with the synagogue, I would run here. . . (*He's at her window.*) I don't care if the whole shtetl burns. I'm fed up with Holeneshti—day after day—

REIZELE. Day after day . . . sometimes I feel that way, too.

LEIBELE. Come out here. I want to tell you something. (REIZELE *comes out; She sits on a raised ledge.*) Give me your hand. (*She complies. He sits next to her.*) Now swear not to tell anyone, and I'll tell you a great secret.

REIZELE. You have my hand. I swear.

LEIBELE. I'm leaving this place.

REIZELE. (*Alarmed.*) Where? When?

LEIBELE. I don't know where, yet. But as sure as there's a God in heaven, and a fire in the shtetl, I'm leaving.

REIZELE. For long?

LEIBELE. Forever.

REIZELE. Forever . . . does that mean I'll never see you again?

LEIBELE. I haven't told anyone except you. I'm leaving with Hutzmach and the theater troupe. He is sure I'll become a famous actor.

REIZELE. And the director Albert Shupak told my father that I can conquer the world. And Sholem Meyer wants to kidnap me to go with them.

LEIBELE. Go with them! I'll be free. It'll be wonderful; you will be free, too. Come with us. To go alone and leave you behind, I'd be miserable. But with you it would be heaven. I'll have enough money—more than enough—You'll have new, beautiful clothes and . . . You must save yourself . . .

REIZELE. And my father and mother?

LEIBELE. I've made up my mind. You can do it, too. We'll be free from this prison. Let this firery sky be our witness that we'll never leave each other. Let's swear to each other that always and forever we'll be together even when we are famous actors.

REIZELE. Some day we'll come back here, both of us, to ask my parents' forgiveness.

LEIBELE. Ah, Reizele. Now we are one. One body and soul. I know that we're doing the right thing. You and I will come back to ask your parents' forgiveness. But I won't come back to my father. I've suffered enough from his beatings. And we'll have enough money. I know where he keeps it and how to open the iron box. . .

REIZELE. *(Horrified.)* Leibele, you don't mean. . .

LEIBELE. You swore to keep my secret. One body, one soul. Only God above will share everything with us.

REIZELE. Look, there's a falling star. It's punished for sinning against the older stars.

LEIBELE. Stars don't fall, they wander. Each star is the soul of a person. A soul wanders, its star follows. Look, the sky is no longer red, the clouds are whiter, soon it will be morning. The sun will rise over the roof of the synagogue. The fire is out. *(They look out over the shtetl.)* People are starting to return home. I see their shadows.

REIZELE. My father and mother will be coming.

LEIBELE. We are one body, one soul. Be ready for me when I call for you. We'll save ourselves for each other. *(Song: They sing a duet, the Jewish folk song, "Dortin, Dortin.")*

SCENE 5

After midnight that Saturday, on the outskirts of HOLENESHTI.

Enter HUTZMACH, LEIBELE, *and a* TEAMSTER. *They are bundled up and carry shabby cardboad suitcases.*

HUTZMACH. Where are the other wagons? *(He coughs.)* Maybe my cough will stop when we're out of this mudhole Holeneshti. Leibele, put my shawl around you. The night is cold.

LEIBELE. Where are the other wagons? Where is Reizele?

HUTZMACH. Shupak and Sholem Meyer have her hidden in their wagon. If your parents come chasing after you, it's better you should be in different wagons. That's what Sholem Meyer said.

LEIBELE. It's so dark. Maybe the wag-ons will be separated. *(He yells to the* TEAMSTER.*)* Hey driver. *(No response.)*

HUTZMACH. Go talk to the wall. *(He takes out a flask.)* How about a schnapps to warm up for the ride? *(The* TEAMSTER *is suddenly alert and approaches and takes a gulp out of the flask.)* When do we start out for Polesti?

TEAMSTER. Are we going to Polesti? I thought we're going to Novoserisk.

HUTZMACH. We cross over to Romania by the road through Polesti. Where does Novoserisk come in?

TEAMSTER. I don't know. Novoserisk is on the way to Bucharest, too.

HUTZMACH. Then why don't we all go by way of Polesti, a cholera should take you?

TEAMSTER. Polesti is Polesti and

Novoserisk is Novoserisk.

LEIBELE. Hutzmach, Hutzmach, what should we do?

HUTZMACH. Don't worry. We'll get there. Where's the money?

LEIBELE. Here. *(He hands a bundle of money to* HUTZMACH.*)* But how about Reizele . . . ?

HUTZMACH. Nothing to worry about. Ah, now we'll know. *(*SHUPAK *and* SHOLEM *enter.)*

SHUPAK. You're still here?

HUTZMACH. We're waiting for you. What's this about Novoserisk? We're supposed to go to Romania by way of Polesti.

SHOLEM. Of course. Get going. It's that Breindele Kossak. She's still packing her junk. We'll give her five more minutes. But you get started.

HUTZMACH. *(To* LEIBELE *and the* TEAMSTER.*)* Let's go. *(*HUTZMACH *exits, followed by a bewildered* LEIBELE *and the* TEAMSTER.*)*

SHOLEM. *(To* SHUPAK.*)* Maybe we should really go to Polesti?

SHUPAK. Are you out of your mind! The minute I cross over into Romania, my first wife will have me arrested. And this is as good a time as any to get rid of that consumptive Hutzmach. A cholera should take him. I taught him everything he knows, now he thinks we can't live without him. I'll show him! We'll go to Odessa, then Kiev. Who needs him. My name shouldn't be Albert Shupak if we don't become the greatest Yiddish troupe.

SHOLEM. Quiet. Here come the others. The wagons are ready. *(The troupe of actors enter;* REIZELE *is bundled in a voluminous coat that is supposed to disguise her. They all arrange themselves like passengers in a carriage, with the driver, and prancing horses. Song and dance of riders—)*

SCENE 6

In Lemberg, HUTZMACH's *quarters, some five or six years later. Trunks, theater posters announcing the great Yiddish actor—*LEON RAPALESCO, *and* BERNARD HOLTZMAN, *Artistic Director. A sofa, a table on which stands a samovar. Old* SARAH BRUCHE, HOLTZMAN's *old Mother (from now on* HUTZMACH *will be known as* BERNARD HOLTZMAN) *stands and pours tea.* ZLATKA, HOLTSMAN's *twenty-year-old sister, walks about with a script in hand as she tries to memorize the role of Judith in* Uriel Acosta.

SARAH. Drip, drip, drip—the Messiah will come before the cup is full. A samovar is like a person, if you drag it from town to town, it gets constipated. Now it's stuck. The cholera should grab it.

ZLATKA. *(Memorizing.)* "What stops me from pressing him passionately to my breast?" *(She repeats the line.)*

SARAH. You memorize and Leibele says when you get on the stage you forget everything. You could have memorized the whole Torah by now.

ZLATKA. I know my lines, but once I get on the stage and Leibele says to me "Judith, Judith," with his hot tears, as is written on each page like fragrant flowers, ". . . we are one and meant for each other," my heart starts pounding with hammers, my hands and feet become paralyzed, and I become tongue-tied. I get dizzy.

SARAH. Your brother is the expert on dizziness, the devil take him. Me too. And this bridegroom he's promoting for you—forget it. Who is the Reizele our Leibele kept calling when he was delirious with fever? I applied cupping to him, and he kept moaning "Reizele, Reizele, where are you?"

ZLATKA. He told me she's his younger sister. He misses her. *(She returns to her memorizing.)* "What stops me from pressing him passionately to my breast?" *(Aside.)* How upset these words always make me. I remember when I sat by Rapalesco when he was burning with fever and he clutched my hand . . . what kept me from trying then to. . .

SARAH. No wonder we get fever. Some gypsy living my Berele found for me! Rolling stones from town to town. All night long we loaf around and sleep all day. Normal people eat breakfast first; with us it's topsy turvy: first lunch and then it's breakfast. A pity on this Rapalesco, such a fine young man. I don't understand how his mother let him get mixed up with these theater charlatans.

ZLATKA. You've become like a mother to him.

SARAH. Orders from my son the great director. And who brings Leibele a glass of milk in bed? Who darns his socks? Who makes him eat regularly? He never wants to eat, just wanders around and talks to himself. We could bust, but Leibele must have the best.

ZLATKA. That's why Berele brought us to him. He could bum around in any hotel, in hell even. But Leibele must have the best of care.

SARAH. What does he want from us? Did we ask him to make you an actress too? You could have become a bride back in our shtetl. So many young men wanted you . . .

ZLATKA. Ah, but some day you'll see signs all over: "Eliza Rapalesco starring in *Uriel Acosta,* with Leon Rapalesco."

SARAH. Dream on, but don't put pretty little birds in your bosom. *(ZLATKA continues memorizing. A knock on the door. SARAH open it to admit IS-AAC SCHWALB, his pretty prima donna sister HENRIETTA, and DR. LEVITT. A pompous medical doctor with cultural pretentions, he carries a medical satchel. ISAAC SCHWALB is very fat, a 5' × 5' roly-poly, actor-manager who has bullied his way into the Yiddish troupe of GETZEL BEN GETZEL's Lemberg Theater. HENRIETTA SCHWALB is the leading lady of this troupe.)*

ISAAC. We came to visit Director Bernard Holtzman and the famous star Leon Rapalesco.

SARAH. Come in. Berele isn't here yet and Leibele is resting. Maybe you want a glass of tea?

DR. LEVITT. No, thank you. We may wait, please?

SARAH. Of course. This is my daughter Zlat . . . Eliza.

HENRIETTA. Of course. We admired you in *Uriel Acosta.* *(Men bow to ZLATKA.)*

ZLATKA. Make yourselves comfortable. I'll see if Rapalesco is ready. *(ZLATKA exits.)*

SARAH. You sure nobody wants tea? *(Silence.)* Then you'll excuse me. I have something in the oven. *(SARAH exits.)*

ISAAC. The way I see it, they should jump at your idea.

DR. LEVITT. If they can be so sensational in Lemberg, can you imagine how they'll triumph in the capitals of the world!

HENRIETTA. But Getzel ben Getzel is our producer. We're under contract with him.

ISAAC. So what? He'll come looking to sue us in Paris or Vienna?

DR. LEVITT. I never saw anything like it in Lemberg or even in Vienna. Wherever you go, all you hear is Rapalesco and Holtzman. They're completely different from shoddy, shabby troupes.

ISAAC. If we can do it, Schwalb, Holtzman and Company will make them all look like a miscarriage.

DR. LEVITT. We're lucky to have them in Lemberg. No one can get near the theater to buy a ticket, all sold out for the next couple of months. From our simple little Jews to generals, students—everybody buys tickets. And all from the speculator.

ISAAC. That damned Getzel ben Getzel, he should drop dead. He works with the speculators and gets richer by the minute.

HENRIETTA. He cut down our operetta to two nights a week and says maybe only once. Our operetta *Hinky Pinky* was a success. Now all he wants to play is *Uriel Acosta.*

ISAAC. If he thinks we'll take a cut in salary, he doesn't know with whom he's dealing. He doesn't fool around with Isaac Schwalb!

DR. LEVITT. The Lemberg Jews don't have an appetite only for cheese. They know art in the theater and come to see it. Owning the only Yiddish Theater in Lemberg gives him a monopoly, but now he'll know what the public wants. The critics say that "our theater isn't worth more than a puff of smoke, it's as dead as a cemetery. Rapalesco has illuminated the lowly Yiddish Theater and raised the masses to new heights. His Uriel Acosta is sublime art." Getzel ben Getzel should make sure the beautiful and talented prima donna Henrietta Schwalb could be saved from her silly roles and play opposite Rapalesco in classics worthy of their genius.

ISAAC. Ah, what we could do in the Yiddish theater if only that Getzel ben Petzel didn't suffocate us! I could play great classic roles. You should see my Hamlet.

DR. LEVITT. You? Hamlet?

ISAAC. Yes, but in my Yiddish adaptation. You see, my Hamlet is a Yeshiva student, son of the chief rabbi. When he comes home from the Yeshiva in Minsk, where he was an outstanding student, he finds out that his father is dead and that his uncle has both married his mother and become the new chief rabbi. Hamlet suspects that his uncle murdered his father, so he starts to make trouble. The uncle needs this! So the uncle complains to the Czar's officials that his nephew is a nihilist and should be deported to Siberia. But the uncle's plot is revealed and he is exiled to Siberia instead. Meanwhile Hamlet's beloved Ophelia dies. The last scene is very touching: in a cemetery, a snowstorm, Hamlet follows his beloved's coffin, and at the end his heart breaks and he falls dead over her grave. That's my wonderful improvement on Shakespeare.

HENRIETTA. I play Ophelia.

DR. LEVITT. It's not a . . . maybe you should change her name, starting with an "O," it should sound more Jewish.

ISAAC. Maybe Oima. *(Irma.)* (BERNARD HOLTZMAN, HUTZMACH, *enters. He now has fashionable sideburns, a cane and gloves, his suit has sharp piping on both vest and jacket—the height of fashion.)*

HOLTZMAN. What's all this? Quiet everybody—you'll disturb Leon Rapalesco. *(He carries a bottle of brandy and a package, both of which he tries to hide from his guests.)*

ISAAC. You invited us to . . .

HOLTZMAN. Welcome, then. I hope you haven't waited too long. You met my mother and sister? Where are they?

ISAAC. Ah, my associate Mr. Bernard Holtzman. Meet one of the stars in Getzel ben Getzel's company, my sister the famous prima donna Henrietta Schwalb. (HOLTZMAN *ogles her and tries to "make time" with her.)* And this is Dr. Levitt, our most prominent medical doctor in Lemberg, a patron of the arts. He is the cultural czar of Lemberg, a pedagogue, a philosophe, a philologue.

DR. LEVITT. *(Acknowledging introductions.)* I wouldn't go that far. I must say the high point of my theatrical exposure is seeing Leon Rapalesco as Uriel Acosta.

HOLTZMAN. No rabbi accomplished more than I when I created such a star for the Yiddish Theater, such a shining light as Leibele, our own

Ralapesco and Zlatka. If not for me who in the world would ever know of Zlatka? When the two of them stand at the end of Act 2 of *Acosta* and he says, "I was born a Jew and as a Jew I will die," and then Zlatka cries out, "Oh, you blind ones. . . ." Have you met my sister? And my mother? *(Not waiting for a reply, he calls out, "Mama" and "Zlatka." Both enter. He secretly passes the brandy to* ZLATKA *with a "Hide it."* ZLATKA *exits and quickly returns.)* Yes, we are true Jews! We'll never forget our Yiddishkayt. *(Song: "Dos Pintele Yid." He embraces his mother.)*

SARAH. Stop tickling me.

HOLTZMAN. *(Handing* SARAH *a package.)* Here, Mama, I brought you some sardines.

SARAH. I don't want it. I made chopped liver.

ISAAC. Dr. Levitt and my sister Henrietta—she's Getzel ben Getzel's prima donna—would like to meet Rapalesco.

HOLTZMAN. Mama, clear the table. Sit down, my friends. *(To* ZLATKA.*)* Is Leon up yet?

ZLATKA. He's been up a long while. He's writing a letter to his mother. (ZLATKA *exits and returns with* RAPALESCO. *He has changed considerably from the adolescent* LEIBELE. *He is handsome, smokes a cigarette in a long holder, every bit the matinee idol.)*

RAPALESCO. We have visitors . . . ?

HOLTZMAN. Yes. Meet Isaac Schwalb, an actor, and his sister, the Prima Donna Henrietta Schwalb. They're in your producer's operetta *Hinky Pinky*. This is Dr. Levitt, a critic and patron of the arts. *(Ad lib introduc-*

tions and acknowledgments.
HENRIETTA, *to* ZLATKA's *obvious annoyance, "makes a play" for* RAPALESCO. DR. LEVITT *gazes at* RAPALESCO.)

DR. LEVITT. He is as impressive here at home as he is on stage. This is the most memorable day in my life. Thank you for the pleasure, nay, the privilege. After your performance, I didn't sleep all night. Your Acosta haunts me every minute—All I see is the Godlike figure of your Acosta. I was, until last night, a renegade, an assimilated Jew. Now I am one hundred percent a Jew.

ISAAC. *(Aside to* HENRIETTA, *gesturing toward* RAPALESCO.)
Look how the color lights up his face.

HENRIETTA. He keeps looking at me. His eyes stab into my heart.

ISAAC. Let him stab away. We'll make a match between you and him.

HOLTZMAN. *(To* ZLATKA, *pointing to* DR. LEVITT.) Be nice to him. Maybe he'll come across with some money.

ZLATKA. *(Aside to* HOLTZMAN.) I think he's only talk. He was the first to ask for free tickets. The first to criticize but not even the last to pay.

ISAAC. *(To* RAPALESCO.) Dr. Levitt is the foremost medical doctor in Lemberg, yet he is a Jew with a Jewish heart.

DR. LEVITT. It would be a great honor to me if all of you would join me after tonight's performance at the Cafe Metropole. We will toast this happy meeting and our new acquaintance. *(He opens his medical satchel and brings out two bottles of champagne.)*

HOLTZMAN. *(Aside, upon seeing the champagne.)* And I had to spend my money on brandy.

DR. LEVITT. Let's drink to Yiddishkayt. My pleasure increases now that I've met you in person. *(Song: "Undzer Yiddish Folk.")*

HOLTZMAN. Mama, Zlatka, bring out some glasses and something for the mouth. *(To* DR. LEVITT.) Maybe you would like some fresh latkes my mother made and some of her wonderful chopped liver. Zlatka, don't just stand there. My sister, even though she's a great dramatic star, she's also a wonderful housewife. (SARAH *hands around glasses.* ZLATKA *passes around plates while she glares at* HENRIETTA. SARAH *exits.*)

DR. LEVITT. Let us drink to the foundation of a glorious Yiddish Theater. No more cheap melodramas and fraudulent biblical operettas. A first class theater with Rapalesco and Henrietta Schwalb on top.

ZLATKA. *(Aside.)* Add free tickets for this loud mouth.

HOLTZMAN. (SARAH *returns, he helps her with the food.)* To the table, my friends. Henrietta, don't be a stranger, come. *(Aside to* HENRIETTA.) You're more beautiful than I heard. You'll be my own leading lady. Why is your brother always watching you?

DR. LEVITT. *(With champagne glass in his hand.)* Ladies and gentlemen. Like Shakespeare and his successor Goldfadn said . . . er . . . er . . . but I will save my speech for tonight at the Cafe Metropole. But now I must say that Rapalesco is greater than my friend Sonenthal in Vienna—he was a poor tailor's son and is now the king of the stage—greater even than Jacob P. Adler and Sir Henry Irving. The new Yiddish Theater lives and you must bring it to shine all over the world, to Paris, Vienna, London . . . long live Rapalesco and the impressario Bernard Holtzman. *(All drink and cheer.)* All over the world Jews will hear Yiddish on the stage and will speak one language forever.

HOLTZMAN. *(Embraces and kisses* DR. LEVITT.*)* My very words. We'll free ourselves from this Pickle ben Flickle with his money-grubbing that suffocates the great art of our Yiddish Theater

DR. LEVITT. I'll send you with my letter to Sonenthal in Vienna. He'll help you get started there. After that—the World!

HENRIETTA. He's always bragging and hacking away like a tea kettle.

ISAAC. Let him. This is our big chance. Now maybe our brother Nissel in London will take notice of us.

DR. LEVITT. Why is our esteemed artiste so quiet? A word . . .

RAPALESCO. Dear friends, the Doctor, the champagne, and your compliments overwhelm me. I'm more nervous now than on an opening night. No matter where I make a speech, I never felt what I feel now. All this is so sudden . . . all your friendly faces . . .

ISAAC. *(Aside to* HENRIETTA.*)* Only friendly. Look at him, my dear sister.

HENRIETTA. More than just friendly.

HOLTZMAN. *(To* ZLATKA, *aside.)* Say something, too.

ZLATKA. Everything stands in my way . . .

RAPALESCO. Everyone wishes me success. But a long way from here is a dear old lady whose eyes look for something else. She thinks always during sleepless nights and worries,

what happened to her Leibele. Did he drown, did a wagon with wild horses run over him—while I travel the world to become a success.

HOLTZMAN. *(To* ZLATKA.*)* Say something. Tell him with God's help he'll soon see his mother.

ZLATKA. *(To* RAPALESCO, *faltering.)* With God's help, you'll see your mother . . . soon.

RAPALESCO. Yes, maybe. But how I miss my frail little, loving mother.

SARAH. *(Weeps.)* A little old mother is still a mother. Even with consumption, she's still a mother.

RAPALESCO. *(Weeps.)* Excuse me . . . I . . .

SARAH. Weep, weep, and you'll feel better.

DR. LEVITT. Dear God! This moving moment will haunt me forever. Such moments are like pearls for the Jewish folk.

RAPALESCO. *(Wiping his tears.)* I miss my mother very much . . . I . . .

ZLATKA. And his sister. *(Others look inquiringly at her.)* He was just writing a letter to his mother . . . and sister . . .

RAPALESCO. *(Song: He sings either "A Brivele der Mam'n" or "Vos Is Gevor'n fun Mayn Shtetele?" At end of his song, he raises his glass.)* I raise this glass to good fortune and to better Yiddish Theater.

DR. LEVITT. United together! I propose that Henrietta and Isaac Schwalb leave director Getzel and join forces with impressario Holtzman and his star Rapalesco.

HOLTZMAN. Hurrah, hurrah! We'll travel to Vienna and Paris, and then to the Pavilion Theater in Whitechapel, London. The producers

Holtzman, Schwalb and Company will be known from . . .

SARAH. Right away you're shlepping to London. The samovar will stay alive, you think . . .

ISAAC. The devil take Getzel. It's a deal. We'll go to London. Maybe Rapalesco will become my brother-in-law.

HOLTZMAN. Brother-in-law? Not on your life. But partners we'll be. *(A knock on the door.* ZLATKA *admits* BREINDELE.*)* This is all we need for a black year—Breindele Kossak.

RAPALESCO. *(Rushes to* BREINDELE.*)* Ah, Madame Cherhiak. Come in. I . . . We're so happy to see you. (HOLTZMAN *and* RAPALESCO *do the introductions.)*

BREINDELE. *(To* RAPALESCO.*)* I thought you were alone so we could talk . . .

RAPALESCO. You were in Holeneshti? You saw my mother?

DR. LEVITT. It's time we left. You're a good audience for news of your mother. Come, friends. Adieu, you great artistes. Remember, tonight after the performance we meet at the Cafe Metropole.

ISAAC. *(To* HOLTZMAN.*)* The doctor is caught in our net. (HENRIETTA *primps.)*

HOLTZMAN. Come, I'll see you out. *(Aside to* ZLATKA.*)* Zlatka, listen in on what that fat witch tells him, and keep your eyes open. Everyone pulls him in every direction. (ZLATKA *winks acknowledgment while* HOLTZMAN *leads others out.* ZLATKA *ushers* SARAH *into other room and hovers unseen near the door.)*

RAPALESCO. *(Kisses* BREINDELE's *hand.)* Madame Cherniak, you'll never know what I went through in last night's performance when I saw you in the audience. Tell me, my dear friend, you were with Shupak's troupe when he left Holeneshti. How is Reizele? You know, the Cantor's daughter with her gypsy dark eyes. Is she still in Shupak's troupe?

BREINDELE. Such a prima donna the Yiddish Theater never saw. When she came on stage in her Hassidic robe and sang "Chaver" or "Friday Night Each Jew is a King," the audiences went wild cheering, they almost wrecked the theater.

RAPALESCO. I knew she'd become famous—a wandering star—*(He pours champagne for* BREINDELE.*)* Here, drink my dear, precious heart. *(He hugs and kisses* BREINDELE. ZLATKA *observes.)* How can I thank you for this wonderful news? What else . . .?

BREINDELE. Wait a minute. Let me catch my breath. Poor Shupak was never meant to have a rich old age from his new star. A Russian Jew, a beggar who became a millionaire managing his son Grisha Stelmach, the famous fiddle player—he plays before kings and princes—this millionaire goes crazy over Reizele's singing, introduces her to the great diva Marcella Zembrick who gets so excited she tears her away from Shupak's troupe and sends her to a conservatory. Now she's the great Rosa Spivak, her name rings around the world.

RAPALESCO. Rosa, Rosa Spivak. . .

BREINDELE. And just think, she and I slept in one bed and shared the same dressing room. We'd sigh together for what we left in Holeneshti: I for that bastard Hutzmach, a cholera should only grab him, and she for a young man who ran off with Hutzmach.

Last night I realized who that young man is.

RAPALESCO. Where is she now?

BREINDELE. The last I heard, they were in London.

RAPALESCO. London! We're supposed to go to London after Vienna and Paris. We'll forget those other cities—we'll run to London! (*He agitatedly paces and espies* ZLATKA.) Zlatka, Reizele is in London. We're going there. Madame Cherniak, you'll come with us. You're my true friend, for life. Zlatka, go study your role. We'll play *Uriel Acosta* in London. And she'll sit with Marcella Zembrick in a box, and my warm tears will be for the years we've been separated. . .

ZLATKA. (*Aside, in tears.*) I'm lost now forever. (HOLTZMAN *enters.*)

RAPALESCO. Bernard, my friend. We're in luck. (RAPALESCO *embraces and dances with a half-drunk* HOLTZMAN.) I've finally found her, thanks to Madame Cherniak, my saint, my angel Breindele here.

HOLTZMAN. Breindele Kossak—a fallen angel, maybe, but a saint only for a Messiah. All right, we can use her in our company. I really had her in mind for our company . . . a contract. Isaac. . .

ISAAC. If you say so, partner. She'll play in the troupe of Holtzman, Schwalb and Company—for life, if you say so.

RAPALESCO. Come, everybody. I'll hire a carriage and we'll drive to the forest. We'll dance in the green fields among the flowers. Today is a holiday with spring in our souls. (RAPALESCO *dons a black fedora, gloves, carries a dandy's cape.*) Ready? Let's go.

HOLTZMAN. Wherever you want, even to the devil.

HENRIETTA. (*Enters with telegram in hand.*) We got a telegram from our brother Nissel in London.

RAPALESCO. London!

HENRIETTA. My brother Nissel is a famous impressario in London. (*She reads the telegram in sing-song.*)

London waits for Rapalesco;
Bring him with our sister.
Gold waits in the streets of
    Whitechapel.
With love, Nissel Schwalb.

RAPALESCO. Bravo. (*He enthusiastically kisses* HENRIETTA.) Hurrah for London! Hurrah for the whole world! (*While all sing and cheer,* HOLTZMAN *provides his obbligato with severe coughing.*)

SCENE 7

MEYER STELMACH's *suite in Hotel Cecil, London. From another room is heard a violin solo of a classic piece. In the room are* MEYER STELMACH, *the very fat* NISSEL SCHWALB, *and* MR. KLAMMER *with a Theodore Herzl–style beard.*

STELMACH. That's how he played when he was only eight years old. I carried him in my arms through the streets of Berdichev and cried, "Dear Jews, don't let him and my seven children starve."

KLAMMER. We know. From all over the world they come to my Cafe National in Whitechapel, and they talk only about Rosa Spivak and Grisha

Stelmach. I couldn't believe them and the newspapers. Now I know. Like the Englishman says, seeing is believing.

NISSEL. When my brother arrives here in London with his troupe, we'll have a banquet in your cafe. And you, Mr. Stelmach, I came here specially to invite all of you to a real Jewish banquet. (ROSA*'s voice is now heard singing an operatic aria.*)

KLAMMER. As the Englishman says, beautiful—real quality.

NISSEL. Ai, ai, ai! A Jewish prima donna. Shame on you, Meyer Stelmach. You should have brought her to the leading Jewish managers, like me.

STELMACH. What, and have you steal her away from me? That's all I need—and lose both the great diva and a golden daughter-in-law.

GRISHA. (*Enters. He is* STELMACH*'s son, in his late twenties.*) Papa, after rehearsal, Rosa likes ice cream. Did you order it?

STELMACH. It's ordered. By now I know what Rosa likes. (ROSA *and her accompanist enter. She is a much more sophisticated and well-groomed* REIZELE.) Ah, Rosa. (*At* STELMACH*'s not-so-subtle urging, the two visitors rise.* ROSA *instructs her accompanist, in French, to come to her home for the next rehearsal.* GRISHA *also speaks in French.*)

NISSEL. She speaks French, too! Ai, ai, ai. . .

KLAMMER. I speak a little French, too.

STELMACH. What don't she speak: Italian, Spanish, German—if you sing in the opera you have to know them all. (*Accompanist exits.*)

ROSA. (*After introductions are acknowledged.*) Oh, where's my ice cream?

GRISHA. Papa, so where's the ice cream?

STELMACH. A cholera should grab these anti-Semites! An hour since I phoned down. (*He phones again and speaks in Yiddish.*) Nu, voo iss de ice cream? Schoen ah shtundeh ven ich hobb. . . (ROSA *laughs.*)

GRISHA. (*Embarrassed, takes the phone.*) Kindly send up the ice cream.

KLAMMER. A born Englishman.

STELMACH. Rosa, Grisha, these gentlemen are London Jews and well known in Whitechapel. Mr. Klammer is an uncle of Theodore Herzl, and Mr. Schwalb is the manager of the Yiddish Theater—you know, a theater for the Jews where they play in Yiddish. . .

ROSA. A Yiddish Theater? In London? Do you go on tour? In what cities? Who are your actors? Are there many other troupes? I used to be a Yiddish actress. I played in Chernowitz, Jassi, all through Bessarabia, even the Ukraine. Ah, it was wonderful. We were poor actors, dying of hunger, but happy and free. (*She sings, "Friday Night Each Jew is a King."*)

GRISHA. Rosa! What are you doing? You forget who you are now.

ROSA. We're in a hotel room among friends waiting for ice cream. Do we have to be famous and non-Jews to enjoy ice cream?

GRISHA. We have to be careful. That's all we need, for the newspapers to connect us with that awful. . .

ROSA. (*Lightly dismisses his snobbery and turns to* NISSEL.) Who is the greatest Yiddish actor?

NISSEL. In America now it's the king of them all, Jacob P. Adler. But in Europe, there is the greatest of the great—Rapalesco.

ROSA.   *(Musing.)*   Rapalesco— Rapalesco. Do you know maybe if he comes from Bessarabia?

NISSEL. I only know he is the best. (*Enter* BELLHOP *with ice cream.*)

ROSA. At last. But it's so little. We should have some for our guests. (*To* BELLHOP.) Please bring some more— oh, three or four portions. (*To* NISSEL *and* KLAMMER *as the* BELLHOP *exits.*) Make yourself at home, my friends.

GRISHA. *(Speaks in French.)* Rosa, it's degrading to fraternize with these lowlifes.

ROSA. *(Also in French)* If you don't like it, I'll leave. Today I am your guest, and I expect gracious behavior from you. *(She dances around and in singsong "I am your honored guest. Her mood abruptly changes to weeping. In English:)* Ah, if only my mother and father could see me now. I'm a queen. . .

GRISHA. Rosa, Rosa.

STELMACH. Go understand artistes. First laughter, then tears. Ice cream and tears.

ROSA. *(More composed. Speaks quietly.)* Mama writes that Papa is very sick. Since my visit home three months ago, he has gotten worse. Excuse me, friends. You, too, must have children. It's hard to shine as a star when in a small shtetl far away a father is deathly sick.

GRISHA. Rosa, please Rosa.

STELMACH. Rosalya, he'll get well. I was sick, I had an operation, and now I'm as good as new. Maybe that's what your father needs. *(He laughs lightly.)*

ROSA. How can you laugh when you know that my father's sickness is because he misses me. Oh, get my things, Grisha.

GRISHA. Please, Rosa. Don't leave. Here, eat your ice cream. . .

STELMACH. I didn't mean anything. All of us older people have our aches and pains. Especially Cantors. . . .

GRISHA. Enough, Papa, enough. I'll have to get out of here. We'll have to have our own place to live, Rosa. After that, Papa, you can invite all the riff-raff from Whitechapel that you want.

STELMACH. I should have known I'd get the devil. You jump on me like Pharoah's plagues. Our guests came to invite us to a banquet at Mr. Klammer's restaurant to honor the Yiddish troupe when they arrive in London.

KLAMMER. We had wanted you to be our distinguished guests.

STELMACH. (*To* GRISHA *and* ROSA.) What do you want from me? I am a Jew, so what harm is it if I like Yiddish songs, once in a while some Yiddish fish? When Fraulein Rosa Spivak sang the Yiddish song, I melted away like a candle. So now I belong to another world. I live in this Cecil Hotel. Suppose I get a few passes to go to a Yiddish play—but no. Because I'm not a famous Jew, because I'm. . .

KLAMMER. As the Englishman says, a social climber. A good for nothing. Goodbye. (KLAMMER *beckons to* NISSEL *for them to leave.*)

STELMACH. What did he call me. . . !

ROSA. Please don't leave, Mr. Klammer. The ice cream is coming. After that, we'll go with you to Whitechapel. I'm dying to be among our Jews again and enjoy a real Jewish meal. And you, Grisha, you'll come, too? *(She coquetishly implores* GRISHA *who succumbs to her.*) And we'll also visit your theater, Mr. Schwalb. I miss the Yiddish Theater. And I miss my father and mother more. I remember when I was a girl, I used to help my mother in the kitchen and hear my father teaching the little boys in the next room. *(Song: She sings "Off'n Pripitchik.")* So long ago and far away. Leibele's mother died. His father has become a religious fanatic and starves himself at a rabbi's home. And I, the poor Cantor's daughter, bought the rich Rapalovich's house and barn so my father could end his days in comfort. And I'm so far away from those I love. . . *(Song: She sings "Home," to the melody of Micaela's song from* Carmen.*)*

SCENE 8

Stage of the Pavilion Theater, lighted only by a lone electric bulb. HOLTZMAN *sits on one of the unpacked, rope-tied steamer trunks that have labels all over them.* HENRIETTA *paces about.*

HOLTZMAN. What a miserable time to come to London! My heart told me that this great London with its fogs would darken my star. London should burn! *(He coughs violently.)* Go figure. London shouldn't have a Yiddish theater? Goldfadn knew—he never came to London, and I let your brother talk me into it. It's dark, it's always raining, and look at this stage with its puny electric light. Electricity! Who needs it. When we had only gaslight we played to packed houses. Your brother Nissel should burn. All he knows is to stuff his mouth like an animal, while our troupe wonders where its next meal is coming from. With no money to pay for their rooms, while the costumes and scenery rot away. Isaac was smart. He got sick and stayed in Lemberg. Six weeks we're waiting—for what? Today there must be an end.

HENRIETTA. Look who's talking. Our director the consumptive. He took this prima donna, who had the public at her feet, and brought me to Whitechapel. And what do I find? Pushcarts, fish peddlers, and their fat wives with big bosoms like cows. I needed Rapalesco on my head? Isaac and Nissel told me Rapalesco would marry me. But the big star has his mind climbing to higheer stakes. He chases around all over London looking for his dream girl. He doesn't know or care if I'm alive. The more I try to get near him, the more he runs away. We play together on stage, we embrace, a kiss on stage, a touch or wink here and there, I do my best to charm him. But when we don't play for weeks—all we can do is starve and play cards. *(She flings a deck of cards toward* HOLTZMAN.*)*

HOLTZMAN. Your brother Nissel is a swindler, a no good louse, a . . .

HENRIETTA. If Isaac heard you, he'd crush you like a cockroach, my friend.

HOLTZMAN. I'd slap his red face so hard he wouldn't know what hit him. A pack of thieves. I know. You're all trying to steal Rapalesco away from me. He's so thick with your brother, and suddenly he looks at me like a stranger. I who made him, who taught him everything he knows . . . *(He coughs himself to silence)*

HENRIETTA. Breindele Kossak had sense. After two weeks, she spit on you and London and jumped on a ship to America. If I had the money, I'd run to America, too.

HOLTZMAN. Why did I drag my old, sick mother and poor Zlatka to this cold bath of a London? If I stayed with Shupak—oi, did I make them laugh! In London everyone has plenty for the Sabbath. They buy beautiful houses, even their cemeteries have beautiful mausoleums, like a bit city. You could move in with all your furniture in one of them. We could play theater for the dead.

HENRIETTA. You're planning to die in London?

HOLTZMAN. I should live so long before I die in London. When there's a funeral here, you can't see the dead man in the fog. You can't even see the cemetery. They tap their way in the dark.

HENRIETTA. When they bury you, the sun will shine, the birds will sing.

HOLTZMAN. Ah, my poor mama and my sister. Zlatka is hopelessly in love with Rapalesco. She cries all night and calls his name in the dark. I feel sorry for him, too. How I hoped to see the day when he would be world famous as a Yiddish actor in his own theater. And I would work with him in my old age. After all, who am I and what do I need? Just Hutzmach, the devil take me. When Rapalesco comes, tell him I'm going to the London hospital. A Jewish doctor there may give me something for my cough. *(He gazes ruefully at the stage.)* London. The theater applauds the debut of Holtzman, Schwalb and Company starring Leon Rapalesco and Henrietta Schwalb. Ah yes—the devil take me. *(He exits.)*

HENRIETTA. All I can do now is play to an empty theater. And Rapalesco was supposed to be my husband. To think I had officers groveling at my feet. Pah! (NISSEL *and* KLAMMER *enter.*)

KLAMMER. You rehearsing a soliloquy?

NISSEL. Henrietta, mazel-tov. There'll be a wedding.

HENRIETTA. I'll fix you with a wedding yet!

NISSEL. Believe me, your wedding will take place, just like Isaac promised. We're going to America. In a few days we sail. Mr. Klammer is my new colleague. He will finance the troupe's trip to the golden land. (*To* KLAMMER.) See, Mr. Klammer. All these trunks filled with costumes, scenic effects, plays, all worth a fortune. Strong ropes for an ocean trip. They all go to America with us. Your name will be known forever. I just got a letter from Breindele Kossak from Columbus's land.

HENRIETTA. From Breindele? What does she say?

NISSEL. In America, just anybody can't get on the stage so easy. They have unions for everything—even for actors. So she's working at another job, but in the theater. She's not married yet—she writes that she can't trust any man and curses them all. But she wants me to come over as soon as I can. Everyone is є says. But we musɬ because he'll be a bigger success than Jacob P. Adler or David Kessler. And that Jacob Gordin will write a play specially for Rapalesco.

HENRIETTA. *(Sighing.)* America, America.

KLAMMER. Did you speak with Rapalesco?

NISSEL. Not yet. But you can be sure I've got him in my pocket. I have another letter from Breindele just for him. Once he reads it, he'll race us to the boat.

KLAMMER. We'll all go to my restaurant to celebrate with a good Jewish meal.

NISSEL. You know, Mr. Klammer, in this very theater I got my start as a poor usher. I was terrific. With me there, no one dared throw orange peels from the balcony or boxes. And if I saw a woman breast-feeding her baby, I buttoned up her blouse and chased her out of the theater. Now after a lifetime, I leave the theater where I worked my way up to be managing director. *(He yells to the wings.)* Hey, janitor. Lock up! We're going to dinner at Mr. Klammer's cafe.

SCENE 9

A small room in HOLTZMAN's *London apartment. The door opens to admit* RAPALESCO. *He appears worried and nervous. He looks into the other rooms, finds no one, and lies down on the sofa. He relaxes and softly whistles. A pale* ZLATKA *enters. She approaches him, turns on a lamp, and sits alongside him.*

ZLATKA. You can tell me. What's on your heart? You'll never have a closer friend. I know everything about you. I want to help you. If I knew where she was, I'd go on my knees to beg her to come to you.

RAPALESCO. I've given up. All my hopes are gone. Today I saw an old, torn poster with two pictures in large print, a couple of months old. "Rosa Spivak and Grisha Stelmach in concert at Queens Hall." I ran there only to find out that she sailed to America a few days ago with Grisha. He's probably her fiance.

ZLATKA. Of course her fiancé. Would she go to America with a stranger?

RAPALESCO. What's left for me? I'll go back to Holeneshti. At least I'll see my mother. God knows how she is. I dreamed that my mother was dead. I saw her lying on the ground with candles around her head. Will you come with me, Zlatka? It will be a holiday. We'll drive to the fair, and then . . . we'll be together again like last year.

ZLATKA. You still love the girl?

RAPALESCO. Oh, how much! How could she break her pledge? It's not possible. Oh, Zlatka, if you only knew her. An angel from heaven. If I saw her once only, we'd never be parted again. *(She comforts him in an embrace. he kisses her hands.)* I would take you with us all over the world. You are devoted to me like a dear sister—aren't you? (ZLATKA *embraces him more fiercely, kisses him wildly, between her tears. The lights dim—their shadows reveal a passionate embrace. Their bodies recline on the sofa—implication of love's consumation. A pause. Stage is in darkness.* HOLTZMAN's *voice.*)

HOLTZMAN. Mama, Mama. *(He lights a match in the adjoining room and lights a lamp.* ZLATKA *steals into the room.)* Where were you? I kept calling . . .

ZLATKA. I was sitting with Leon. he has a bad headache. (HOLTZMAN *looks at her suspiciously. He coughs.)* You're so pale. You're fading away to nothing. I should have spoken up sooner. I know the doctor said you should go to Switzerland.

HOLTZMAN. The doctor is an idiot. What good is fresh air and sunshine without a theater, without a stage— *(He coughs again.)*

SARAH. *(Enters from outside; she carries a heavy basket.)* Either they laugh or they cry, while I have to climb these stairs with this heavy basket. (HOLTZMAN *coughs violently, wipes his mouth with a handkerchief that shows blood.)*

ZLATKA. Mama! He's coughing up blood . . . !

SARAH. Woe is me! Go, quick, get the doctor.

ZLATKA. God help me! While I'm running I'll get run over and die. (ZLATKA *exits.)*

SARAH. Lightning and thunder have struck us. (HOLTZMAN *raises himself and follows* SARAH *to door of the other room. They encounter* RAPALESCO.) Oh, Leibele, we're cursed.

HOLTZMAN. What curse? What are you carrying on and worrying Leon?

RAPALESCO. What happened? Bernard, you look so sick . . .

HOLTZMAN. Sick? Ha, when was I ever healthy? It's nothing. I've been busy all day. Looks like the theater will open soon and you will play. Zlatka can count on it. (*To* SARAH.) Where's Zlatka? Don't you dare call a doctor. I don't need a doctor. Get something to eat for Leon. (HOLTZMAN *exits to other room.* SARAH *picks up her basket, looks at* RAPALESCO, *then exits, weeping.* RAPALESCO *paces nervously, fingers shabby curtains and furniture with revulsion. He is obviously depressed, then gazes with pity and sorrow toward direction of* HOLTZMAN's *exit. A knock on the door. He opens door and* NISSEL *and* KLAMMER *enter.)*

NISSEL. Hello, Leon. This very moment, the whole world is waiting for your answer. Yes or no. If yes, we're all lucky. But if it's no, God forbid, then you and we are kaput. But, you can be sure we'll find a new star. Actors are two for a penny.

KLAMMER. Like the Englishman says, for money you can even buy a king.

RAPALESCO. What's this all about? What's going on?

NISSEL. Leon, I'm only thinking of what's good for you, or I should drop dead on this spot.

RAPALESCO. Quiet down, please. Holtzman is very sick.

NISSEL. Sick? Very sick? A pity. The very reason for you to leave him, because a sick manager is unlucky for the Yiddish Theater. You told me yourself your wings are tied up with him.

KLAMMER. As the Englishman says, from a sickness you'll catch the disease.

NISSEL. Rapalesco, look. *(He shows* RAPALESCO *the ship's tickets.)* See.

We're going to America. Your ticket is right here. We sail tomorrow from Liverpool. Everyone goes to America: prize fighters, English actors, singers, even the famous Yiddish singer Rosalya Spivak has gone to America. With Mr. Klammer's money we go to America the golden land.

KLAMMER. I'm even leaving my wife to go to America. Like the English . . .

NISSEL. The trunks are already on the train to Liverpool. Your Uriel Acosta costumes are half way to America.

RAPALESCO. Add Holtzman? Bernard . . . ?

NISSEL. Just read what Breindele Kossak writes to you. (*Hands letter to* RAPALESCO.) American directors are strong, healthy. They wear stovepipe hats and ride in carriages while actors . . .

RAPALESCO. (*Reading.*) "The managers will go crazy about you. Union or no union, for a star there is no union—they make a deal. Everyone says your place is here in the golden land, but don't bring . . . (*His voice falters.*)

NISSEL. (*Reading over* RAPALESCO's *shoulder.*) That's what it says, "Don't bring that old skeleton. He'll poison the Yiddish Theater in America." That's what it says. (*They stand quietly as they observe* HOLTZMAN *enter.*)

RAPALESCO. Bernard, are you feeling any better?

HOLTZMAN. Better. Much beter. Tomorrow I'm going to Switzerland. I heard the plans about America. You must go with them. You'll bring the best of Yiddish theater to the new world.

KLAMMER. Like the Englishman says, a true friend is really a friend.

HOLTZMAN. A sick managing director is unlucky for the Yiddish Theater. I'm through, finished.

RAPALESCO. Don't talk foolish. You'll always be my managing director. Just let us have a success in America, then I'll send for you, Zlatka, and Mama to come to America.

KLAMMER. Nothing like trying says the . . .

HOLTZMAN. Zlatka should really go with you.

NISSEL. Not on this ship. If you paid a million pounds, you couldn't buy another ticket. All gone, I should live so.

SARAH. (*In tears at the door.*) How could you have the heart to leave him when he's so sick? He's already half dead. Woe is me. The angel of death is waiting for him. Woe is me.

HOLTZMAN. Mama, get in the kitchen. (*To the others.*) Ha, I'm Bernard Holtzmann, the one and only Hutzmach. Sick as I am, I could still be a success in America. Whom do they have in American to equal me? There are only two real Yiddish actors in the whole world—Rapalesco and Holtzman. That's why Rapalesco must go first and prepare them for Holtzman who comes later. And when I step out on the stage in America with my song and dance as Hutzmach or Kuni Leml, or as Bube Yachne, America won't have a chance to catch its breath. There are no sick actors. An actor doesn't dare be sick. I'm not a manager—I'm an actor! Only to promote Rapalesco did I give up the stage for a while, to train him, to take care of him, to stand in line to applaud him and cry bravo,

Rapalesco! My Leibele from Holeneshti. I stole him away from his father and mother, because the world was waiting for him. Now America needs him! (RAPALESCO *weeps.*) I'll sing and dance again, in America.

(Song: Reprise of HOLTZMAN *singing "Romania, Romania." He falters, while* ZLATKA *enters with a doctor as the curtain falls.)*

CURTAIN

ACT II

SCENE 1

LEAH's *apartment on Rivington Street,* MEYER STELMACH *and the* BEADLE *of the neighborhood synagogue are busily tacking up mezzuzahs on the various door frames.*

STELMACH. How many mezzuzahs have you put up already?

BEADLE. Plenty. Don't worry, mister, evil spirits won't come here.

STELMACH. The main thing is to have plenty near her bedroom. Don't be stingy. Her daughter says that everything must be Kosher. It's a world-shaking event for Leah, the wife of the late Cantor of Holeneshti, may he rest in peace, for her to be in America. For her we should make all New York Kosher. *(His sarcasm is wasted on the* BEADLE.*)*

BEADLE. Such a pious woman. She sits all day in the synagogue. And charity, no one ever gave so much.

STELMACH. I got pictures of saintly rabbis. Hang them up, too. These pictures of Moses and Aaron, hang them up nice. Ach, such a foolish woman. She could live like a queen with her daughter in the Hotel Plaza. But no, for her it's Rivington Street next to the synagogue. Her husband, long years to us, her daughter says wasn't

so fanatic. Moses should hang near the door facing East. *(The* BEADLE *complies.)* That's fine. How many telegrams we had to send her before she said she'd come to America! Only when we sent a delegation to her—did we convince her. That's me, Meyer Stelmach to do the dirty work. Suddenly, she screams she forgot her brass candle sticks in Holeneshti. Our American sterling silver aren't Kosher enough for her. Soooo, Meyer Stelmach, impressario and father of the famous violin virtuoso Grisha Stelmach, has to schlepp himself all over Allen Street to find brass candlesticks. *(He unwraps package of candle sticks on table.* LEAH, *well dressed, carrying a prayer book, enters.)* Talk about the Messiah. Good morning, Hazenteh. You finished your morning prayers, so now you can have breakfast.

LEAH. Breakfast again? Every day the same thing, so fancy. By us back home when we got hungry, we had a nosh. Here it's breakfast.

BEADLE. Look, Hazenteh. These mezzuzahs are really Kosher. I bought them from our chief rabbi. They're the real McCoy.

LEAH. American rabbis, tfui! Go believe them. I should have brought my own mezzuzahs from the old country.

STELMACH. *(He gives money to the* BEADLE.) Thank you. Go in good health. You should come around once in a while and keep the Hazenteh company. (BEADLE *ad libs exit.)* My dear in-law—oh, excuse me, we're not in-laws yet.

LEAH. So long as your son plays the fiddle, we're not in-laws. My daughter will get the right one without a fiddle. My husband, may he rest in peace, never played a fiddle. And his father and his father's father didn't know from fiddles either.

STELMACH. We'll be in-laws yet. Our children love each other. They want to get married and they will, either here in New York or Paris or London, or on the moon.

LEAH. Paris, London! When you fly high, you land on a pig.

STELMACH. How long must their love-sickness drag out. *(A knock on the door.* STELMACH *opens door to* ROSA *and* GRISHA. ROSA *kisses her mother.)*

ROSA. How do you feel, mama? More comfortable here? The neighbors on the sidewalk crowded around my automobile and praised you to the sky. They think you're wonderful.

GRISHA. She knows that. How about breaking the news to her?

ROSA. Mama, we saw a beautiful house uptown, right across from a synagogue. As long as you're going to stay in America, you'll live with us. Because . . .

LEAH. Nu, because what? What are you talking about?

ROSA. I told Grisha that yesterday you agreed . . .

STELMACH. You agree? Wonderful! So why am I standing like a dumb Golem . . . ? Mazel-tov, children—mazel-tov, Hazenteh. So now you're an in-law. *(He kisses* ROSA *and wipes his tears.)*

GRISHA. Why the tears, papa?

STELMACH. Who's crying? We'll send a cable to your mother in London . . .

LEAH. Don't send your cable yet. It's the eve of lamentation month for the destruction of the Temple. We mustn't be joyful this month, so no wedding yet. We must spend this time in prayer and remember the woes of our people. The story is . . .

ROSA. Leave the sad stories to Yom Kippur. We're not getting married right away, Mr. Stelmach . . .

STELMACH. Maybe now you could call me Papa?

ROSA. Grisha has been patient for my answer for so long. The truth is that I resolved never to get married.

LEAH. An old maid yet? Did you ever hear of such a thing . . .

STELMACH. It's God's will. Grisha Stelmach and Rosa Spivak were meant to be a pair.

LEAH. If it comes from God, why stop it? So, mazel-tov. If your God's holy father were still alive, he'd have plenty pleasure. (LEAH *kisses* ROSA.) Right after the wedding, you should buy me a ticket on the boat so I can go home. I swore on your father's grave that I would be buried next to him in Holeneshti. *(She places a hat on* STELMACH's *head.)* We're practically in-laws. So now you can wear a hat, like a real Jew. And a special favor, please grow a beard. *(They all laugh.)*

STELMACH. Even with curly sideburns like a real Hassid. Anything for you.

How wonderful, my son's bride earns the biggest salary, and when you hear her sing . . . *(He tries to imitate her coloratura.)*

ROSA. I'd love to take all of Verdi's music, with the orchestra and the whole ensemble and throw them out. Then I'd stand center stage and sing . . . *(She sings a few phrases from "From Hasilovitch to Leibovitch.")*

STELMACH. Ah, how a Yiddish song touches the heart! Children, tonight we'll eat in a Yiddish, Kosher restaurant—Sholem's Roumanian Restaurant. You'll see Yiddish actors, writers, editors. And tomorrow, we'll go to the Yiddish Theater on the Bowery. A great star from Bucharest is opening in *Uriel Acosta.* They say the Queen of Romania shook hands with him. And the great Adler, Sonenthal, Mogulesco, even Sir Henry Irving are fit only to shine his shoes. We'll celebrate this happy occasion. I'll buy a box at the theater—the devil take everything else. Starting today, only Jewish things, Yiddish Theater, Jewish pastrami—no more turkey, no more . . .

GRISHA. Jewish hot pastrami is good, Papa, but our publicity agents warn us not to be identified with the Yiddish Theater.

ROSA. *(Musing.)* Yiddish Theater . . . *(Song:* ROSA *sings, "I Have a Cottage Without a Roof.")*

SCENE 2

In the apartment of the LOMZER CANTOR. *He is attired in a Prince Albert coat and a stove-pipe hat. Children, dressed in white as waiters are rehearsing their roles as waiters and in the choir. The* LOMZER CANTOR *supervises them.*

LOMZER CANTOR. No, you have to make it much nicer. This isn't London. A blessing on Nissel Schwalb who brought us to America from that dark cellar where we starved in Whitechapel. Here I'm not only a Cantor, I'm a reverend who can perform weddings. Now I associate with high class people. Once again, let me hear you . . . *(He sounds his tuning fork; choir starts to sing. They are interrupted by entrance of* NISSEL *and* KLAMMER.*)*

NISSEL. Everything in order, Cantor? They'll be ready to come in soon.

CANTOR. Ready. One surprise will be bigger than the other.

KLAMMER. As the Englishman says, a good beginning makes a smashing end.

CANTOR. How do you like my idea? My children are both waiters and the choir. For each dish, they'll sing my own musical composition. This will be an engagement party that will make history!

NISSEL. Sha, sha. We don't want Rapalesco to know yet. You warm my heart. Thank God, you're such a success in America. My heart told me America needs a genuine, heimisch Cantor like you. Now you can repay me for all I did for you. Remember, today my sister Henrietta and Rapalesco must be engaged to marry according to Jewish tradition— whether he wants to or not. When he makes his American debut tomorrow in the Bowery Yiddish Theater and becomes a success, I want to be sure he's tied to my sister. So when I nod and wink to you, according to Jewish law, you say, "The voice of the Groom and the voice of the Bride," and right away break the plate. That does it—a legal, binding betrothal.

CANTOR.So good. Now, boys and girls, the guests and the happy couple are in the next room drinking schnapps and eating sponge cake with pickled herring and . . .

NISSEL. They've already drunk plenty. Rapalesco can hardly stand up. *(He goes to the door and calls out.)* Ladies and gentlemen, our famous Lomzer Cantor invites you to come sit at the tables. *(As the guests— among whom are* RAPALESCO, HENRIETTA, BREINDELE KOSSAK, AC- TORS—*come in, the* LOMZER CANTOR *conducts the choir.* RAPALESCO *is quite drunk.)*

CHOIR. *(They sing.)* Welcome dear friends, Welcome to the Cantor's home, Welcome, Dear, dear friends. Sit down at the tables And begin to eat. *(The altos sing, "Begin to eat," then the bassos repeat, "Begin to eat," followed by the entire choir, "Begin to eat." The guests applaud. The choir embark on their roles as waiters, carry in plates, and sing.)* Here comes the fish, Here comes the fish. Beautiful fish, wonderful fish.

CANTOR. *(To* KLAMMER.*)* My own com- position.

KLAMMER. Unbelievable.

NISSEL. Friends, this is a celebration. Not only of the Lomzer Cantor's great success in America, but also the debut tomorrow night of our Yid- dish troupe in America. But we have more for you, and that will be a sur- prise later. The manager of the the- ater told me that he is having a very distinguished audience tomorrow night: The governor is coming from Albany, Jacob Schiff and Gug- genheim will be in the front row. Also, their friend the president of the Pennsylvania railroad. Our benefac- tor Mr. Klammer will make a curtain speech. The main thing is our shining star, Mr. Rapalesco, will put across our success.

CHOIR. *(After applause, the children serve soup and sing.)* Soup, soup, soup, Sweet soup, chicken soup with noodles. *(Altos and bassos sing the last line alternately, then the entire choir sings the same.)*

CANTOR.My own composition.

CHOIR BOY. Three cheers for the Lomzer Cantor. *(Cheers.)*

KLAMMER. I'll make my big speech to- morrow at our company's American premiere. But on this occasion we must reflect and rejoice. A man's life consists of four epochs, Spring, Sum- mer, Fall, and Winter. Spring, said Moses, is the most poetic time of the year, when everything blooms and comes to life and the heart is filled with love—ah love, said Tolstoy. Love and Sympathy. Our immortal Shake- speare said that the world stands on three things: Love, love, and love. I say in the words of King Solomon, "Sing bridegroom, sing bride." *(*RAPALESCO *is drinking unre- strainedly and getting more drunk.* NISSEL *nods and winks to the* CAN- TOR. *The* LOMZER CANTOR *takes his place and intones a prayer.)*

CHOIR. We wish you good luck, Good

luck, good luck, Good luck, good luck and a happy life. *(CANTOR breaks a plate and exlaims Mazeltov.)* (NISSEL *kisses* RAPALESCO *and then his sister* HENRIETTA. *"Mazeltovs" all around and gaiety.)*

BREINDELE. *(To* NISSEL.*)* Mazel-tov. Maybe soon for us.

NISSEL. Enjoy, everybody. Come, let's have some music. We'll dance. *(Choir sings and one of them plays an accordian.)* Come, Breindele. Dance at another's then you'll dance at your own. (NISSEL *and* BREINDELE *dance. Others also dance.)*

RAPALESCO. *(Staggering to his feet.)* I want to dance. They say I'm a groom. So where's the bride. *(He weaves toward* HENRIETTA *and tries to dance with her.)*

NISSEL. Aha, he wants to dance with the bride. It's a good sign.

RAPALESCO. *(Drunkenly.)* You think I can only play Acosta? I can dance, too. Hutzmach taught me everything, even to dance. Nobody has such a golden heart like Hutzmach. He gave up everything to make me a great star—his career, his mother, his sister, everything. None of you are worth the mud on his shoes. He is a true folk artist. I'm from our Jewish people, from Holeneshti. I had a dear mother, but she's dead. My father gets charity from a rabbi and eats leftovers. My brothers and sisters— all far away. Even my dog Terkish died because he misses me.

HENRIETTA. *(Disengaging herself from his arms amidst confusion.)* He's dead drunk. Ugh, he's sweating. Somebody take him home.

RAPALESCO. Get away from me, all of you. Acosta goes by himself. Breindele, where are you? You gave my letter to Reizele? Did she read it? We swore by the stars even though we wander we'll always be one. Who is this Grisha Stelmach? He thinks he's a bridgegroom! No! I'm the bridegroom. Play, more music. Everybody dance . . . *(He dances drunkenly as lights dim.)*

SCENE 3

London, in a small room. A sick HOLTZMAN *lies on a small bed.* ZLATKA *sits near him, nursing a baby.* SARAH *is mending. A warm sun shines through the window.*

HOLTZMAN. *(Reading a newspaper. He coughs intermittently)* All New York is raving about the new star, Leon Rapalesco. They say "he's descended from holy rabbis and a distinguished family going back to the Baal Shem Tov. His debut will be at the Yiddish Bowery Theater in *Uriel Acosta*, as directed by Bernard Holtzman." How could I direct it when I'm lying here sick as a dog? Maybe they want me to come over for the first night. Where is Sholem Meyer? What date is it today? *(He looks at top of the newspaper.)* In ten days is his debut. I can still get there.

ZLATKA. If the doctor will let you. The trip takes two weeks.

HOLTZMAN. But with a faster ship it takes six to seven days.

SARAH. (*To* ZLATKA *who quietly sings "Rozhinkes Mit Mandl'o".*) Why did you have to show him the newspaper? To my trouble there's no end. You see in the paper the picture of your little bastard's father. . .

HOLTZMAN. Mama, don't you ever use that word again! His child is the most beautiful gift he could have left us. The baby is completely him, his face, his eyes. We'll bring him up and I'll train him to be a bigger star than his father. He'll never leave us because he's our very own blood. Oh, you little artiste. Look at the way he smiles and twinkles his eyes. Just like his father. Soon I'll get out of my sick bed and we'll all go to America. Zlatka will marry Leon, I'll be his director again, Mama will cook delicious dishes. . . (SHOLEM MEYER *enters.*) Quick, tell me, Sholem Meyer, when is there a fast ship to America. I want to be at Rapalesco's opening night.

SHOLEM. The fast ship leaves Liverpool tomorrow, six days to New York. (*The women look at him worriedly; He winks to put them at ease.*)

HOLTZMAN. So. I'll get ready. You'll lay out the money for the tickets, Sholem Meyer. Once I'm in America, with Leon's help, I'll pay you back. We'll get decent clothes for Zlatka, a warm coat for mama, and an outfit for our little bird. He should look like a little gentleman when he meets his father. You see, Mama, a person shouldn't worry. Great brains made marvelous inventions, a fast ship. When we're at our greatest need, not enough money even for a little milk, along comes our angel, Sholem Meyer, and saves all of us.

SARAH. Take a spoonful of medicine, Berele. Sholem, let him rest. (ZLATKA *weeps as she rocks the child.*)

HOLTZMAN. My medicine is the fast ship. How I miss Leon! The moment I first saw him my heart knew he'd be a great star. (*He has slumped down on the bed. Coughs. He's bewildered.*) Zlatke, Mama, Sholem Meyer, where are you? Where have you all gone?

SARAH. Woe is me.

SHOLEM. Don't cry. You mustn't upset him in his last moment.

HOLTZMAN. (*Sings: "I am a little Hussidl" or "Romania, Romania."*) The fast ship arrives Friday before his debut. I'll be there. . . (*He takes up his song again as his voice weakens and he expires in death.*)

SHOLEM. He has earned his peace.

SARAH. (*Rocking herself.*) Let him sleep in peace. (*Lights dim.*)

SCENE 4

Two adjoining boxes in a theater. STELMACH, GRISHA, *and* ROSA *in one box. In the adjoining box sit* HENRIETTA *and two other women.*)

ROSA. (*Studying her program.*) According to the European critics, he's an extraordinary actor. "He adds to the great reservoir of rich Jewish talent.

Each expression comes from his heart and soul." I never heard of him. He's from Bucharest.

GRISHA. A superficial talent. The American stage has many better ones.

HENRIETTA. (*To her companions in the adjoining box.*) Just look how the audience is excited. Not an empty seat.

ROSA. (*To* HENRIETTA *in the next box, as the house lights dim.*) Please don't talk during the performance. It's disturbing.

HENRIETTA. I could talk. Rapalesco the star is my fiancé.

GRISHA. An audience of idiots. (*Enormous applause as the stage is dark. Darkness to bridge a lapse of time. Lights on stage on full for end of Act I of* Uriel Acosta, *as actress playing Judith declaims her speech. Curtain falls, house lights on so that boxes are now lighted.* ROSA *applauds.*)

ROSA. Too bad she ends the act. She spoils the effect. Her hands are gross and red. Her voice is like a peasant's. Too bad the star is surrounded by such poor talent. They ruin the atmosphere. (NISSEL *and* KLAMMER *appear in* HENRIETTA'*s box*)

NISSEL. Do you know who that lady is in the next box? She's Rosa Spivak, the famous diva.

HENRIETTA. (*Excited, loud.*) Really?

NISSEL. Don't scream, you cow. Just look how Meyer Stelmach is hiding. He doesn't want anyone to know he likes Kosher food and Yiddish theater. Don't say anything or give him away. Remember.

ROSA. (*She leans over toward* HENRIETTA'*s box.*) Excuse me. You say the star is your fiancé?

HENRIETTA. Yes, that's right. My fiancé.

ROSA. He's from Bucharest?

HENRIETTA. He's from Bucharest as much as I am, hah.

ROSA. Are you an actress too?

HENRIETTA. Am I an actress! You never heard of Henrietta Schwalb who won first prize in the Lemberg beauty contest? I and my fiancé are different kinds of stars. I play in operettas and he in classic plays. Our manager won't let us appear together.

ROSA. The program says he was born in Bucharest.

HENRIETTA. That's just publicity. He was born in a little Bessarabian shtetl called Holeneshti. An actor stole him away from his family and made him an actor. Hutzmach trained my Rapalesco.

ROSA. (*Stammering.*) Holeneshti! Hutzmach! Leon Rapalesco! He must be Liebele. I knew there was something about him. . . Rapalesco from Rapalovich. . .

GRISHA. What's wrong, Rosa? These people are staring at you . . . (NISSEL *and* KLAMMER *leave* HENRIETTA'*s box as house lights dim.* STELMACH *and* GRISHA *whisper to each other.* GRISHA *turns to* ROSA.) Papa says those two men who came to the next box recognized us. You remember them from London. We'd better leave quickly. The newspapers mustn't report we attended the Yiddish Theater.

STELMACH. Sha, sha. Look how the audience is tense. Rosa, don't lean over the rail, you'll fall out. Here, use my opera glasses. (ROSA *focuses the glasses on the stage as* RAPALESCO *is heard in Act 2 of* Uriel Acosta.)

ROSA. How beautiful his eyes are. How much painful love they've seen. I can't believe it's really he. This must be a dream. No—it's not a dream.

GRISHA. Rosa, people are staring at you more than at the stage. What's happened to you?

ROSA. After this act we must see him in his dressing room. I want to tell him everything that has been locked up in my soul.

GRISHA. What are you talking about? What's locked up . . .?

HENRIETTA. The lady must be crazy. She keeps chattering away like a parrot.

STELMACH. Look how he embraces his blind mother. He's wonderful, the devil take him. He touches my heart. Sha. He falls, now he rises. Sha.

ROSA. Grisha! Just see his eyes. He's looking at us, at our box. (*She tries to rise as she applauds with the audience as the lights dim on the stage. A spotlight focuses on* KLAMMER *before the curtain on the play of* Uriel Acosta.)

KLAMMER. Ladies and gentlemen, worthy public. No wonder we need the police to hold back the crowds. How do you like our Acosta? (*Applause, bravos, whistling, cheers.*) Yiddish Theater marches ahead, with better theater worthy of our traditions. I wish officially to thank the distinguished guests who patronize

our theater. In the first box on my left is the famous Yiddish Prima Donna, Henrietta Schwalb. (HENRIETTA *rises and takes a bow to the applause.*) In the box next to her is the world renowned opera diva Rosa Spivak with the greatest fiddler Grisha Stelmach who are as popular as Edison and Lincoln. (ROSA *rises to acknowledge the applause but stammers.*)

STELMACH. It's an outrage. Only by the Jews can this happen. (*He frantically hands coats to* GRISHA *and* ROSA *while he tries to usher them away.*) This is the first and last time. From now on no more gefuehlte fish and no more Yiddish Theater.

GRISHA. It's a scandal, Papa. For this night I'll never forgive you.

STELMACH. Our chauffeur is waiting. Let's go. (*Applause for them as they hurry out.* NISSEL *blocks their exit.* STELMACH *pushes him aside.*) I don't know you. This has been a big mistake. A scandal . . .

NISSEL. You're ashamed of your fellow Jews! You parasite. You live off your son's fiddling. I wouldn't trade you for a fish peddler on Hester Street. (*Blackout. Song:* ROSA *sings alone, spotlighted before curtain, a song of longing for her Liebele* [*there are half a dozen available*].)

SCENE 5

RAPALESCO's *dressing room. Agitated,* RAPALESCO *enters and throws himself onto a chair.* KLAMMER *enters.*

RAPALESCO. Who asked you to make a speech! What kind of stupidity is this with speeches! I played my part and

the audience applauded. Friends of mine came to see me. Who asked you to announce their names?

KLAMMER. Nissel told me it's a custom in America. If tomorrow the President of the United States came, I'll announce him too. America is built on publicity. (HENRIETTA *enters.*)

HENRIETTA. Such chutzpah from that woman! And the two idiots with her . . . They are given tribute, respect, they are applauded, so they grab their coats and run out. When I told her you're my fiancé, her eyes almost popped out of her head.

RAPALESCO. *(Tosses his clothes around and kicks his chair.)* Who asked you to sit in the box! Who needed you there? You distract my performance with your shining false diamonds. You're driving me out of my mind, I'm going crazy from you!

HENRIETTA. What have you got against my diamonds? Is it my fault if those idiots ran away? (NISSEL *enters.*)

NISSEL. I should have fixed him, given it to him right between the eyes. That barefoot bum is ashamed of the Jews! What can we do without Jews? Can a Jew make a living without Jews? *(Knock on the door.* KLAMMER *opens it and a voice announces, "Ready for Act 3.")*

RAPALESCO. I have to lengthen my beard. Where is my dresser?

NISSEL. The theater is going wild. Such acting New York never saw.

RAPALESCO. Stop crowding into my dressing room? I can't breathe. *(He glowers at* HENRIETTA.*)*

HENRIETTA. What do you want from me? Is this the way you thank me for announcing in the theater that you're my fiancé?

RAPALESCO. What kind of fiancé? Since I came to New York I've been in a daze. Fiancé? What nonsense.

NISSEL. Hey, what did you say? "What fiancé?" You forgot already the ceremony at the Lomzer Cantor when the plate was broken? It's a legal engagement.

RAPALESCO. *(Adjusting his makeup.)* You did it all. Did I know what was going on? I was dead drunk.

NISSEL. You were drunk? You think that because you're a big shot actor you can ruin my sister? She's a bigger star than you and brings in more money in the box office than you.

HENRIETTA. The greatest Yiddish prima donna you don't find so easy . . . *(She storms out.)*

KLAMMER. As the Englishman says, a breach of promise is a strong case. (NISSEL *holds the door against an intruder.*)

SHOLEM. *(From outside the door.)* Tell him Sholem Meyer brings him regards from London, from Hutzmach—from Bernard Holtzman.

RAPALESCO. *(Dashes to the door.)* Let that man in.

SHOLEM. Leibele, it's me, Sholem Meyer from Shupak's troupe. Remember?

KLAMMER. Get out of here . . .

SHOLEM. I'll pull out that pretty beard of yours one hair at a time.

NISSEL. The audience is disgusted. The intermission is too long.

RAPALESCO. Sholem Meyer, wait for me here.

SHOLEM. I'll go with you. I'll stand in the wings. (RAPALESCO *and* SHOLEM *exit. Lights dim to indicate short passage of time. Lights go on.* KLAMMER *sits alone.* HENRIETTA *rushes in.)*

HENRIETTA. It's terrible. He's ruined the act. He's acting like he's out of his mind. It's not Acosta he's playing. People are running to the box office to get back their money. Where's

Nissel? *(She runs out. A shot is heard. Much noise off.* KLAMMER *rushes to the door; he's blocked by* NISSEL.)

NISSEL. We're ruined. He forgot his lines and kept looking up at the boxes. When the audience started to hoot at him, he took out a gun and shot himself and fainted. Someone ran for a doctor. *(*RAPALESCO, *supported by* SHOLEM, *enters.)*

RAPALESCO. No doctor . . . not necessary.

KLAMMER. We need a lawyer. We'll sue you for damages. *Uriel Acosta* is scheduled for the complete week. We used up the money from the advance sale. How can we refund any money?

NISSEL. *(*HENRIETTA *returns.)* We need a lawyer, too. We have a breach of promise case.

HENRIETTA. *(To* RAPALESCO *who is reclining on setee.)* Lie quietly and rest. Look how perspired you are . . .

RAPALESCO. Be so kind, Henrietta, leave me alone. Please go. Sit down, Sholem Meyer. I want to close my eyes for a few minutes.

HENRIETTA. I'll come for you tomorrow with a carriage. We'll take a ride in Central Park. *(*HENRIETTA *exits, followed by* NISSEL *and* KLAMMER.)*

SHOLEM. *(Wiping* RAPALESCO's *face with a towel.)* Who is that woman?

RAPALESCO. They tell me she is my fiancée.

SHOLEM. Fiancée? No. How about Zlatka and the baby?

RAPALESCO. Zlatka? Baby? What are you talking about?

SHOLEM. That's why I came to America. I brought with me Zlatka, the boy, and Sarah Bruche. You should see him, long should he live. Looks just like you. Zlatka is so dear to me, and the boy—I feel like he's my own child.

RAPALESCO. A child? Looks like me? What are you talking about? And Hutzmach? Didn't he come, too?

SHOLEM. Alas, he's in a cemetery in London.

RAPALESCO. *(Bursts into tears)* Bernard . . . *(Song: He sings "Vi Ahin Zol Ikh Geyn?")*

SHOLEM. He died with your name on his lips. Until the last moment he believed he would sail to be at your debut in America. Zlatka was so dear to him, and loving.

RAPALESCO. *(Removing his beard and makeup, washing.)* Where are they now?

SHOLEM. I rented a room on Cherry Street. We only arrived at Castle Garden yesterday.

RAPALESCO. Let's go. We're going to them.

SHOLEM. Not so fast. They'll be embarrassed if you bust in on them. Actually, Zlatka is shy about you, afraid to see you. You're a famous star and she's a simple girl. Give her a few more days to get used to all this. But my oh my, her baby . . . !

RAPALESCO. He's my son. I won't deny it. Depend on me. I'll do what's right. *(He lights a cigarette, looks in mirror, then starts to weep loudly, as music rises and lights dim.)*

SCENE 6

RAPALESCO's *rooms in a cheap hotel; it has an anteroom, and a door leads off to a bedroom. Walls covered with old-fashioned flower designs of wallpaper, and the furniture is old-fashioned. At rise, noise of arguments. Seated at a table are* KLAMMER, NISSEL, *and* HENRIETTA. KLAMMER *reads a newspaper while* NISSEL *squirms in discomfort because of the heat.*

NISSEL. A donkey he played, not Acosta. An Acosta like his you could get two for a nickel. I could play it better. (*He grimaces and mimics* RAPALESCO.) "I was born a Jew and I'll remain a Jew," and when I finished the monologue, they'd cheer me from the top gallery.

HENRIETTA. Such a scandal, such a disaster! But I'm glad that she gave him the fig and ran out of the theater.

NISSEL. So what does the *Herald* say?

KLAMMER. The *Herald* says the Jews in New York are to blame for this failure, for allowing their theater to be under an elevator train.

NISSEL. Bad dreams and a black year on their head.

KLAMMER. So where is he, this Bucharest star? Where is he, our murderer! The theater is closed—kaput!

NISSEL. Really closed, huh? I told you they'd close the theater.

HENRIETTA. But I'm supposed to play Shulamith next week.

KLAMMER. The sheriff will play it. Who ever expected such a calamity! I owe nine months' rent. Not even a year, and I begged the landlord, but he threw me out.

NISSEL. That bloodsucker. Between him and the Union, we don't stand a chance. A black year on all of them. America gonnif!

HENRIETTA. (*Sings.*) "I'm sailing back, I'm sailing back." They may be swindlers, but you're no better, you're also fakirs.

NISSEL. My heart told me she'd sail back. I'm sailing with her.

KLAMMER. Where in hell are you sailing? In Romania you'll starve, and in Poland and Russia you never know when the next pogrom will catch you. Let's sail to London. Unless the sheriff already took over my National Cafe . . . we could have enough to eat . . . (SHOLEM *enters from bedroom.*)

SHOLEM. Mr. Rapalesco told me to tell all of you to leave.

NISSEL. That's all we need, for that barefoot clown to throw us out.

HENRIETTA. No one throws me out. I sail away on my own power.

SHOLEM. Sail in good health. Give our regards to Getzel ben Petzel.

NISSEL. (*As* SHOLEM *edges away from him to outer door.*) You dare talk that way to my sister! I came to talk business with that faded star . . . (NISSEL *swings at* SHOLEM *just as the outer door opens and* BREINDELE KOSSAK *enters. His swing lands a slap on her as* SHOLEM *ducks and runs out into bedroom.*)

BREINDELE. I'm only an orphan. Whoever lifts a hand to me should be paralyzed that way! (NISSEL *relents, withdraws as he wipes his perspiration.*) So that's the thanks I get for running to a lawyer to arrest Rapalesco for breach of promise and get him to marry Henrietta, you slap me . . . !

KLAMMER. Who asked you to tell us to come to America?

SHOLEM. *(Re-enters)* Mr. Rapalesco says unless you will all leave in a nice way right now, he'll phone the police to take you away in an ambulance.

BREINDELE. *(Shrieking.)* In an ambulance! He'll need an ambulance before I'm through with him! I imported him to America . . . *(To* SHOLEM.*)* You and your ugly face, go tell your friend no one treats Breindele Cherniak like . . . (RAPALESCO *enters. She attacks him.)* So, that's the way you repay me for telling you where your darling Reizele is? For me being the first one to tell you about your mother's death? The cholera should grab you!

RAPALESCO. My friends, I asked you in a nice way to leave me.

KLAMMER. Because of you I lost my money, my natioal pride, and maybe my restaurant. Who knows, maybe even my wife. I won't argue with you, but where can I go, how can I go home? Where?

NISSEL. Where can a man go when he's so tied up in the theater? All right, I won't manage you any more. I'll manage my sister the beautiful prima donna. I'll even manage my brother Isaac; he's a better Uriel Acosta than you, even a Hamlet. We in the theater can even go back to the circus. But where can this poor man go, the man who had faith in us, our Mr. Klammer?

BREINDELE. So he lost his money. Why should I care. He didn't want to give me, Breindele Kossak, a chance to act. He can go to the devil. That goes for all of you. Have a big "success" and goodbye! *(She stalks out.)*

KLAMMER. That's the theater. When you work together you're inseparable comrades. But after that, no one else exists except the next role. As the Englishman says, like a ship they come and go.

NISSEL. *(At door, referring to* BREINDELE.*)* She's a good actress. I'll need her. *(Turns to* RAPALESCO.*)* Well, the devil take you, I think you're the best Uriel Acosta they'll ever get in America.

KLAMMER. This entire business is like a big joke. I'm a joke. Shakespeare said, "The world's a stage and we're all actors." *(He points to* RAPALESCO, HENRIETTA, *and* NISSEL.*)* He's an actor, she's an actress, and you're a manager. And I am only a restaurant keeper—all in fun. *(Weeps.)* Once I was . . . *(Song: He sings "Vos Iz Geven Iz Geven Iz Nito."* RAPALESCO *gives him money.)* Thank you, you are a gentleman.

NISSEL. Whatever else, I knew he's a gentleman. (KLAMMER, NISSEL, *and* HENRIETTA *exit.)*

RAPALESCO. I pity all of them.

SHOLEM. A pity on Henrietta, too. It's not your fault that you have such a great love instead of her. I, too, suffer from the same sickness. Everytime I see Zlatka, look into her eyes, and now the baby—such a beautiful boy, he lies in his cradle and laughs. I love him as though he were my own.

RAPALESCO. I'll do the right thing. But my heart is with someone else.

SHOLEM. Why should the world stand in your way? You're an artiste, and your heart yearns for another. With her, God will help you. But the child must have a father. Leibele, your son will never find anyone who loves him more than I do. I will raise you an Acosta who will stand like the strongest tree. Mama Sarah is willing. Zlatka herself believes it's for the best. She's lonely, I'm lonely. I'll find something to make us a living, for Zlatka and the child, and, long should she live, for Mama Sarah. I don't care if I work in the theater or not . . . for my new family I would . . . *(A knock on the door.)*

RAPALESCO. Come in.

BELLHOP. *(Enters and holds a letter.)* Mr. Rapalesco, I have a letter for you. *(RAPALESCO takes letter, tips BELL-HOP who exits, tears open envelope nervously, and starts reading.)*

RAPALESCO. "My dearest wandering star," . . . it's from her, from Reizele . . . *(Quietly at first, then agitatedly, he reads, sits, rises, while SHOLEM looks at him as though he were mad.)*

SHOLEM. Nu, good or bad news?

RAPALESCO. *(Reading aloud.)* "The ridiculous fantasies of the worst romantic novel couldn't tangle up one event with another as does life itself. The events of last night upset me so that I don't know how I lived through it. Would that I could tell you one hundredth of what lies in my heart. If my heart hasn't broken when I found you to be the real Acosta, it must mean that my heart is made of steel. How I wanted to jump from my box onto the stage, embrace you and shout, 'Leibele, my Leibele.' But I had to escape from the theater because of the scandalous speech by your idiotic manager who identified me, and because—I am pained to write this—because you are pledged to another.

SHOLEM. That Klammer and Nissel should sink into hell.

RAPALESCO. *(Continuing to read.)* "I came home and wept. I cried all night . . . I cried for our happy life long ago, for our youth that has fled, for our early love. As I write, I kiss you— we owe each other so many kisses. Do you remember the night of the fire? Our vows to each other? Alas, all that now must be buried. For it is too late. Grisha, my fiancé, insisted he won't wait any longer. With grief I consented, for now I know I must not stand in the way of your happiness, too. I saw her in the box next to mine. She is beautiful and talented. I hope you will be very happy with her. What use is it for me to dwell on what might have been. At Grisha's insistence, my mother consented to set aside her religious scruples for this month of lamentation so that we will be married tomorrow. The ceremony will be at the residence of the famous Lomzer Cantor, so that my mother will be happy with a real Kosher affair. I may be wed to another, but my heart and soul are yours forever. You, too, may be wed to another by the time this reaches you. I kiss you, do you hear, I kiss you, dear wandering star. With heavy heart, your falling star, Reizele." *(Agitated, tearful.)* I kiss you, too. *(He suddenly springs into action, grabs his outer coat and prepares to leave.)* Sholem, kiss Zlatka for me, the child too, and Mama Sarah. Be a good father to the boy. You'll never regret it, even if I have to steal to do it.

SHOLEM. Where, what . . . ?

RAPALESCO. I'm going to a wedding. Wish me luck . . . *(He quickly exits as curtain falls.)*

SCENE 7

At the home of the LOMZER CANTOR. *Down stage right is a small room in which* ROSA, *dressed in a simple bridal gown, is being arranged by her mother* LEAH. *The rest of the scene is the large room we visited at* RAPALESCO'S *"engagement party." It is now festively decorated with flowers, and a "chupah," the traditional canopy for a Jewish wedding. Chairs are arranged for guests. The* LOMZER CANTOR *in his splendor stands at the ready under the canopy. His children—the choir—flank him in readiness. The* CANTOR *is giving last minute instructions to the choir.* MEYER STELMACH *leads* GRISHA *in, both are attired in formal afternoon wear, topped with stovepipe hats.*

They exchange greetings with the CANTOR. *The* CANTOR *nods to the choir, one of whom starts playing the "Wedding March," on his accordian.*

Suddenly the scene is invaded by NISSEL, KLAMMER, *and* HENRIETTA.

NISSEL. Oh. We'll wait outside.

STELMACH. As long as you're here, stay for this happy occasion. Today I want everybody to be friends—my son is getting married. *(Ad lib acknowledgments,* NISSEL, KLAMMER, *and* HENRIETTA *seat themselves, when* BREINDELE KOSSAK *enters. She also is greeted and invited to stay.* NISSEL *speaks to her.)*

NISSEL. We're going back to England. We came to say goodbye to the Lomzer Cantor. At least I made him a success. *(Accordian again takes up the "Wedding March.")*

BREINDELE. *(Weeping.)* Excuse me, I always cry at weddings.

LEAH. Come, my darling. If only your God's holy father was here . . . (ROSA *steels herself, and* LEAH *and she walk, in step with the music, out of the small room and approach the canopy.* GRISHA *steps forward, takes her arm and the two of them walk to stand before the* CANTOR. *The accordian stops playing. The* CANTOR *sings the appropriate wedding hymn. The ceremony progresses to the point when the* CANTOR *speaks.)*

CANTOR. *(To* GRISHA.) Do you take this woman to be your lawful, wedded wife, to love, cherish, in sickenss and in health . . .

GRISHA. I do.

CANTOR. *(To* ROSA.) Do you take this man to be your lawful . . . (RAPALESCO *bursts in.)*

RAPALESCO. Stop. *(Consternation and confusion.)* Rosa, no, don't do it!

GRISHA. Who the hell do you think you are! Get out of her, you . . . you . . .

ROSA. *(Thrusting her bouquet of flowers upon* LEAH, *she rushes into* RAPALESCO'S *eager arms.)* Leibele . . . oh, Leibele . . .

RAPALESCO. *(Between kisses, and oblivious to those around them.)* Rosa, I love only you. Will you marry me?

ROSA. Yes, yes, yes . . . oh, my Leibele . . .

GRISHA. I knew all along that your heart belonged to another. I might as well be a good sport. Good luck. *(ROSA and RAPALESCO whisper to each other.)*

RAPALESCO. As long as the Reverend Cantor is ready, we'll be married now.

LEAH. With an actor! Oi gevald! My Reizele—did you ever hear of such a thing!

ROSA. Mama, I love him. I wont' marry any one else but Leibele.

LEAH. I know him?

ROSA. Yes. He's Ben Rapalovich's son Leibele.

LEAH. Oh. A fine family. Your father, may he rest in peace, he always said

he was a good scholar. Maybe he'll become a rabbi . . .

RAPALESCO. We'll talk about it, but right now the cantor is waiting, and so are we.

CANTOR. It's God's will.

LEAH. If it's God's will, then go ahead. *(The wedding ceremony continues with RAPALESCO as the groom. When RAPALESCO ritually crushes the glass with his foot, all cry "Mazel-tov." Kissing, handshaking, congratulations all around. The accordian plays typical Jewish wedding music, the choir sings, all is joy as ROSA and RAPALESCO sing "Dortin" as reprise. Then all dance.)*

THE END

THE FLATBUSH FOOTBALL GOLEM

It takes brave, adventurous minds to reconcile medieval mysticism with twentieth-century reality. David Lifson and Martin Kalmanoff have blended shtetl mores with mainstream America in this roisterous, rollicking musical comedy, *The Flatbush Football Golem*.

The legend of the Golem has for centuries beguiled champions of Jewish survival and afficionadoes of folklore. The contemporary, almost fanatic devotion of the orthodoxy now centered in Brooklyn is explored in this musical. Lifson and Kalmanoff celebrate a wholesome American football tradition and Judaic orthodoxy.

When I first read *The Flatbush Football Golem*, I was determined to stage it and create its choreography, and partake of its certain success. I particularly like the play's affirmation of traditional Judaic values coming to terms with the enthusiastic aspirations of American youth.

David Lifson has been my close friend all our lives. I've watched him grow this past century. My enthusiasm for *The Flatbush Football Golem* is manifest in my determination to direct its production.

Anna Sokolow

Anna Sokolow is a distinguished director and choreographer. Her dance has been seen throughout the world. She currently directs at the Julliard School.

THE FLATBUSH FOOTBALL GOLEM

A Musical Comedy

Book by David S. Lifson
Music by Martin Kalmanoff
Lyrics by Lifson and Kalmanoff

CHARACTERS

BORUCH LOEW, a yeshiva student steeped in Kabala
JOSHUA STEIN, his friend, All-Scholastic football star
MILLIE, Joshua's girl friend, a premed student
RACHEL, Joshua's sister, a student nurse
JACOB STEIN, father of Joshua and Rachel, a widower
SAMSON AGRONSKY, the Golem
REBBE RABBI SCHNITZER, Chief Rabbi and Yeshiva President
COACH SCHWARTZ, Yeshiva football coach
DOCTOR (doubling as Schwartz and Schnitzer)
YESHIVA STUDENTS, CHEER LEADERS, FOOTBALL PLAYERS (Hassidic students to double as the players), GIRLS, VOICE OF ANNOUNCER

MUSICAL NUMBERS

ACT I

"Havdalah; Hamavdil; Have a Good Week; Hassidic Dance," BORUCH AND COMPANY

"Moon Over Brighton Beach," JOSHUA AND MILLIE

"Behold, Thou Art Fair, My Love" (Song of Songs), JOSHUA AND MILLIE

"In the Torah It Is Written" *(Duet),* BORUCH AND RACHEL

"Moon Over Brighton Beach" *(Reprise),* JOSHUA, MILLIE, BORUCH AND RACHEL

"Don't Try to Fix Me Up," JACOB

"Go Bring Up Children," JACOB

"We're the Yeshiva Beavers," THE YESHIVA FOOTBALL TEAM

"Incantation" *(Creation of the Golem),* BORUCH

"We're the Yeshiva Beavers" *(Reprise),* THE YESHIVA FOOTBALL TEAM

"Behold, Thou Art Fair, My Love" *(Reprise),* SAMSON

"Do the Shuckle," BORUCH AND COMPANY

ACT II

"Sunday Brunch," JACOB AND COMPANY

"In The Torah It Is Written" *(Reprise and duet),* JOSHUA AND MILLIE

"The Way of a Man With a Maid," BORUCH

"Nothing's Sadder Than a Fallen Jock," SAMSON

"Who Asked for Love?" *(Duet),* BORUCH AND SAMSON

Finale: "We're The Yeshiva Beavers" *(Reprise)* and Hassidic Dance, PRINCIPALS AND COMPANY

The musical score for The Flatbush Football Golem is available from the composer, Martin Kalmanoff, 392 Central Park West, New York, N.Y. 10025.

Acclaimed by critics, Martin Kalmanoff's musical theatre pieces, in more than two thousand performances, include collaborations with Saroyan, Ionesco, and Eric Bentley. "Kalmanoff's Opera Hit of Evening," said the *New York Times* of his Gertrude Stein work. He conducted the Detroit Symphony in two of his ten operas. The Bentley libretto of Chekhov's *Harmfulness of Tobacco* with Kalmanoff's music was a triumph at Lincoln Center. His musical comedy version of *The Fourposter* was cheered on its successful tour. His concert music was the vehicle for NBC, CBS, and ABC TV and radio performances by Robert Merrill, George London, Gladys Swarthout, Licia Albanese, and Donald Gramm. More than two hundred recordings of his popular songs feature Mario Lanza, Elvis

Presley, Humperdinck, Dean Martin, Tony Bennett, Pat Boone, Robert Goulet, Vic Damone, and La Rosa. Kalmanoff conducted performances for Edie Adams, Genevieve, Robert Goulet, Doretta Morrow, Robert Rounsville, Gordon and Sheila Macrae, among others. The Little Orchestra Society performed his musical *Young Tom Edison* at Avery Fisher Hall and on radio. His *Mod Traviata* appeared on the "Mike Douglas Show" with Mike Douglas, Jack Klugman, Rich Little, and Margaret Whiting. Kalmanoff's *Give Me Liberty* succeeded at the New York Edison Theatre and on an extensive tour. His articles appeared in *Opera News* and in *Music Journal.* Crowning his outstanding career is his *Sacred Service, The Joy of Prayer,* with Sherill Milnes on Vox Records, a work commissioned by New York's Temple Emanuel.

PROLOGUE

The Sanctuary in the Flatbush Yeshiva. The setting is stark, containing the Ark of the Torah. Students, dressed in the black caftans, black hats, white shirts without ties (the typical garb of the Williamsburg-Flatbush Hassids), prominent, curled sideburns (payesses), *and prayer shawls across their shoulders, are swaying as they pray. Their age averages between 18 and 22.*

As They pray, the Voice of the pious BORUCH *rises above the Others. It is sundown of a Saturday in June, and the ritual is the "Havdalah" and the "Hamavdil," which proclaim the end of the Holy Sabbath.*

BORUCH. *(He raises the cup of wine and chants like a Cantor.)* Blessed Art Thou, O Lord, Ruler of the Universe, who createst the fruit of the vine. *(He drinks and then passes the goblet to the others who sip the wine.* BORUCH *continues singing.* BORUCH *holds up the spice-box.)* Blessed Art Thou, O Lord, Ruler of the Universe, Who Createst All

Spices. *(He replaces the spice-box.* BORUCH *then holds up a lighted candle.)* Blessed Art Thou, O Lord, Ruler of the Universe, Who createst the light of fire. *(At the end of each blessing, the others chant "Amen.")* Be with us, O Lord of Hosts, now that the Sabbath Day departs, As the sun dwindles down to a dying ray, part of us dies with the dying Sabbath Day. We thank Thee for the Blessings of the Sabbath we have shared. The water we have drunk from Thy wells hath made us whole. We give thanks unto Thee for the gifts the Sabbath hath brought: rest for the body, peace for the soul. As we start a new week, may the comfort of the Sabbath stay with us, Inspiring all we do, let it be there ev'ry day with us, Something of the Sabbath, to make our spirits soar, Bringing hope and sustenance till it's Sabbath Day once more. *(As the others in unison chant an "Amen,"*

BORUCH *speaks the start of the "Hamavdil."*)

Just as this braided candle has two interwoven strands, even so are our lives an intertwining of the secular and the Holy.

STUDENTS. *(Chanting in chorus.)*
Blessed Art Thou, O Lord, our God,
Ruler of the Universe,
Who hast created the separation of
our six days of labor from the
seventh day of rest,
Even as light from darkness.
Blessed Art Thou, O Lord, Ruler of
the Universe,
Who separatest the secular from the
sacred, the profane from the Holy,
Amen.

BORUCH. *(Spoken.)* The sun is down. The service is over. Shavua tov, a good week to all!

STUDENTS. *(Singing and shaking hands in greeting as they go from one to another.)*

Shavua tov, have a good week, ein
guter woch, have a good week.
Shavua tov, have a good week, ein
guter woch, have a good week.
May you find peace of mind and all
the good things you seek,
Shavua tov, ein guter woch, have a
good week!

(The song is repeated with an obbligato and continues instrumentally underscoring ensuing dialogue.)

A STUDENT. Ach, if I had a voice like yours, Boruch, I'd become a cantor.

BORUCH. I'm not interested.

A STUDENT. Such a wonderful career! You can sing in one of the important synagogues, you can teach, sing at concerts, Bar Mitzvahs and weddings—why, you might even become an opera star and sing at the Concord. Look at . . .

BORUCH. *(Impatient.)* I'm not interested.

A STUDENT. Don't bite my head off. At least you can thank me for being enthusiastic about your talent.

BORUCH. Talent? What good is talent when the mysteries of the Kabala remain elusive. I try and try—nothing!

STUDENT. You are prying into mysteries not meant for us. Only the holiest may be initiated. For the rest of us, it is forbidden.

BORUCH. And if enemies threaten our people, may not a sinner like myself come forth to save us?

STUDENT. Always with your hypothetical problems. Soooo, how many angels can dance on the head of a pin?

BORUCH. Sneer and laugh, but don't deny that our people have always been threatened. Yet, we survive. Why? How? Somewhere in the vast, hidden depths of the Kabala philosophy lies the answer.

STUDENT. And what would you do with the knowledge?

BORUCH. I'd do what my ancestor the holy Rabbi Loew of Prague did centuries ago in saving the Jews from pogroms that were destroying them. He formed a massive man figure out of the earth, and with the aid of mystic Kabalistic incantations, he breathed life into this being, this Golem. The Golem had no brains, no soul: he responded only to the bidding of the Rabbi. This Golem went forth and destroyed the enemies of the Jews.

STUDENT. You'd better not let our Rabbi hear you. Our salvation lies in prayer, good deeds, the pious life. (*He looks about and observes the singing of the other* STUDENTS.) Why must our songs be so lugubrious? Why not joyful?

BORUCH. Practically all Jewish music—popular or religious—is in a minor key only, except for one or two which are in a major. Maybe it's because our Jewish problems are really major, soooo, our songs are in a minor key.

STUDENT. I should think a happy song like "Shavua Tov" should ring out in a major . . .

BORUCH. Why not! (BORUCH *leads the* STUDENTS *in a chorus of* "Shavua Tov" *in a major key. He indicates his dissatisfaction with it.*) You see! Jewish music just doesn't sound right in the major. Enough already. Shabbas is over. Let's dance. (BORUCH *and the* STUDENTS *break into a spirited Hassidic dance. Lights Fade.*)

ACT I

SCENE 1

A June evening, Brighton Beach. Two young couples stand at the water's edge and join the chorus of "Ohs" and "Ahs" from thousands on the beach and boardwalk at each spectacular burst of fireworks that illuminates the sky over nearby Coney Island.

JOSHUA STEIN *has his arm around* MILLIE's *shoulder. He is a tall, handsome youth with an athletic build. He wears white slacks and a T-shirt.* MILLIE *is a delicious-looking girl, dressed in yellow shorts and a matching, sleeveless jersey that succeeds in doing justice to her provocative bosom. Her short cropped hair, her unpainted and suntanned, laughing face has an irresistible impishness. The other couple is an incongruous contrast, for the young man,* BORUCH, *is a throwback to a medieval ghetto, with his black hat, a tieless white shirt buttoned to the top button, a black suit, and a pale, somber face framed by the orthodx payesses— all suggest the ascetic scholar. He stands decorously near the other girl,*

RACHEL STEIN, *who wears a skirt and blouse (with sleeves) and whose face, despite its seriousness, is pretty beneath her glasses.*

A specially spectacular fireworks display illuminates the sky.

BORUCH. Pagan ritual.

MILLIE. C'mon, Boruch. Admit it's beautiful. It's exciting.

RACHEL. (*Conciliatory.*) It is . . . pretty . . .

BORUCH. Bread and circuses.

MILLIE. I like circuses. Doesn't orthodoxy allow for any fun?

JOSHUA. Aw, knock it off, Millie. Boruch won't change, and that may be a good thing. There's virtue in tradition that . . .

MILLIE. Since when have you gotten religion?

JOSHUA. I guess I always had it. It must have been suppressed. Thanks to Boruch, I now understand how important it is.

MILLIE. (*Turns to* RACHEL.) How about

you, Rachel? Has Boruch bewitched you the way he has your brother?

RACHEL. I think I understand him. At least, I have an open mind . . .

MILLIE. But Boruch hasn't got an open mind. He . . .

JOSHUA. Let's not get into a religious hassle again. Just look at the moon over the water . . . (JOSHUA *takes* MILLIE'*s hand and leads her aside toward the water's edge.*)

"Moon Over Brighton Beach"

Moon over Brighton Beach,
Where the stars seem within easy
    reach.
Our hearts are full of love,
As full as the full moon above.

We know the pleasures that love can
    teach,
And now we pledge ourselves each
    to each.
We feel our hearts take flight tonight
Up to the bright moon over Brighton
    Beach.

MILLIE.

Here far from the subway crowd,
Where car horns blare, but not quite
    so loud
Midst the sweet perfume of gas,
We stroll through broken glass.

We hear the soothing sound of a
    disco drum,
As we stumble over some wino bum.
You can kiss your girl, and, as you
    hug her
You hope you're not stabbed by a
    moonlight mugger.

JOSHUA. (*Spoken.*) Millie, don't keep your eyes on the ground. Just look at that beautiful moon up there.

Moon over Brighton Beach,
No need to make a speech,
That night we fell in love
As fast as the falling star we saw
    above, my darling,

I know our hearts will reach
The greatest heights that a heart can
    reach.

BOTH. (*In harmony.*)
Holding you tight seems oh so right
Beneath the bright moon over
    Brighton Beach.

MILLIE. Honestly, Josh, I don't understand you. I respect Boruch. I believe he's one of the most brilliant scholars I know. Maybe he's a saint. But his knee-jerk reaction to anything he thinks is frivolous or doesn't conform to his prescribed ritual is a bit much. I don't interfere or criticize his mysticism or Kabala hang-up. Why must he always criticize me?

JOSHUA. You're either too sensitive or paranoid. He's an unusual person. I respect his wisdom and our traditons. (*Meanwhile* BORUCH *and* RACHEL *have seated themselves on the sand and are quietly talking.*)

MILLIE. I think he's hooked your sister. Do you think he's as passionate about her as he is about his religion? Would he say a prayer before he kissed her? Is kissing allowed?

JOSHUA. Must I again repeat "The Song of Songs" to you?

"Behold, Thou Art Fair, My Love"

Behold, thou art fair, my love,
How fair and how pleasant thou art.

Thou hast the eyes of a dove,
Thy neck is a tower of ivory.

Thy belly is like a heap of wheat
Set about with lilies,
They breasts are like clusters of
    grapes.

They navel is like a round goblet
Which wanteth not honey.
They mouth is like the best wine
That goeth down sweetly.

MILLIE.
    A bundle of myrrh is my beloved to
        me,
    Ye shall lie all night betwixt my
        breasts.

JOSHUA. *(Spoken.)* That's the best offer
I've had today. *(Resumes singing.)*

Set me as a seal upon thine arm,
    upon thine heart
For many waters cannot quench
    love,
Neither can the floods drown it,
For love is cruel as the grave,
And love is strong as death.

Behold, thou art fair, my love,
My love, how fair. *(They kiss.)*

MILLIE. You said, "That's the best offer
I've had today." You've had others?
JOSHUA. Yes.
MILLIE. What were they?
JOSHUA. Well, there were the offers
from Alabama and Notre Dame.
MILLIE. Let's get married before you go
off to college.
JOSHUA. But how about your premed?
MILLIE. I'll take it at the university you
attend.
JOSHUA. It's very likely that I won't be
going away to college.
MILLIE. Oh, Josh, but you had your
heart set on it. It's not money be-
cause . . .

JOSHUA. Of course it's not money. My
father has more than the mint. And
the football scholarship would see me
through anyway.
MILLIE. So tell me already! What's the
big secret?
JOSHUA. You must first promise you
won't interrupt.
MILLIE. I promise.
JOSHUA. I've decided to go to the Flatbush Yeshiva. (MILLIE *opens her
mouth in amazement and is about to
speak.)* You promised not to interrupt.
MILLIE. *(She starts to laugh almost
hysterically.)* You . . . you . . . you
are what?
JOSHUA. I've a good mind not to tell
you. You promised . . .
MILLIE. I didn't interrupt. I'm just
laughing because I think I heard you
say that . . .
JOSHUA. You heard me right. I'm going
to register at the Yeshiva.
MILLIE. I've got to ask you a questiion.
O.K.?
JOSHUA. Go ahead and ask.
MILLIE. How about your football career? You are city-wide All-Scholastic. You've got offers from almost all
the Big Ten. More important, you've
had your heart set on it. And your
father . . . oh, my God, does he
know?
JOSHUA. I haven't told him yet.
MILLIE. Well, don't tell him when I'm
around. *(She walks a few steps away
from* JOSHUA, *stops suddenly and
looks signnificantly at* BORUCH.) I
see. It's Boruch's work. *(Silence
while she looks back and forth from*
BORUCH *to* JOSHUA.) You mean you're
going to grow side-locks, payesses,
wear those ghastly black clothes,
and . . .

JOSHUA. If you knew the true history of the Jews, you wouldn't sneer at the traditions and ritual that sustain the torch bearers like Boruch . . . and me, I hope.

MILLIE. I'm more religious than any girl I know. At premed school they think I'm a weirdo, with my kosher lunch bag from home. But I don't go around dressed as though I'm in a medieval ghetto. Hey, I bet when we're married you'll expect me to shave my head and wear a wig. *(Disconsolately, she sits on a log.)*

JOSHUA. *(He approaches the log tentatively, sits beside her.)* You've got to understand. There are thousands of years behind what I'm doing.

MILLIE. We're not living thousands of years ago. This is the tail end of the twentieth century—it's today! So let Boruch live in his own spiritual ghetto, but why can't we be devout and modern—American?

JOSHUA. I know what I must do.

MILLIE. And what will your father say when you tell him?

JOSHUA. It's my life. He embarrasses me with his bragging about me. When I meet any of his buddies from his office or from his golf club, all they talk about is football. They must think I'm an idiot savant. He's got a sports page view of life.

MILLIE. He's proud of you, and so am I. He has visions of you making a ninety-yard run for a touchdown in one of those New Year's Day Rose Bowl or Orange Bowl or whatever bowl games. You're New York's hero with your All-Scholastic and all the big colleges chasing after you—so, who can blame him? You better be prepared for a different kind of fireworks when you tell him.

JOSHUA. But he's religious, too. He's president of our synagogue; he gives a fortune to it. Oh Millie, I hoped you'd understand . . . *(He puts his arm around her and they quietly talk. Our attention is now drawn to* BORUCH *and* RACHEL *who have been sitting on the sand.)*

RACHEL. It's a beautiful night. In northern Europe, it's a festive holiday. Midsummer night.

BORUCH. At the Yeshiva, we celebrate it, too . . . not always exactly on June 21 . . . it's Shavuoth.

RACHEL. Is your family also religious?

BORUCH. I have no parents. They died in Poland during . . .

RACHEL. Please don't tell me. I know it's painful for you—it's painful for me, too.

BORUCH. I live with my sister. She escaped in time. She took me with her.

RACHEL. Is she as . . . religious as you are?

BORUCH. She is. But, possibly not exactly in the way I am.

RACHEL. How are you different?

BORUCH. She doesn't understand my interest in the Kabala.

RACHEL. What is the Kabala? I always thought it was part of Hebrew teaching.

BORUCH. So it is. But it is available only to those who are of an exemplary way of life, those who have led a pure enough life to have the mysteries of the spiritual essence of God. It goes back to the sainted Rabbi Ben Yohai two thousand years ago, and he derived his doctrines from Adam, Noah, Moses, and David. Its writings go back to Abraham. During the darkest days of the Inquisition, it sustained our martyrs. It played a role in the founding of Hassidism. Even the goyim resort to it to understand their concept of the Trinity.

RACHEL. It sounds very complicated, sort of a specialized scholarship.

BORUCH. I've been studying it as far back as I can remember. I hope some day to be worthy of it.

RACHEL. And can a girl, a woman, be a devotee of Kabala?

BORUCH. I suppose so.

RACHEL. But it's revealed only to the devout orthodox.

BORUCH. Yes . . . ?

RACHEL. But the orthodox proscribe what a woman's place is in the scheme of things, in the home, in society, in religion, in . . .

"In the Torah It Is Written"

BORUCH.
In the Torah it is written
When a youth by love is smitten
She must serve him faithfully,
Accept his ways religiously.

RACHEL.
But the Torah's too permissive
In making the female sex submissive
Yet, believe me, I'd rather be spayed
Than treated like a serving-maid!

BORUCH.
There's a reason for tradition,
Don't regard it with suspicion
But when push comes to shove
The Torah says O.K. to love.

RACHEL. *(Spoken.) God* forbid we should be atheists! *(Sung.)*
What's the Torah got to say
About a woman's role today?
To marry for kinde, kirche, and kuche,
Shave her heard and wear a peruke,
Before making love, have to say a boruche,

I'd really have to be a dumb palooka.
I would never wear a wig
Just to please some chauvinist pig!

BORUCH. *(Spoken.)* Please! Let's keep is Kosher! *(Sung.)*

There's nothing wrong with orthodox ritual,
It can make love more spiritual.

RACHEL.
But to make me stick to strict orthodoxy
You would have to be pretty foxy!

BORUCH.
After all, what's right is right.
I think you're being a bit uptight.

RACHEL.
If you behave, some day you'll see
I'll consider giving *you* full equality!

BORUCH. *(Spoken.)* Gee, thanks! Let's not quarrel. All it boils down to is the simple formula whereby orthodox women are no different from orthodox men in being shielded from contamination in wanton traffic with a frivolous, irreligious world. As simple as that.

RACHEL. Saying it with such sincerity almost convinces me.

BORUCH. Why "almost?"

RACHEL. I must decide whether it's my emotions that are guiding me or my honest reason.

BORUCH. Emotions?

RACHEL. Yes. Even though I don't understand much of your religious hang-up, and believe me I want to, there's something about you that makes me want to believe, and actually to believe everything you say. (BORUCH *takes her hand.)*

BORUCH. Oh, Rachel . . . *(He stammers and falters.)*

RACHEL. Isn't there anything in your Kabalistic ritual that has words for love? (*Instead of answering,* BORUCH *buried his face in her hands.* JOSHUA *and* MILLIE *are once again heard.*)

MILLIE. And will we be able to get married before you finish Yeshiva?

JOSHUA. I'd like to get married tomorrow. But how about your med school?

MILLIE. We can get married whenever you say.

JOSHUA. Maybe we should wait until I finish Yeshiva.

MILLIE. Maybe we can meanwhile live together like . . .

JOSHUA. Like nobody, period.

MILLIE. Ho, ho, you've become a puritan.

JOSHUA. It is against orthodox principles. And how about your family and mine? They'd disown us.

MILLIE. Does orthodoxy also prescribe when husband and wife may sleep together?

JOSHUA. As a matter of fact, yes.

MILLIE. It's like the rhythm business of the Catholics, I suppose. My God, isn't life complicated enough without . . . ?

JOSHUA. It's simple and comforting within the life of the devout. Of course we'd easily sail through life if I took the football scholarship, finished my B.S. in business administration, and went into my father's business.

MILLIE. And I'd leave my premed at Einstein, enroll for the premed at your college, we'd get married . . .

JOSHUA. But we'll see each other all the time here. Einstein and my Yeshiva are right here in New York . . .

MILLIE. Oh, Josh, be sure what you're doing. I only want you to be happy.

JOSHUA. Look, Millie. Wow, isn't it beautiful! *They stand in awe of the splendid illumination of the fireworks.* BORUCH *and* RACHEL *have risen and gaze out at the fireworks.*

BORUCH. The moon should be exciting enough for all of us.

"Moon Over Brighton Beach"
(*Reprise.*)

(ALL FOUR *reprise last stanza.*)

SCENE 2

The next morning; the living room of the opulent JACOB STEIN *home in Flatbush. When the scene opens, the telephone is ringing.* JACOB STEIN *is heard from another room; he is loudly yelling for someone to answer the phone.* RACHEL *hurries in, en route to the telephone that is on a small table in an alcove of the room;* STEIN *is immediately behind her. He is about 50 years old and is dressed in the leisure fashion of a suburbanite on a Sunday morning.*

STEIN. Remember, if it's a woman, just get her name. Tell her . . . tell her I'm not in.

RACHEL. When should I say you'll be back.

STEIN. I'm out of town, and you don't know when I'll be back.

RACHEL. (*At the telephone.*) Hello . . . No, Joshua Stein is not in, but I'm expecting him any minute . . .

STEIN. (*Tugging at her arm.*) Who is it?

RACHEL. (*Waving* STEIN *away, while she*

writes on a pad adjacent to the telephone.) Yes . . . yes . . . Coach O'Connell, with two ns and two ls, area code 219, yes, I've got it, yes, operator 51. Thank you. (RACHEL *replaces the receiver.)*

STEIN. O'Connell? Who is it? Why didn't you let me talk with him?

RACHEL. It wasn't for you. It was *not* a woman. It was for Josh.

STEIN. So tell me already. Who is this O'Connell?

RACHEL. The coach of the Notre Dame football team. He wanted . . .

STEIN. I know already what he wanted. It's wonderful. They want our Josh!

RACHEL. But does Josh want them?

STEIN. What are you talking about! Of course he wants one of them. All the big colleges want our Josh. He's the hottest thing . . .

RACHEL. Talking of hot things; who's this woman you're running away from. You can tell me, Dad. Did you get her . . . in trouble?

STEIN. What are you talking about? Me, get a girl in trouble! Of course not. And what's more, young lady, mind your own business.

RACHEL. If you want me to lie for you, then I'm entitled to know.

STEIN. What kind of talk is that? My children don't lie. I didn't bring you up to . . .

RACHEL. But you just told me that if a woman is on the phone and asks for you, I'm to say, a) that you're not in, and b) . . .

STEIN. Enough with your As and Bs. That's not lying. It's business.

RACHEL. You mean to say you have to lie in business—tsk, tsk, tsk, tsk, Daddy, you disappoint me.

STEIN. I'm the biggest man in ladies'

underwear, and I didn't get there without . . . Hey, what is this? You putting me on the witness stand or something?

RACHEL. I simply think that I'm entitled to know what you're doing if you ask me to . . . what other word can I use except "lie" for you?

STEIN. All right. Sit down and be calm, so I'll tell you. *(They both sit on the sofa.)* Your mamma died three years ago last Purim. So ever since then, all my supposed good friends have been trying to marry me off. Now it's that sister of Lazarus. Her husband was a doctor and he left her with half the tenements in Boro Park. She calls me at the office, she calls me when I'm playing pinochle with her brother and some of the boys. He's her private detective—she always knows where I'll be.

RACHEL. Maybe she's a nice lady. You can't live the rest of your life being celibate.

STEIN. What's this celibate? What does it mean . . . and don't tell me. You kids nowadays are too fresh. You talk dirty. And what's more, if and when I decide I want to get married again, I'll let you know. Till then the subject is closed.

"Don't Try to Fix Me Up" *(Verse.)*

"I must admit I used to try to match
    you up
With accountants, doctors, lawyers,
    men like that,
And now you want to do the same to
    me,
Paying me back tit for tat, but no
    thank you!

(Chorus.)

Don't try to fix me up, don't try to
  mix me up. I'm happy the way I
  am.
Once you tie the knot you soon find
  out
You got a lion by the tail you
  thought was a lamb.

Don't try to fix me up, I'm not a
  lonely pup,
From women I could stand a little
  vacation.
Don't make me take the leap, I need
  my sleep,
And who needs all that aggravation?

If young people can't make a go of
  marriage
What do you expect from us alte
  kockers?
How little you young people know of
  marriage.
If you think I'll go to some lady's
  home
And knock at her knocker, you're off
  your rocker!

Don't try to wed me off, don't try to
  bed me off,
Like a candle, I've burned out all my
  wicks.
Little miss fix-it, I'll have to nix it—
I've had it up to here with chicks,
I know when I've had my last licks,
You can't teach an old dog new
  tricks!

RACHEL. You don't want us to worry
  about you, Daddy. Josh and Millie
  will get married one day, and I . . .
STEIN. Oh ho, so that's it. Who's the
  lucky boy? I should be asking questions instead of you accusing me of
  God knows what.
RACHEL. No one special.
STEIN. You go out on dates. Say, why do
  you wear such plain clothes? You're
  Jacob Stein's daughter; you should
  dress classy when you go to a dance
  or to a show.
RACHEL. The boy I go out with doesn't
  take me to dances or shows.
STEIN. *(Suspiciously.)* Where does he
  take you? Who is he? Do I know
  him? What's his name?
RACHEL. Loew.
STEIN. I mean what's his Christian
  name?
RACHEL. Oh, Daddy! It's Boruch.
STEIN. I asked you where does he take
  you? Is he ashamed of you or something?
RACHEL. Oh, Daddy, you always answer
  your own questions. He's a very serious young man. He's an orphan, but
  he lives with his sister. I was out with
  him last night, we had a double date
  with Josh and Millie. We went to . . .
STEIN. Oh, he goes to school with Josh.
  Does he play football, too?
RACHEL. *(Laughing.)* Hardly. He goes
  to the Yeshiva. He's an orthodox Jew,
  a Hassid.
STEIN. Oh my God! You mean one of
  those fanatics! Oh no, Rachel, my
  darling, you can't mean it. Do you
  realize what kind of a life you're letting yourself in for? *(The outside
  door is heard slamming shut.)* Since
  when does Josh hang around with
  such characters . . . !
JOSHUA. *(He enters, dressed in a warm-
  up suit, sneakers on his feet.)* That
  was great. Hey, Dad, when are you
  going to take up jogging with me? Do
  you a lot of good.

STEIN. I get plenty exercise on the golf course.

RACHEL. And chasing away designing widows.

STEIN. *(Glaring at her).* You're someone to talk when you're going out with that creep. *(He turns with anger upon* JOSHUA.*)* Who's this Jewish Billy Graham you introduced to your sister . . . ?

RACHEL. *(Quickly interrupting.)* There's a phone call for you. The operator wants you to call back. They're waiting.

STEIN. *(Enthusiastically and with a cheerful tone.)* It's one of the colleges. O'Connell, with two *n*s and two *l*s, from Notre Dame. If he calls you on a Sunday, it must be important. A frummer Catholic to call on Sunday . . .

RACHEL. *(Handing the note to* JOSHUA.*)* The operator said it was urgent.

JOSHUA. *(Crumpling the note and putting it on an ash tray.)* Forget it. I'm going up for my shower. *(He starts for the door.)*

STEIN. *(Spluttering.)* But they're waiting. Even I know about that Notre Dame. Oy, wait till I tell that Gottlieb that my son got a scholarship to Notre Dame.

JOSHUA. Forget it, Pop. I'm accepting no scholarship from any college.

STEIN. What are you talking about? Everybody knows you're going to one of the big colleges on a scholarship for football. You're the hottest thing in American football—you'll be All-American. You're better than Red Grange ever was, and Joe Namath is a bum compared with you. They got a special committee at my golf club to be ready to run a pool on your passes, your yard runs, your scoring

when the time comes. We've got this planned better than any sales campaign I have in ladies' underwear. Why, I even . . .

JOSHUA. I'm sorry, Pop. It means a lot to you, I know. But it's my life. I'm not going to play football anymore. I'm going to study.

STEIN. So, you want to go in for law, or for medicine. You still have to go to pre-law or premed. Take your time, but you can play football while you're . . .

JOSHUA. You don't understand, Pop. I don't want to go to any college, that is the kind of college most guys go to. I want . . . *(He hesitates.)*

STEIN. So tell me. It's not a barber's college, so what other kind is there?

JOSHUA. The Flatbush Yeshiva.

STEIN. *(He stares incredulously at* JOSHUA, *looks at* RACHEL *who tentatively smiles back. He seems shattered as He crumples into a chair.)* Go bring up children. You slave for them, you spend sleepless nights worrying about them . . .

JOSHUA. Hey, Pop, you're stealing the lines from my Bar Mitzvah speech.

STEIN. Don't be such a smart-assed chump. You always trusted me. You always took my word about what's best for you. Trust me. I've given you the best of everything. Don't spoil it now. This idea of yours, it's just a passing whim. Every young man goes through a phase of uncertainty . . .

JOSHUA. I'm certain. Now let's talk sensibly, Pop. What's more important, my flash-in-the-pan glory of a football season or the glory of our people over thousands of years? That's what is important to me. I'm not saying it should be for all Jewish boys. But I know what I must do. After all, you believe in our religion. You're president of the synagogue. It'll be an honor to you that your son turned to a devout life.

RACHEL. It's not a whim for Joshua, Dad. He's . . .

STEIN. Aha! Now I see where the dog is buried. It's your fanatic boy friend. First he tries to make a rebbitzen out of you, a good Jewish girl, and now he tries to made a tzadick, a saint, out of my son. Gevald! What's happening to us? We're Americans. We're not living in a ghetto in a shtetl.

JOSHUA. And what has happened to the shtetls? They're all gone.

STEIN. They're still alive in your mind . . . in the mind of Rachel's boy friend.

JOSHUA. Exactly. And all that Yiddishkeit means mustn't die or remain only a memory in somebody's mind. It has lasted for thousands of years, and it's important that we carry the torch.

STEIN. You sound like a romantic nut. All our Jewish laws, traditions, morality are in the American way of life.

JOSHUA. All the more reason I should identify with it. Sorry to upset you, Pop. But right now I want to take a shower and get ready for a date with Millie . . .

STEIN. At least go to the Yeshiva University. God knows. I donate plenty to them. After all, they have a law school, even a medical school. Your Millie is attending their premed. You can . . .

JOSHUA. They've become too secular. Boruch says . . .

STEIN. Stop! I don't want to hear what that fanatic says! So go where you like. Only don't say I didn't warn you.

(JOSHUA *exits.*) Go bring up children.

"Go Bring Up Children!"

You give your son just ev'rything
But he turns out a religious fanatic
He's like a loony moony freak
With bats up in his attic.

(Chorus.)

Go bring up children, it's a thankless
    job at best.
You work for them, you slave for
    them, you're always
    secondguessed.
Go bring up children, knock yourself
    out and what have you got?
You give 'em the best of ev'rything
    and still they go to pot.
        (*Last time:* "Oy, Gevalt!")

You bring your girl up proper,
You do all you possibly can
But when she brings home a
    roommate
It isn't even a man!

(Spoken.) "A Les-bi-an! Is she
    Jewish?"

(Chorus.)

You spend your hard-earned shekels
To get your child a Ph.D.
But after ten long years in college
He doesn't know from A B C!

(Chorus.)

You kill yourself to help 'em
But they end up a walking
    catastrophe.

You wonder why you bothered to   When they make such an ass o' me!
    whelp 'em
                                                          (*Chorus.*)

SCENE 3

The interior of the Flatbush Yeshiva.   "shape up," as you might say it, in
The prologue to this scene is a dance   their studies, but they must demon-
fantasy. Some Yeshiva STUDENTS *are*   strate their devotion, their dedication
standing in prayer. One of them ap-   to our Holy Torah.
proaches a window, becomes excited by   STEIN. I've seen enough to be con-
what he sees, and beckons the others   vinced that this is an outstanding
(all of whom are dressed in the same   center of learning, not only theologi-
fashion as BORUCH *whom we encoun-*   cally, but also in its awareness of the
tered in the first scene) to look out upon   real world.
what he has seen. From their gestures   RABBI SCHNITZER. I couldn't have put it
we learn that they are seeing boys play-   better myself. Our sages tell us that
ing ball on the street outside. They   our real world is guided by our spir-
dance a pantomime of a football scrim-   itual world, and our spiritual world is
mage.   inspired by the real world.
                                                      STEIN. Tell me, Rabbi, or should I say
Suddenly, the REBBE *enters, is aghast*   Rebbe?
at the frivolity, admonishes the stu-   RABBI SCHNITZER. Suit yourself.
dents, and they return to their ritu-   "Rebbe" is the colloquial, a sort of
alistic swaying.   affectionate address, while Rabbi is
                                                      more formal. Between the two of us, I
At the conclusion of this ritualistic   wold be honored if you said "Rebbe."
dance of the Hassidm, the STUDENTS   STEIN. So, tell me, Rebbe, my son en-
seat themselves, seminar-fashion,   rolls here, he goes through his course
around a large table, and the REBBE, *at*   of studies, then what?
the head of the table, holds forth on the   RABBI SCHNITZER. What, you ask? Pos-
day's lesson.   sibly a more fulfilled human being.
                                                      Possibly a Jew who is at peace with
STEIN *and the Chief Rabbi (*RABBI   himself and with his world. More
SCHNITZER*), who is head of the*   likely a young man who has dis-
Yeshiva, enter the scene as though they   covered, who has learned eternal
are on an inspection tour, which in fact   truths that will guide him toward the
they are. RABBI SCHNITZER *is most dig-*   Socratic "good life." Oh, you raise
nified, dressed in the usual black, but   your eyebrows at the mention of a
he wears a yarmulka rather than a hat.   pagan sage other than our Judaic
                                                      magids or lamden. The world of
RABBI SCHNITZER. These are our ad-   knowledge, of eternal truths, is uni-
    vanced students. Not only must they   versal.

STEIN. Look, Rebbe, I'm a practical man, but I'm a good Jew. I'm not as pious as you, nor as devout as your students. I now find out that I'm not even as devout as my son.

RABBI SCHNITZER. Your son, Joshua. I've met him. You should be proud of him.

STEIN. Yes, I'm proud, all right. But I think not for the reason you have in mind.

RABBI SCHNITZER. Oh, yes, I am proud of him not only because he's a good Jew, but for the fact that he's an outstanding athlete.

STEIN. So you know about him being the outstanding, most promising football player in the country?

RABBI SCHNITZER. Don't be misled by our religious way of life, Mr. Stein. We are very much part of the world. Yes, I know about Joshua's great promise as a football player. The fact that he wants to give up all that glory because of his religious dedication is rare. It is an indication of a strong yet humble character.

STEIN. Tell me, Rabbi, I mean Rebbe, do the students in the Yeshiva spend all their time studying and praying. How about sports?

RABBI SCHNITZER. Oh, no. I assure you, they are normal, wholesome young men. We have a fine chess team.

STEIN. And football?

RABBI SCHNITZER. Alas, no. Perhaps we may be able, one day, to add soccer to our intramurals, but football is not conceivable.

STEIN. Why not?

RABBI SCHNITZER. It really never occurred to us. But suppose it did, we'd need a football stadium, additional personnel such as coaches, uniforms, travel expenses to compete with other colleges, and so on. Then, most college games are on Saturdays, and that is absolutely impossible.

STEIN. Let's take the last item first: nowadays, with lighted stadiums, many games are played at night. So the games can be played on Saturdays after sundown, after Havdalah. As for the expenses, the cost of equipping a team and training it, let us say that would be my department. I'm ready to make a substantial endowment to the Yeshiva for a football team.

RABBI SCHNITZER. It's very tempting. But I cannot decide unilaterally. We have a board of trustees, an academic council. Of course, I can consult them quickly and give you a decision in a week or, at the most, ten days.

STEIN. You might tell them that my endowment would cover at least four years. I believe that will give the Yeshiva time to develop an outstanding team, get enough money in gate receipts so that the program will be self-sustaining. After all the Catholics are very religious, and their colleges have outstanding football teams. The Yeshiva team will be able to play them, even Notre Dame.

RABBI SCHNITZER. Did you have any dollar figure in mind? The trustees and the academic council will ask me . . .

STEIN. Of course they will. Before I tell you, I want you to know that my figures are based on a survey I made as to the cost. That will include scholarships to attract good players . . .

RABBI SCHNITZER. We have a scholarship fund. But the recipients must meet our admission standards.

STEIN. Naturally. My grant will have no strings attached except that the money must be devoted to a football program. Now I figured $250,000 per year for four years, or a total of one million.

RABBI SCHNITZER. I assume you have thoroughly investigated it. I am optimistic about the program. Our orthodoxy does not close our minds to the new. It is a new idea for us, but it does fit in with the mainstream of the land, of these times, and of our youth.

STEIN. *(Withdrawing an official document from his breast pocket.)* I've had my attorneys draw up the deed for the endowment grant. You'll find attached to it my check, certified, for $100,000 as earnest money.

RABBI SCHNITZER. I will present this to my board. *(They shake hands as the lights dim.)*

SCENE 4
A SERIES OF SPOT BLACKOUTS.

The locker room of the stadium of St. Ignatius College. The Football team of the Flatbush Yeshiva is getting dressed for the first game of the season. Their uniforms are black with the religious fringes protruding below their vests, with black helmets fringed with fur—the effect of their uniforms resembles the traditional garb of the Hassidm.
COACH SCHWARTZ *is delivering a pep talk to the team.*

COACH. *(He mounts a bench.)* Quiet everybody. *(A hush falls upon the* PLAYERS.) Over five thousand years of history will be looking down on you. You are going out on the field not only to play the game as honorable Jews, but in the sportsmanlike standards that have made our nation great. I'm proud of each one of you the way you have shaped up in training. Remember, teamwork is the formula for success. When Joshua stood before the walls of Jericho, his faith and that of his followers brought victory, but a victory that caused no injury or death to any participant. Before you go out to certain victory, Boruch will lead you in prayer. (BORUCH *intones a prayer in Hebrew; the others join him.)* Exactly as the trumpets of Joshua caused the walls of Jerico to fall, so will we celebrate our coming victory now with the blowing of the Shofar. *(At a signal from the* COACH, *one of the students produces the Ram's Horn and blows forth upon it.)* Now get out on that field and kill them!

"We're the Yeshiva Beavers"
(Sung by the entire football team)

We're the Yeshiva Beavers
And we'll fight to win today
We'll hock 'em so hard
Fighting for ev'ry yard
They'll schrei "Oy vay! oy vay!"
  Rah, rah.

We're the Yeshiva Beavers
Battling hard as any Maccabee

So all you true believers
Pray us on to victory.

(Interlude.)

Down with the Eli Bulldog,
Kill the Army Mule,
Schlug the Princeton Tigers,
Show them we're no one's fool.

We'll tame the Columbia Lions
Till they lie down like lambs.
Then Harvard and Dartmouth and
    for dessert
We'll swallow the Fordham Rams.
    Burp!

(Repeat.)

We're the Yeshiva Beavers
And we'll fight to win today
We'll hock 'em so hard
Fighting for ev'ry yard
They'll schrei "Oy vay! oy vay!"
    Rah, rah.

We're the Yeshiva Beavers
Battling hard as any Maccabee
So all you true believers
Pray us on to victory. Rah! Rah!
(Blackout. When the lights go on again,
MILLIE *is alone, pacing nervously.*
JOSHUA, *helmet in hand, limping and*
distraught, panting and staggering,
enters. MILLIE *rushes to help him*
and leads him to a bench.)

JOSHUA. What are you doing here?
    You'd better beat it before the others

come in. They'll be here in a second.
MILLIE. In a second. Are you hurt? Oh,
    Josh, you were wonderful. You were
    the whole team. What happened to
    the rest of them?
JOSHUA. They haven't got the experi-
    ence, they haven't got the weight,
    they just aren't ready.
MILLIE. Don't worry. Next season you'll
    win every game . . .
JOSHUA. If we survive this season.
    (Noise of approaching PLAYERS.*)*
    Thank you, darling. We haven't lost
    yet. *(They kiss;* MILLIE *hurries out.)*
    What am I saying? "Haven't lost
    yet." They've scored 45 to our
    nothing . . . *(He's interrupted in his*
    thoughts as the rest of the team
    drags itself in.)
COACH. *(Enters and busily encourages*
    various members of the team.) Well,
    men, that was your baptism—Oh,
    what am I saying? Let's say you got
    your feet wet . . .
JOSHUA. We were drowned.
COACH. That's no way to talk. Where's
    your spirit! Remember the Mac-
    cabees. It's not going to be a push-
    over, but I promise you the second
    half will be different. Now, move
    about slowly, don't sit still, not too
    much water, get some cold water on
    your faces, rub each other's muscles.
    This is only the beginning . . . we're
    going to come out on top by the end
    of the season and play in the Cotton
    Bowl . . .
A PLAYER. You mean the matzoh bowl.
    (Blackout.)

SCENE 5

The strand at Brighton Beach. The following evening.

BORUCH *and* RACHEL *are sitting on a wooden trestle that projects out from the boardwalk.*

RACHEL. The effect on my father was pitiful. He just sits and stares, mumbles to himself, and then suddenly gets up, realizes that he got up for nothing and sinks down again in his chair.

BORUCH. As King David said, "This too shall pass."

RACHEL. But till it passes, he's suffering.

BORUCH. It's expected for people to suffer when their objectives, their values are so shallow, so transient, so . . .

RACHEL. I'm losing patience with you. You expect people to live according to a remote philosophy. How about their feelings, their normal passions, their . . . (BORUCH *reaches out to her.* RACHEL *impatiently turns away from him.*)

BORUCH. That's the point precisely. Even the pagan Plato believed that the eternal idea was what counted.

RACHEL. Our minute by minute life isn't what the books tell us to do. We have feelings. We train for a purpose, we hope to succeed. Yes, we hope even to win in what you might think is a very "transient" or frivolous "objective." (*She has used the words "transient" and "objective" sneeringly. They sit silently. He is about to say something, then rejects the idea and sits quietly.* RACHEL *rises and walks a few paces away, then she turns upon*

him.) And you say that Joshua is your closest friend. How can you be so aloof from his suffering!

BORUCH. Some day you'll look back on what you just said. You sound so melodramatic about someone "suffering" because of one football game. You've seen one, you've seen them all. People watch the games each week, by the millions they watch, either in the stadiums or on TV. I'll bet that if they switched channels or accidentally arrived at the wrong stadium, they wouldn't know the difference.

RACHEL. Haven't you any idea what loyalty means? All sports are partisan. You are either loyal to your team, or you are thrilled by the performance of a personality whom you admire. All of us can't play football or baseball or soccer or whatever sport. So we get vicarious pleasure out of watching a favorite who is playing for us. I'll bet even you have your philosophic heroes like Spinoza or Maimonides. Well, my hero is my brother. I want him to play well, and I want him to win. And if you were half the friend you claim to be, you'd feel the same.

BORUCH. I've a surprise for you. (*She looks at him expectantly.*) I agree with you. But we've got to plan how to help Joshua. Here they come. Give me your hand, please, so they won't know we argued—we should cheer him up. (*Hand in hand, they greet the entrance of* JOSHUA *and* MILLIE.)

JOSHUA. (*He has a bandaid on his forehead, another on his chin. He limps.*) Did you loverbirds miss us?

MILLIE. I hope they didn't.

BORUCH. To be perfectly honest, no. Ruchele helps me forget the world.

JOSHUA. I wish I could. You're the wise philosopher, Boruch. Tell me, why must the goyim always win?

BORUCH. Not always. In the golden days of antiquity, of Biblical times, we prevailed and we survived.

JOSHUA. We can't live on yesterday's cake. We need the food of victory once in a while at least.

BORUCH. It wasn't so long ago, the Jews of Prague, in the seventeenth century, won a sensational victory.

RACHEL. I never heard about it.

MILLIE. Neither did I.

BORUCH. A simple but gratifying story. *(While he tells them, they seat themselves.)* Prague was "enjoying" one of its periodic pogroms. Jews were being slaughtered, women raped, children murdered, the synagogues pillaged and burned. The desperate, frantic remnants of the Jews thrust themselves upon the comfort of Rabbi Loew. One night, he formed out of the earth, the figure of a massive man. Then he uttered the mysterious words known only to a few, a formula that had been handed down through the millenia. Accompanied by his incantations and other trappings of his ritual, the figure of clay formed out of the earth, rose as a living man. Call it hypnosis, or what-ever modern term you fancy, he was able to control the thoughts and actions of this massive man whom he named Golem. This golem towered over ordinary men, was powerful of muscle, and completely impervious and insensitive to physical pain.

MILLIE. A secret weapon.

BORUCH. Exactly. Needless to say, the Rabbi directed the golem to protect the Jews from the anti-Semitic pogromists. The golem scattered the murderous goyim, destroyed many of them, and the Jews survived.

MILLIE. Until the next time in another country the pogroms raged again.

BORUCH. We must not succumb to cynical despair.

RACHEL. What happened to the golem?

BORUCH. According to the legend, he fell in love with the Rabbi's beautiful daughter. The Rabbi had no choice but to return him to his original state of clay.

RACHEL. How awful—how ungrateful!

JOSHUA. I wish I had a golem on our team. Wow! If I had him to run interference for me, I'd make ten ninety-yard runs in each game. Wow!

BORUCH. Perhaps our faith may prove to be our golem to guide us to victory. Meanwhile, it's late, we have eight o'clock classes, so let's get going. *(They ad lib their exit as the lights dim.)*

SCENE 6

The same scene: almost midnight.

Enter JOSHUA *and* BORUCH. *They are furtive as they look around to make certain there are no interlopers lurking about.*

JOSHUA. But are you sure?

BORUCH. For the umpteenth time, yes! Anyhow, what's the difference, we've got nothing to lose and so much to gain.

JOSHUA. It's a scary idea.

BORUCH. Look here, Joshua. Maybe I shouldn't have told you about it. I could do all this without you. All you would have to do is cash in on the glory.

JOSHUA. I'm sorry. It's just that I'm nervous. Do you realize we're actually going to create a life?

BORUCH. Such as it will be. We can't give it a soul, however.

JOSHUA. Why can't we . . .

BORUCH. You're like a child with his "Why, Daddy?" Just stop with all your questions and let's get to work. (BORUCH *starts pacing off a measurement in the sand.*) We can't have him grotesque. If we make him too tall we'll run into problems. Let's say around six and a half feet.

JOSHUA. That's reasonable.

BORUCH. Weight?

JOSHUA. Not too much or he'll be sluggish in running. Let's say not less than two hundred pounds. Over that is your guess.

BORUCH. Start in on his feet, I'll work above his hips. (BORUCH *and* JOSHUA *silently work at sculpting a figure in the sand. The lights dim briefly to indicate the passage of perhaps an hour. The lights rise—they are rays from the arc lights on the boardwalk—to reveal* BORUCH *and* JOSHUA *who have finished the figure in the sand.*)

JOSHUA. (*Rising and appraising his work.*) That doesn't look bad at all. I wish Millie and Rachel were here. They'd give me some pointers in anatomy.

BORUCH. That would have spoiled it all. Women are not permitted to these secret rites. And it's a secret. They mustn't know. (BORUCH *rises and looks at the completed figure.*) That's it. What do you think?

JOSHUA. Looks like Michelangelo's Moses without the horns.

BORUCH. That's not a beard, it's the shadow.

JOSHUA. Now what?

BORUCH. You must leave me now. You can go home and the golem—hey, what shall we name him?

JOSHUA. That's easy. Samson Agonistes.

BORUCH. It can't be "Agonistes." Let's make it Samson . . . Agronsky. So, you can go home and tomorrow morning, Mr. Samson will register at the Yeshiva. Between now and then I will instruct him and he will do everything exactly as I tell him.

JOSHUA. Gosh, can't I see him, talk to him, when he stands up?

BORUCH. All right, we'll meet you in half an hour in front of the delicatessen at the BMT station. (JOSHUA *exits.* BORUCH *removes, from a pouch he had been carrying, his phylacteries, and accompanies himself in a chanted prayer as he places them on his forehead and wraps them around his forearm. He chants the incantation.*)

"Incantation at the Creation of the Golem"
Boruch ataw Adonoy, Elohenu, melech ho-olum
Blessed art Thou, O Lord
King of all creation,
Help us now, O Lord, to overcome
Those who seek our annihilation

We humbly acknowledge that Thou alone hast the right
To breathe the fire of life into mortal clay

Thus we invoke Thee now in our
darkest night
To let this creature see the light of
day.

For the glory of Thy people in this
hour of need
We beg Thee our most fervent prayer
to heed
Bring forth tonight from this lifeless
sand and stone
A mighty being made of flesh and
bone

Let him be a giant among men.
Let him, like Samson of old, have
the strength of ten!

O Lord, take fire, air, water, and
earth,
Combine them now in this mighty
Golem's birth!

*(He then goes into a trancelike dance,
chants the secret words to invoke the
spirits that will breathe life into the
clay figure, and soon ghost-like figures appear and join him in a dance
of mystic character.*

*There is a moaning and a stirring by
the clay figure, and the spirits huddle
in awe. A fainting* BORUCH *falls ex-
hausted down upon the sand.*

The GOLEM *rises, waves his arms and
the Spirits fade out of the scene. The*
GOLEM *helps* BORUCH *to his feet.)*

SAMSON. Who are you? Who am I?
Where are we?
BORUCH. You are Samson Agronsky, a
pious Jewish student. I am Boruch
Loew, your fellow student. (BORUCH
*stands away from Samson, and
speaks in a ritualistic, portentous
voice.)* Samson Agronsky, you are a
devout, orthodox Jew. Your age to be
registered at the Yeshiva is twenty.
You are a serious and accomplished
scholar of the Torah. Henceforth you
will think, speak, live only as I direct
you. If you have any problems, you
will consult me, and me only, and not
do anything without my instructions.
Do you understand.
SAMSON. Yes, Boruch Loew.
BORUCH. We will now go to meet your
fellow student, Joshua Stein. He is
Captain of the Yeshiva football team.
In the game of football, which you are
to play, you will follow his instruc-
tions only.
SAMSON. Yes, Boruch Loew. (JOSHUA
breathlessly rushes in. He is awed by
SAMSON. JOSHUA *frantically draws*
BORUCH *aside.)*
JOSHUA. Boruch, the most terrible thing
. . . I formed him below the hips . . .
BORUCH. Looks good to me.
JOSHUA. Millie should have helped me.
She knows anatomy from premed.
BORUCH. So tell me already.
JOSHUA. I forgot to circumcise him.
BORUCH. And a belly button . . . ?
(Blackout.)

SCENE 7

*The locker room of the Fordham Sta-
dium just before the Fordham-Yeshiva
game. The Yeshiva* PLAYERS *have just*
*about completed dressing into their
uniforms.* MILLIE *and* RACHEL, *dressed
in cheerleading outfits, enthusiastically*

lead in singing the team "We're the Yeshiva Beavers," followed by a cheer.

ALL. Alamem, alamem, alamem kochtechho / Yitzhek di boom-boom, rah, rah, rah! Yay Team! (JOSHUA *and* COACH SCHWARTZ *are standing out of earshot of the others. They are arguing.*)

COACH. I'm the coach and I'm entitled to know what's going on. You take too much on yourself. I'm responsible.

JOSHUA. Please trust me.

COACH. I trusted you. I even let your girl friend and your sister form a cheerleading squad. The Rabbi will chew me up.

JOSHUA. Every team has cheerleaders.

COACH. I'm in the doghouse with the administration. They're screaming murder—NO WOMEN! On top of that, now you pull in a ringer. I know nothing about your friend Samson.

JOSHUA. Just this once, just trust me, please. I'll never ask you for another favor. I worked all week with him. You saw both of us in scrimmage yesterday. Well, what did you think?

COACH. (*Grudgingly.*) So, O.K., he was wonderful. So what happens when he gets up against the real McCoy? Those goyim from Fordham will murder him. At least, with his size, let's put him in the line, center or tackle.

JOSHUA. He'll amaze you. He's the perfect fullback. I worked out all the plays with him. He'll be the perfect running interference for me.

COACH. But when I tell him anything, he stands there like a dunce, like a golem.

JOSHUA. What do you want, a braggart who's a phoney or a silent man who delivers? I know we'll make history today. Fordham is the number one team in the East. They won't be after today.

COACH. But fullback? Just look at his weight.

JOSHUA. He's as fast as an eagle. Just wait and see . . .

COACH. What have we got to lose! We can't do worse than we did with St. Ignatius. (*He turns from* JOSHUA *and calls out.*) Hey, Samson, come over here. (SAMSON, *bigger and more formidable in his padded uniform, approaches* JOSHUA *and the* COACH.) What do they feed you? My God, you're big.

SAMSON. Boruch says that's good for football players.

COACH. "Boruch says." Don't you think for yourself? This is football, man. You've got to be quick and make quick decisions—by yourself. Now listen, I've watched you all week. I think you'll be excellent in the line as center or tackle. Joshua wants you in the backfield. I'm going to take a chance with you. You'll play fullback. But on one condition: Joshua carries the ball and you run interference only. Get it?

SAMSON. (*Vacantly nodding his head.*) Yes.

COACH. (*Feeling* SAMSON's *muscles.*) Doesn't feel too flabby to me. Anyhow, you're to go on a diet. The human body is 93 percent liquid. Cut down on salt and spices; they help liquid remain in the system. No booze of any kind. More proteins, no sweets. I'll get you a mimeographed diet.

SAMSON. I like kishke.

COACH. That's the first thing you cut out. You need more muscle and less fat. (*He turns to* JOSHUA.) It's your show. Remember, if they slaughter us today, you'll take the blame.

JOSHUA. (*To the* COACH *who leaves him and* SAMSON.) No sweat. I'll gladly take the blame for winning the game. (COACH *takes his stand to give his pre-game pep talk.* SAMSON, *who has found a paper cup, starts spitting into it.* JOSHUA *observes* SAMSON.) Hey, what are you doing?

SAMSON. Losing weight.

JOSHUA. Don't do it when other people are around. It's not polite.

COACH. Well, men, you're going out to the big test. So we lost last week. What's passed is past. Forget it. We're going to win today. Fordham is leading the Eastern conference. We win this game and we'll sail right into the Cotton Bowl game on New Year. We learned our lesson last week. Today it's a new ball game. You've got the stuff. Now get out there and fight as you've never fought before. We're going to make history today. Up and at 'em! (*All the men exit. The stage is empty for a moment.* SAMSON *rushes back in, finds a cup, spits into it, and quickly exits. Lights dim, then come on accompanied by the offstage cheering in the stadium. Loudspeaker blares the sounds and the voice of the* ANNOUNCER.)

ANNOUNCER. What a ball game! This game will go down in the annals of football history. The invincible Fordham Rams have been stopped in their tracks. There he goes . . . Joshua Stein is carrying the ball. What speed! His one-man interference is an unknown; here's his name, Samson Agronsky. Tomorrow the world will wake up with a new football hero. It's been like this all evening. Stein has been famous for his passing. But in this game he's passed only once, in the first quarter. He's been making line drives, end runs, and gosh, I'd even say he's hurdled over the Rams. There he goes! Agronsky mows them down out of his path. Stein could make it in a walk behind him. It's uncanny. Zowie! Another touchdown. Yeshiva 42, Fordham 0. I can't believe it. The Rams are stunned. If you must know, I'm stunned. Two minutes to go in the last quarter. If I didn't see it with my own eyes, I wouldn't believe it. Only a miracle can save Fordham from a shut-out. There's the kick-off. Stein is getting ready to receive. Wait, there's an accident. He slips. He's down. His teammates rush to him. Agronsky is under the ball. He's got it. He's standing still with the ball. Go on, man, don't you know which way to run! What's that, there's this guy on the sidelines yelling at him. He's just another penguin in black. He's motioning to Agronsky to run with the ball. There he goes! Wow! That's not running, that's flying! He's over the fifty yard line—the Fordham backfield stand like a phalanx to keep him back. Thirty seconds to go. What a ball game! Agronsky has ripped through them, all four are down and he's away like a bullet. He's got the last twenty-five yards with no opposition. Fifteen yards to go, ten, five, he's over! Listen to that crowd . . . I never saw anything like it. I never expect to see anything like it again. There's the gun, the game is over, Yeshiva 48,

Fordham 0. Ladies and gentlemen, I saw history made today . . . *(The* AN-NOUNCER'*s excited voice fades away as the lights dim. The lights rise as the jubilant Yeshiva team comes in. All hug* SAMSON, *cheer him with slaps on the back.* COACH *pushes his way through the* PLAYERS *and congratulates* SAMSON, *then seeks out a tired-looking* JOSHUA, *extends his hand to him.)*

COACH. I was wrong and I admit it. I hope you won't hold it against me.

JOSHUA. (*Vigorously shaking hands with the* COACH.) Thanks, Coach. I'm glad you went along with my suggestion. But I'm sorry I fumbled the ball, especially with less than a minute to play.

COACH. It can happen to the best of us, we're all only human. Just look at Samson. Did you ever see someone who's more of a decent human being? He's so quiet, no arrogance, nothing of the show-off about him. Some players I've known would be strutting around like the prize champion. But a modest, decent, human being—that's our Samson! (*The* COACH *turns away from* JOSHUA *and becomes businesslike and addresses all the* PLAYERS.) All right, men. Let's go. I'm proud of you. You've all been the best team I've ever coached. We've won a crucial game . . . but it's only the beginning. We're going to go on and beat the daylights out of all our opponents, and then on to the Cotton Bowl (*Cheers from the* TEAM.) Now, I know you're all going out to a victory celebration. Joshua and Millie are throwing a party. First, everybody shower HERE—I don't want any of you going away from here all sweated

up and catching pneumonia. Next, remember you're all in training, so get to bed early. AND, remember, no whiskey, and not even beer. Now get going. (SAMSON *has gone off by himself to a corner and is methodically spitting into a cup.* BORUCH *enters, is joined by* JOSHUA, *and they both quietly confer with* SAMSON. JOSHUA *and* SAMSON *don their coats and are about to leave when they are intercepted by the* COACH.) I thought I told you guys to shower before going out. You're all sweated up.

JOSHUA. We figured we'd shower at my place and dress for the party there . . .

COACH. No special characters on this team. What goes for one goes for all. Now, off to the showers. (*He stands ominously at the door.*)

JOSHUA. O.K., Coach. (JOSHUA *surreptitiously signals* BORUCH. *The two of them hustle* SAMSON *between them into the shower and contrive to have his front unobserved by the others.*)

BORUCH. (*Standing guard at the shower door.*) I wish this football season were over already.

JOSHUA. We have seven more games— and, then the Cotton Bowl. When we're through with this season, they'll call it the Borscht Bowl.

BORUCH. If we last that long. Not only didn't you circumcize him, you didn't even give him a belly button!

COACH. (*Aproaches* JOSHUA.) Tell me, Josh, how come I never heard of Samson before? We scouted the country for the best players, and we never heard of him.

BORUCH. (*Hastily.*) He's a refugee from the Middle East.

COACH. He talks—when he does open

his mouth—better English than I do. A refugee, you say?

BORUCH. From one of those oil Emirates that used to be part of the British Empire. He went to English schools, even to one of the prep schools in England.

COACH. I'm only asking because after that ninety-yard run of his, all the sports reporters are gonna corner him. I'd like to know more about a member of my team before I read about him in the papers. I don't like surprises.

JOSHUA. I bet you like the surprise Samson gave you tonight.

COACH. It could be a fluke. But I can't understand how he just mowed them down. I never saw anything like it in my life.

JOSHUA. Neither did I—ever.

COACH. He's a valuable piece of property. Hey, Boruch, he's your buddy. Keep an eye on him. And you, Josh, you might as well know that I was gonna bawl the piss out of you for that fumble. But, next time you fumble, be sure Samson is there to scoop up the ball. He's a real credit to the Jews. (COACH *walks off.*)

JOSHUA. So, if he's such a credit to the Jews, "how come" he likes that pigskin?

BORUCH. Maybe our golem is a reform Jew.

SCENE 8

Later that night, at the home of the Steins. A party. When the curtain rises, a few girls are seated around the living room, RACHEL *and* MILLIE *are circulating with platters of food, a stereo is playing a Hassidic dance, a few of the Hassidic youths are seated and in conversation with the girls, while a few of the youths are dancing dervishlike in an Hassidic routine.*

The music and the dancing stop. BORUCH *intercepts* RACHEL.

BORUCH. Here, let me help you. And while I find customers for this herring, you bring out the vodka—and some glasses.

RACHEL. But Joshua said the Coach warned that there was to be no drinking. The football men are in training.

BORUCH. Do I look like a football man? Are you, Millie, and the rest of the girls football men? (SAMSON *approaches them.*) Hey, Samson, help Rachel.

SAMSON. What should I do?

BORUCH. *(Gaily.)* Anything she tells you. She's your boss. (RACHEL *and* SAMSON *exit—apparently to the kitchen.* MILLIE *encounters* BORUCH).

MILLIE. I heard you. You seem to be pretty sure of Rachel.

BORUCH. Wha . . . What?

MILLIE. You told Samson to do anything Rachel tells him. You're so smug. A typical male chauvinist.

BORUCH. As long as you don't say "chauvinist *pig*." That's not kosher.

MILLIE. You may laugh at it and sneer at the clichés. You're not married to Rachel yet, and you assume she'll be the dutiful, monogamous female who will only breathe according to her lord and master.

BORUCH. Look, Millie, get off the barricades. Everyone, whether he knows it or not, lives according to tradition . . .

MILLIE. You're wrong. We are going to make our own traditions. And I want you to know, not only won't I shave my hair, I will continue to bathe as I always have. When Josh and I get married, and go on our honeymoon, the mihkva in which I'll immerse myself will be in a nice soft, warm bath in our honeymoon suite at a Holiday Inn or a Sheraton Hotel.

BORUCH. When King Solomon knew the Queen of Sheba, in the Biblical sense, she didn't go to a mihkva.

MILLIE. At least you compare me with a queen.

BORUCH. Millie, when you and Josh are married, and when Rachel and I are married, too, you will be my sister. As sister and brother we should not quarrel. Our faith has survived and triumphed over time for thousands of years. I hope it will survive our relationship.

MILLIE. You always seem to win an argument by invoking religion. You know something, you're like the goyim when they say "the devil can cite scripture for his purpose."

BORUCH. You mean I'm a devil?

MILLIE. No, of course not. But you certainly are devilish. Rachel must think so. (JOSHUA *has entered*.)

JOSHUA. I heard that. Don't you think I'm devilish, too, Millie? (JOSHUA *embraces* MILLIE *and gives her a kiss*.)

MILLIE. Sometimes you are. But Boruch is more like Mephistopheles, a Faustian devil. (RACHEL *and* SAMSON *return. He carries a tray with glasses and she holds a bottle of vodka. They circulate and dispense drinks among the guests*.)

JOSHUA. Hey, what's this? The coach said no booze.

BORUCH. It's a victory celebration. What harm can a little drink do? Let's drink and be merry. (*Drinking and general conviviality. Soon* JOSHUA *and* MILLIE *are alone with* BORUCH.)

MILLIE. Joshua, you should set your buddy straight about a few things. He thinks that after you and I are married, I'm going to become a docile house cat, a rebbitzen. You may as well know right now I'm not going through with this mihkva jazz, I'm not going to shave my hair and wear a wig—or a "sheitelle" or whatever it's called . . . and what's more . . . (Their conversation fades away and RACHEL *and* SAMSON *are heard in an intense conversation*).

RACHEL. Your life must have been very interesting . . .

SAMSON. Oh, I don't know. Very ordinary, I think.

RACHEL. What got you interested in football?

SAMSON. I suppose I always was interested.

RACHEL. You've got the build for it. I never saw such a physique.

SAMSON. Too heavy. I'm trying to lose weight.

RACHEL. How? I'd love to know a good diet—a football man's diet.

SAMSON. It's not exactly a diet. You see, a person's body consists of 93 percent water . . .

RACHEL. I never knew that. You're very intelligent, too.

SAMSON. So, I figure that if I cut down on the liquid, I wouldn't be so heavy. That's why I make sure to spit four times every hour.

RACHEL. You're not serious! *(She looks at him with amazement, then begins to laugh. He is puzzled by her reaction.)*

SAMSON. Did I say something funny? *(She continues to laugh.)* I've got to go to the bathroom. It's time for me to spit. *(As he starts to rise, she restrains him.)*

RACHEL. I can't believe you're serious. Whoever gave you the idea must have been playing a joke on you. Now sit here and talk to me. Forget that nonsense about spitting. My, for a football hero you're mighty serious.

SAMSON. I'll do as you say, what you tell me. Boruch said so.

RACHEL. You admire Boruch, don't you?

SAMSON. Oh yes. I don't know where I'd be without him.

RACHEL. That's interesting. I thought Joshua was your close friend, the one who brought you to the Yeshiva.

SAMSON. Oh no, it was Boruch.

RACHEL. He is brilliant. Very serious, like you.

SAMSON. Oh no, I'm not like him. He's very smart. I do anything he says.

RACHEL. He is brilliant, but you should have a mind of your own. You can't go through life being someone else's puppet.

SAMSON. How about yourself? You're his girl. You'll marry him and have to do what he says.

RACHEL. I don't know. I'm not married yet, not to Boruch at any rate. I may meet someone else who won't demand that my life become eclipsed by his. I am a person, too, and I won't become a shadow of my husband. And you—you shouldn't be a shadow of anyone, even Boruch, as brilliant as he is.

SAMSON. What can I do?

RACHEL. You said you do what he tells you. Well, he told you to do as I tell you, didn't he?

SAMSON. Yes.

RACHEL. Well, I'm telling you to stop giving all your time to sports, to football. With your wonderful appearance, I can visualize you standing before a congregation, a regular King David leading his people. But you have to have something to say to them. Start concentrating on learning, on scholarship.

SAMSON. I will, as long as you tell me to do it. Will you help me?

RACHEL. I'd love to. The Yeshiva library is open tomorrow. I'll meet you there around one o'clock. Will you be there?

SAMSON. It's a date. I'll be there.

RACHEL. *(Reaching for a book which she hands to* SAMSON*).* This is one of my favorite song-books, Hebrew and Israeli songs. *(She leafs through the book.)* Here, look at this one from the Bible. "The Song of Songs."

SAMSON. *(Reads, looks at* RACHEL *ardently.)* "Behold, thou art fair, my love . . ." (SAMSON *sings to her*).

"Behold, Thou Art Fair, My Love"

Behold, thou art fair, my love,
How fair and how pleasant thou art.
Thou has the eyes of a dove,
Thy neck is a tower of ivory.

Thy belly is like a heap of wheat
Set about with lilies,
Thy breasts are like clusters of
  grapes.
Thy navel is like a round goblet
Which wanteth not honey.
Thy mouth is like the best wine
That goeth down sweetly.

A bundle of myrhh is my beloved to
  me,
I would lie all night betwixt her
  breasts.

Set me as a seal upon thine arm,
  upon thine heart,
For many waters cannot quench
  love,
Neither can the floods drown it,
For love is cruel as the grave,
And love is strong as death.

Behold, thou art fair my love,
My love, how fair.

BORUCH. (BORUCH *approaches them.
He has a a a tumbler of vodka in his
hand.*) That's good. You two are getting nice and chummy. But not too
chummy, I hope.

SAMSON. We have a date for tomorrow
afternoon.

BORUCH. (*To* RACHEL.) But . . . but you
and I have a date for tomorrow afternoon.

RACHEL. My date with Samson is important. You and I can meet tomorrow night, if you wish.

BORUCH. "If I wish!" No, I don't wish.
You can't . . .

RACHEL. Can't what? I can do as I
please!

SAMSON. Oh, Boruch, I have something

I want to ask you . . .

BORUCH. Not now. (*He waves* SAMSON
away and glares at RACHEL.) You
can't talk to me that way, you
can't . . .

RACHEL. No one tells me what I can or
can't do. I'm not your slave, con-
cubine, nor submissive wife—if I'll
ever be your wife.

BORUCH. What's happening? What's
made you change like . . .

RACHEL. You're the one who changed.
You were always so charmingly gentle, so sweet, patient, and kind. Now
you're screaming at me. I suppose it's
the vodka you've been drinking.

BORUCH. I have not changed. You have
changed. It's a good thing I see you
now the way you really are, before
we're married and it's too late. So,
O.K. Have your date with Samson.
You can have your date with him tomorrow night, too, and tomorrow,
and tomorrow, and tomorrow all the
time. (BORUCH *gulps down a shot of
vodka. He turns to the assembled
guests.*) Hey, everybody. This is a victory celebration. Let's have some real
fun! Let's dance the way the Hassidm
pray. We'll call it the Shuckle dance.
(BORUCH *leads the others in a song
and dance. During the dance,*
RACHEL *and* SAMSON *are paired. She
snuggles in his arms.* BORUCH *observes them; this makes him dance
more furiously.*)

"Do The Shuckle"

Do the shuckle, do the shuckle,
Do the shuckle till your knees begin
  to buckle.
Oh, the goyim are a pious sect,

When they pray, they always
  genuflect,
But the Hassid pounds his heart
  with his knuckle
And does the shuckle, does the
  shuckle, does the shuckle.

Do the shuckle, do the shuckle,
It's as succulent as sucking
  honeysuckle,
Yes, the Zulu does a lulu of a dance,
He whoops it up like mad, throws a
  crazy lance,
But the Hassid taps his heart with
  his knuckle
And does the shuckle, does the
  shuckle, does the shuckle.

Oh, the Parsees kneel to gods of fire,
The Balinese pray and sway in scant
  attire,
And the Muslim bows his face to
  Mecca,

But the Hassid knocks his chest like
  woodpeckers,

Doing the shuckle, doing the
  shuckle,
Don't give a hoot if squares who
  watch you start to chuckle.
Oh, the Quakers when they all
  assemble
Sit around until they start to tremble,
But the Hassid has no truck with all
  that truckle,
He does the shuckle, does the
  shuckle, does the shuckle.

(BORUCH *tries to cut in on* SAMSON *to dance with* RACHEL. *She shrugs* BORUCH *off and leads* SAMSON *by the hand out of the room. A crestfallen* BORUCH *gazes after them. He takes another shot of vodka, and then frenziedly joins the dancers as the curtain falls*).

CURTAIN

ACT II

SCENE 1

Same, next morning. A large table is set for Sunday brunch. No one on stage. A doorbell is heard. STEIN *hurries through en route to the front door. He is casually dressed.*

STEIN. (*Offstage.*) Ah, hello, Millie. Come in.
MILLIE. Hello, Mr. Stein. How are you?
STEIN. Never better. What a game yesterday, no?
MILLIE. I never saw anything like it.
STEIN. Put your coat in the closet. It's

time you should know your way around a house. (*A brief pause.* STEIN *and* MILLIE *enter.*)
MILLIE. Isn't anyone else here yet?
STEIN. No, not yet. Josh is out jogging with Samson. I expect Boruch any minute. How did you enjoy last night?
MILLIE. It was a wonderful finish to an exciting day.
STEIN. This Samson is an amazing fellow. He ran like the wind with that ball. They showed film clips of it on TV this morning. Say, do you know

what he did after everybody left from the party? He and Rachel cleaned up, perfect.

MILLIE. But, Mr. Stein, I helped, too.

STEIN. Don't you think it's time you started to call me something a little less formal than Mr. Stein? I think a future daughter-in-law has a license to call a future father-in-law, Pa, or Pop or something. But not Dad. I never liked the sound.

MILLIE. (*Approaches* STEIN *and lightly kisses his cheek.*) Thank you, Pop. And here's a kiss to make it official.

RACHEL. (RACHEL *has entered in time to see the kiss.*) Naughty, naughty, Poppa. What will that widow say, the one that's always phoning you?

MILLIE. Poppa has just invited me into the family. I'm so happy, I had to kiss him. And you too, Ruchele . . .

RACHEL. (*As* MILLIE *embraces her.*) Ugh, not Ruchele. I know it's the endearing way to say Rachel, but it sounds strictly from the ghetto.

STEIN. (*Busy checking items on the table.*) The ghetto did pretty good yesterday. I got to know that Samson better.

MILLIE. Ask Rachel. She's getting to know him, and how.

RACHEL. Now, Millie. No gossip.

STEIN. Something I shouldn't know, about my own daughter?

RACHEL. He's a very interesting person. Interesting background, but sounds very mysterious. From the Middle East and England where he was educated.

STEIN. He's a quiet fellow. He walks and looks like a golem, but when he's playing football, my oh my, he's like a dancer. What I want to know is what's he doing studying in a Yeshiva.

RACHEL. He doesn't talk much, but he's a very serious person. And very pious. When he talks, I could swear I'm hearing Boruch's words.

MILLIE. You seem very interested in him.

RACHEL. He's an interesting person. I want to know him better.

MILLIE. And what will Boruch say to that?

RACHEL. Boruch is just too possessive. It'll do him good if he sees me interested in someone else.

STEIN. What a family. Thank God for you, Millie. At least, you'll be a doctor. I hoped Josh would be a lawyer or something like that. Sick we are some of the time—lawsuits, all the time. Now Rachel finds a fellow, so it's a malamud, a scholar. Maybe she'll change her mind, at least an accountant—no. It's another scholar, yet an imported one from the Middle East. (*The outside door is heard slamming shut.* JOSHUA *and* SAMSON, *dressed in jogging clothes, enter. Ad lib greetings,* JOSHUA *kisses* MILLIE.)

JOSHUA. Hello, everybody. Hey, you haven't eaten all the food! I'm starved. Here, let me have your jacket, Samson. (JOSHUA *takes off his jacket, takes* SAMSON*'s, exits briefly with them, and quickly returns.*) Where's Boruch? Samson, wait till you eat this food, a real Flatbush shore dinner, lox, herring, bagels, cream cheese, blintzes—the works! C'mon, Samson, let's wash so we can start as soon as Boruch gets here. (JOSHUA *and* SAMSON *exit.*)

STEIN. That Josh is like lightning. You'll

have to slow him down, Millie.

RACHEL. If you want a lawyer and an accountant in the family, why don't you find out what the widow's sons do for a living, Pop? After you marry her, you can adopt them.

STEIN. Millie, you talk to her. Lately she's getting very fresh. The simple fact is, the bottom line is that I don't want to get married to that widow or anybody else. Every time the phone rings, I'm scared it's that pest Gottlieb trying to fix me up with a date. If he didn't play such good golf and didn't stand in so good with the Union, I'd lose him, but quick.

RACHEL. I'll put the bagels in the oven. (RACHEL *exits.*)

STEIN. You're a nice girl, Millie. What do you want with a crazy family like mine.

MILLIE. You're a lovable family. And don't you try to discourage me. (JOSHUA *enters, followed by* SAMSON.)

JOSHUA. What happened to Boruch? He's always on time. (*Doorbell rings.*) Talk of the devil. (JOSHUA *exits and quickly returns with* BORUCH. MILLIE *takes* BORUCH's *coat and takes it out and quickly returns.*)

STEIN. So, Boruch, how's the malamud?

BORUCH. I'm sorry I'm late. They had a rabbi on the WEVD Jewish Hour who spoke of the life of the Bael Shem Tov. I had to hear it all, even though I found him wrong fifty percent of the time.

RACHEL. *(Returns.)* Hello, Boruch. (BORUCH *returns the greeting.*) Why don't you wash your hands while I bring out the food? The rest of you, please sit down. (BORUCH *exits to wash,* RACHEL *exits to bring in food, the others take places around the table.* BORUCH *returns and joins others at table.* RACHEL *brings in food, finally ALL are seated.*) Boruch, will you say the prayer, please? (BORUCH *intones the appropriate prayer. He then rises, looks at the other men in expectation. None moves.*)

BORUCH. We now wash our hands. *(None of the others moves.)* Washing of the hands is part of the sacred ritual of . . .

MILLIE. But, you washed just a moment ago . . .

BORUCH. There is a traditional ritual that . . .

MILLIE. But it all seems so . . . so . . . Oh, damn, so ridiculous!

BORUCH. Doctors wash their hands, I'm sure, before examining a patient. Yet, when they proceed with their more sophisticated examination, or surgery, they wash again to be sure they are sterile. Perhaps our ritual is inspired by the same principles of . . .

RACHEL. So, O.K. already. Go make yourselves sterile before the bagels get cold. (JOSHUA, SAMSON, *and a reluctant* STEIN, *rise and troop out to wash. When they are out of the room,* MILLIE *indignantly turns to* RACHEL.)

MILLIE. God knows, I respect Boruch, I'm actually almost intimidated by his brilliance. But this blind fanaticism is just too much. I hope Joshua won't become a slave to Boruch's code.

RACHEL. Something's got to give. I know you'll handle Josh. But I've got to do something about Boruch before we get married.

MILLIE. He's very persuasive. Just look, even your father has succumbed.

RACHEL. Pop is a good host. He doesn't want to make waves. But I think I've got a plan that should . . . (*The men start trooping back and seat themselves. The two girls wink knowingly to one another.* STEIN *rises. He leads the company in a waltz production number.*)

"Sunday Brunch"

STEIN AND COMPANY.
Sunday brunch, Sunday brunch,
When it's too late for breakfast and
    too soon for lunch.
Sunday brunch, Sunday brunch,
When you don't have to face the
    weekday crunch.

You can fill your belly with belly-lox
Till you can hardly move and you
    feel like an ox!

When you munch Sunday brunch,
Oh, you feel so lazy and grand.
When you've hardly started, you
    can't believe how much you've put
    away
And you feel so full you've got to
    rest up the rest of the day.
Thanks a bunch, thanks a bunch,
To the guy who invented Sunday
    brunch.

(*Interlude.*)

You gorge on khally,
A bagel, a bially,
Wash 'em down with a nip of
    schnapps.
You'll agree that cream cheese
Is a real dream cheese

And matjes herring is tops, no one
    stops.

Your twentieth blintz
Will make you wince,
But the first to quit's a party-pooper.
That heavenly whitefish
Is a real out-of-sight fish,
You eat yourself into a stupor! (Soft-
    shoe.)

Sunday brunch (Sunday brunch),
    Sunday brunch (Sunday brunch)
When it's too late for breakfast and
    too soon for lunch.
Sunday brunch (Sunday brunch),
    Sunday brunch (Sunday brunch)
On the day you escape the subway
    crunch.

You have time to fill your belly with
    belly-lox
Till you can hardly move and you
    feel as fat as an ox!

When you munch Sunday brunch,
Oh, you feel so cozy and warm.
When you've hardly started, you
    can't believe how much you put
    away
And you feel so full you've got to
    rest the rest of the day.
Thanks a bunch, thanks a bunch,
To the Lord who gave us Sunday
    brunch! (STEIN *brings forth a bottle of whiskey and offers some to the others. None take any.*)

JOSHUA. We're in training.

MILLIE. Ho ho! How about last night?

JOSHUA. Only one as a celebration.

STEIN. I'm in training, too. For golf, this gives me courage. You're not in training, Boruch?

BORUCH. I'll have a little one, please.

STEIN. (Pouring for BORUCH.) And you ladies? Maybe I should make for you Bloody Marys?

RACHEL. I'll have some vodka in my orange juice.

MILLIE. Me, too. (*The two girls hold up their orange juice glasses into which* STEIN *pours a shot of vodka.*)

STEIN. (*Holds up his schnapps and poses for a toast.*) Here's to my children, their friends, to my family's additions, and to the Yeshiva's winning season.

JOSHUA. I can toast that with my orange juice. (*They lift their glasses and drink.* SAMSON *does not drink, instead he sits contemplating his glass of orange juice.*)

BORUCH. Drink up, Samson. (SAMSON *hesitates.*) Don't you like orange juice?

SAMSON. I do. But why should we toast only a winning season for the Yeshiva? Why can't we toast the learning of its students, toast our becoming learned men to enrich the lives of our people, and to . . .

BORUCH. That, too. So drink up. (SAMSON *still hesitates.* RACHEL *quickly speaks up.*)

RACHEL. He's right. The triumphant survival of our people was not won on the playing fields of Flatbush or any gridiron. It's in learning where we've succeeded far beyond any other people. Samson should give his thoughts, his efforts, his brain to learning.

JOSHUA. We have to live within the mainstream of our nation's culture. Healthy body—healthy mind. And football is the main current in the mainstream.

BORUCH. He's absolutely right.

RACHEL. Ho ho, look who's talking. I thought you called such things "bread and circuses."

BORUCH. You wouldn't understand.

MILLIE. Why wouldn't she understand?

BORUCH. A man must find his place, his moment, his fulfillment in . . .

MILLIE. There you go again. "A man must" do this or do that. Why can't you include women?

STEIN. (*Bewildered by the belligerence in the conversation.*) Have some lox, everybody.

JOSHUA. Here we go again. The battle of the sexes. Why can't we . . .

STEIN. Yes, why can't we have a nice breakfast with no arguments? Rachel, get the coffee.

RACHEL. (*Mimics her father.*) "Rachel get the coffee." Why don't you say, "Joshua, get the coffee"?

STEIN. Well, because . . . Well, if your mother were still with us, may she rest in peace, I wouldn't have to ask anybody. She'd bring it.

RACHEL. Exactly. You're the MAN, the lord of the manor, the big shot. And your women have to wait on you.

STEIN. What's this all about? We are supposed to be enjoying a nice, a peaceful Sunday brunch. Can't we just eat and enjoy without settling the world's problems? Look how nice and quiet our guests are. Let's change the subject. Tell us, Samson, what were you thinking when you made that terrific run yesterday?

SAMSON. I wasn't thinking. I just did what I was supposed to do.

BORUCH. You hear that, Rachel? He did what he "was supposed to do." We all have our roles to play in this life. Samson's is to play football and do it well.

MILLIE. Oh, I see. And Rachel's role is

to play the scullery maid, to serve the men.

STEIN. What is this, a debate? Twenty questions? Let's eat, drink, and be merry. We're all close friends, more than friends. And we have an affection for each other. What's more, we're all happy about Samson's sensational play yesterday. So let's not argue. Let's enjoy . . .

JOSHUA. Pop is right. Let's enjoy.

MILLIE. It would be nice to have coffee with breakfast. (*She looks meaningfully at* JOSHUA.).

STEIN. What's the big deal—so your poppa will get the coffee. (STEIN *exits toward kitchen and soon returns with a steaming pot of coffee. He pleasantly pours while walking around the table. He tries to interrupt each argument with a jovial offer of coffee.*)

MILLIE. Your father is really a gentleman—of the old school.

JOSHUA. Wow! You want it both ways. You want women's lib and independence from male domination. Then you expect the man to cater to your femininity.

RACHEL. There are certain traditional rituals that make sense. Ask Boruch, he knows all about tradition and ritual.

JOSHUA. But you are trying to break with tradition, with the woman's place in society . . .

MILLIE. Yes, tell us, Joshua, what is the woman's place? You mean to be subservient to her lord and master, to be . . . oh, what's the use.

RACHEL. But what has all that to do with love? When you're in love, do you stop to make a legal contract?

BORUCH. Marriage is a contract . . .

JOSHUA. And it protects the woman.

MILLIE. No. It protects the family, and the man is part of that family.

"In the Torah It Is Written"
(Reprise duet.)

JOSH.
First you ask for independence,
Then you want us to dance
    attendance
And cater to your femininity,
Such behavior's asininity.

MILLIE.
You think women are disasters,
You think you're our lords and
    masters,
But we girls have minds of our own,
Of you men we're not a clone.

JOSH.
You seem to think that our
    tradition's
Nothing else but superstition
And that we try to save face
By keeping women in their place.

MILLIE.
What's your great anxiety
About our place in society?
I'll never consent to be a slave,
To be stashed away in your crummy
    cave.
If you think my hair I'll agree to cut,
My dear little man, you're off your
    nut!
For my part, a healthy pox
On ev'rything orthodox!

(*Spoken*). Do you realize the old orthodox Jews had a special prayer thanking God they weren't born women, God forbid!

JOSH.
Now, listen here, my pretty Millie,
I think you're being pretty silly.

MILLIE.
Then just give us liberty
And you will have no quarrel with
me.

JOSH.
Most gals who're glib on women's lib
Behave like they still belong in the
crib.

MILLIE *and* RACHEL.
Don't be so macho, you boys, and
we
Will consider giving *you* full
equality!

JOSH *and* BORUCH. *(Spoken.)* Gee,
thanks! (SAMSON *and* STEIN *have
been toasting one another with the
schnapps.)*

JOSHUA. Samson is lucky all right.
Nothing but football on his mind.

SAMSON. No more football.

JOSHUA, BORUCH, *and* STEIN. Wh—
wha—what!!!

SAMSON. No more football.

JOSHUA. You can't give up the team
now! We all depend on you.

SAMSON. No more football.

JOSHUA. Don't just keep saying that.
What do you mean? What brought
this on?

SAMSON. Rachel told me.

STEIN. What did Rachel tell you?

SAMSON. I should learn from books, be
a scholar like Boruch, be a respected
man.

BORUCH. That's all very flattering. But
I'm telling you that you must continue to play football.

SAMSON. You told me last night to do
what Rachel tells me.

BORUCH. Now I'm telling you to forget
that and . . .

MILLIE. What is he, your slave? Don't

let him bully you, Samson . . .

RACHEL. *(Putting her arm around* SAM-
SON*'s shoulder.)* That's right, Samson.
Don't let them bully you. (SAMSON
reacts to RACHEL*'s embrace.* BORUCH
*approaches him and tries to lead him
away from the table. The two girls
hold* SAMSON. *There is a tug-of-war,*
BORUCH *pulls at* SAMSON, RACHEL
and MILLIE *pulls at* SAMSON *from opposite the men.* STEIN *helplessly
jumps back and forth between the
contestants.)*

STEIN. What's happening here? This is
supposed to be a peaceful, happy
feast, a celebration with our hero
Samson, my two children with their
future husband and bride. Stop it,
now! Joshua, why are you sitting like
a golem? Stop them!

MILLIE. Just let him dare butt in . . .

JOSHUA. Oh yeah? You girls are starting
to throw your weight around too
much . . .

MILLIE. Oh yeah, it's about time we did.

SAMSON. I never had people fighting
over ME.

RACHEL. I won't let them take advantage of you, Samson. From now on
I'll protect you from their bullying.
What's more, I'll help you with your
studies. I'll coach you.

SAMSON. *(He stands and puts his arm
around* RACHEL*'s shoulder.)* I'd like
that . . .

JOSHUA. And how about your football
schedule?

SAMSON. Whatever Rachel says, I'll do.

BORUCH. *(Ominously to* RACHEL.*)* Well,
what's your plan? You want to ruin
the team's chances? And what's
more, are you going to let this . . .
this . . . Samson come between us!

RACHEL. Just listen to him. We're not even married yet and he's giving me ultimatums, laying down the law!

MILLIE. Don't let him or any man bully you, Rachel.

JOSHUA. You, my love, can help matters by simply keeping quiet.

MILLIE. Oh, I see. I'm to shut up when you tell me.

JOSHUA. At least when I think it reasonable for you to shut up.

MILLIE. And I have nothing to say about it? You decide what's reasonable for me to do? I'm glad I found out in time.

RACHEL. Come, Millie. We don't need these male chauvinists.

MILLIE. But we can't leave Samson to their whims. What are you going to do, Samson?

SAMSON. I . . . I . . . I don't know.

RACHEL. Let me tell you, then. Become your own man. Tell Joshua and Boruch to go play their own games, football, and whatever. You start being a serious student and make something of your life that's worthwhile.

JOSHUA. Look, Rachel, you don't know what you're saying or doing. Knock it off. If Samson doesn't play football, he loses his scholarship.

RACHEL. I'll see him through. Pop will help, won't you, Pop?

STEIN. I don't know.

RACHEL. I never asked you for anything. What happens to Samson means a lot to me. (*She crosses to* STEIN.)

BORUCH. Now I know. So that's that.

"The Way of a Man with a Maid"
(*Verse.*)
Four things are a wonder,

According to Proverbs, thirty:
eighteen & nineteen:
The way of an eagle in the air,
The way of a serpent on a rock,
The way of a ship upon the sea.

But the way of a man with a maid
Is the greatest wonder of all to me.

(*Chorus.*)

For Rachel my hopes still burn
Though I see my chances fade
I guess I still must learn
The way of a man with a maid.

Though I try to get through to her
It's like running a blockade.
What is it I do to her
To spoil the way of a man with a
maid?

It's not enough to really care,
You must possess great finesse.
If your technique just isn't there,
What a mess! What a mess! What a
mess!

When it comes to gals I've got few
talents,
It's time to call a spade a spade.
I've been weighed and found
wanting in the balance,
Don't know the way of a man with a
maid.

(*Second chorus.*)

I see my girl slipping through my
hands,
Despite the best plans I've laid.
Oh, when will I ever learn
The way of a man with a maid?

Many a man has had to sing a sad
   love-song,
I guess I'll have to join the parade,
It's been asked, "What does a
   woman want
And what's the way of a man with a
   maid?"

It's not enough to really love her.
I can't make her understand
'Cause though I really love her
This whole affair is getting out of
   hand.

I've got to put my thinking skull-cap
   on
Before the last card is played
And maybe I'll learn just in time
The way of a man with a maid.

STEIN. This is absolutely crazy. Now
I'm ordering everybody to sit down
and act like sensible people. Samson
is a football hero and he's got to
play . . .

RACHEL. Not if he doesn't want to.

STEIN. Hold the wire with your big
mouth for a while. Let me finish. You
and Boruch were happy together. So
what now? Is it all over? And you,
Millie, how about you and Joshua?
I've been counting on a doctor in the
family. You can't spoil your chance,
Joshua's chance at happiness? *(The
two couples square off and refuse to
look at each other.)* Soooo, it's all
over. I won't have it, I . . . *(They all
start arguing and quarreling. The
phone rings again and again.* STEIN
holds his head). I can't talk to anyone
now. You take it, Rachel.

RACHEL. Why me? Always ordering me.
Why don't you tell Josh to answer it.

STEIN. So all right! Anybody, answer
the phone . . . please?

RACHEL. *(She picks up the receiver,
says hello, and listens. "Yes," she answers, smiles and replaces the receiver.)* What were we saying . . .

STEIN. So, who was it on the telephone?

RACHEL. Your friend Gottlieb. He'll be
here in fifteen minutes with the
widow he's got for you.

QUICK CURTAIN.

SCENE 2

The classroom at the Yeshiva. SAMSON
sits alone, isolated from the other STU-
DENTS. *Some furtively look toward him,
but quickly turn their heads when he
smiles at them.*

SAMSON *rises and approaches them,
one at a time, with an open Sidar in his
hand and points to a passage as though
to ask for clarification. Each turns his
back to* SAMSON *and shuns him.*

The disconsolate JOSHUA *and* BORUCH
enter. They nod to SAMSON, *but do not
join him. The two edge toward the window and silently look out. The* STU-
DENTS *sit around a long table over
which the* RABBI *presides and intones
while reading from his Sidar. It is a
tableau much like a Rembrandt painting of medieval Jewry.*

BORUCH. Joshua, stop brooding. You

must get back to your studies. After all, that's why you're here. No matter what, our studies are more important than anything.

JOSHUA. Not more important than Millie.

BORUCH. Give it time. You're both so hot-headed. When you both cool off, in a few days, you'll call her and everything will be as it was before.

JOSHUA. Can you say the same for yourself and Rachel?

BORUCH. Yes. Even though our quarrel is very fundamental, I have faith in the truths of our traditions.

JOSHUA. Then you don't know my sister. Hey, you ever think she'd fall for that big golem Samson?

BORUCH. That's one of the reasons I believe that Rachel and I will make it up.

JOSHUA. You have something in mind?

BORUCH. No. But I have faith in our traditions.

JOSHUA. The way I feel right now, I wonder if I did the right thing when I gave up playing for one of the Big Ten colleges.

BORUCH. Have faith, Josh. So what if Samson doesn't play? The team has confidence, you're still the wonderful player you've always been.

JOSHUA. But we're coming up against the toughest game, with Notre Dame. If we win, we're a cinch for the Cotton Bowl. And if we lose—

BORUCH. Don't even think it! Make up your mind you're going to win. Have faith in whatever you choose. And sort out your values. Millie and your studies or football. Study, Joshua. Study the Torah. It will bring you understanding, peace, and the good life.

RABBI. (*To* BORUCH *and* JOSHUA.) What do you think you're doing! You're supposed to be studying. Is this proper behavior for dedicated scholars? For Talmudists? You are here to study the holy words of centuries of sages who kept alive the word of God, to be inspired to carry on the cherished traditions of our fathers. You will be leaders. In you will live our history and our culture. Back, back to your studies! (*The* RABBI *points at* SAMSON.) You, start reading the passage. (SAMSON *falters through a passage of Hebrew. The* STUDENTS *jeer at him.* SAMSON *sings.*)

"Nothing's Sadder Than a Fallen Jock"

When the frantic cheers are over,
When you've made your final block,
An athlete has few supporters,
Nothing's sadder than a fallen jock.

All they've written of your glory
Now is just another crock,
Today you don't rate a back-page
    story,
Nothing's sadder than a fallen jock.

Today who remembers Fran
    Tarkenton,
And who now nameth Joe Namath?
Once they would dazzle, now they're
    worn to a frazzle,
They're too lame to cut the gameth.

Oh, once you were the greatest,
Now you're just a laughing stock.
Oh, how are the mighty fallen,
And nothing's sadder than a fallen
    jock

      (*Second chorus.*)

Once the world was yours for the
    asking,

Now how low has fallen your stock.
Once in the limelight you were
  basking,
Today you're just a fallen jock.

No use to yearn for the old days,
You can't turn back the clock.
Nothing ahead for you but cold
  days,
Nothing's sadder than a fallen jock.

One day you're a hero,
From coast to coast, a great big star.
Next day: "Samson who?" that's
  you, a zero.
They can't even recall who you are.

Once you were the sportswriters'
  darling,
Now they bat you around like a
  shuttlecock,
You can't get out of your state of
  shock,
Nothing's sadder than a fallen jock.

(*A beaten* SAMSON *flees out of the classroom.*)

JOSHUA. Where's he going? Why don't you stop him?

BORUCH. I don't feel like it. I don't care if he never comes back.

JOSHUA. Just because you're jealous? Rachel isn't serious about him. She's just teasing you.

BORUCH. She knows how I feel. I don't see why she plays games with me.

JOSHUA. Just because you can't see, because you're jealous, you're hurting the team. You could simply order Samson to play. He has to do what you tell him.

BORUCH. I don't know what would happen then. Only confusion. I told him to do exactly what Rachel tells him. How was I to know she'd tell him to forget football?

JOSHUA. But you can still tell him what to do.

BORUCH. It's more complicated than that. If Rachel really loves me, she'll come back to me on her own without my ordering Samson to defy her. But what are you worried about? You can win. You must have confidence, faith in yourself. (BORUCH *and* JOSHUA *are again at the window.*)

JOSHUA. (*There he sees* SAMSON *in the street.*) There he goes. He doesn't even know how to cross the street.

BORUCH. What do you expect from a golem?

JOSHUA. The light's against him. I hope he doesn't try to cross. There he goes, oh my God . . . (JOSHUA *screams through the window.*) Watch out, don't go . . . wait . . . (*Sound of brakes of a truck. Offstage screams.*) He's hit. Let's go, Boruch. (BORUCH *and* JOSHUA *dash out.*)

SCENE 3

Waiting room in a hospital. BORUCH, JOSHUA, MILLIE, *and* RACHEL *are worriedly impatiently holding vigil.* JOSHUA *paces,* BORUCH *reads from a Sidar,* MILLIE *and* RACHEL *are huddled in animated talk.*

MILLIE. Shouldn't his people, his family be notified of the accident? (JOSHUA *looks helplessly toward* BORUCH.)

BORUCH. (*Matter-of-fact.*) I've taken care of that.

JOSHUA. He was star-gazing in the middle of the day.

MILLIE. He isn't used to New York traffic. I should think you two would have kept an eye on him.

JOSHUA. Go on, blame us. There are thousands of accidents every day. Are we to blame for them, too?

RACHEL. But you know that Samson is naive, like a great big baby and needs . . .

BORUCH. Needs tender, loving care. Too bad you weren't there to mother him.

MILLIE. I've listened to you two going at each other long enough. Now cut it out. Sooner or later, you'll kiss and make up. Please make it sooner, because it's getting on my nerves.

BORUCH. Look who's talking. How about you and Joshua? Doctor, use your own medicine.

MILLIE AND JOSHUA. *(Simultaneously.)* We . . . it's different . . .

BORUCH. Everyone thinks he's different. (*Enter hospital resident* DOC-TOR.)

DOCTOR. Are you the friends of the man hit by a truck?

BORUCH. Yes, Doctor. How is he?

DOCTOR. The strangest thing. We examined him from head to toe. Not a scratch on him. It's unbelievable. He still seems dazed.

MILLIE. How about internal injuries?

DOCTOR. We went into all that. Not a sign. But we think we had better keep him here for another day or two. You never know how these things have residual effects. We want our neurologist to give him a once over.

RACHEL. I'm so relieved. That poor thing . . . (RACHEL *and* MILLIE *converse with one another. The* DOCTOR *draws* BORUCH *and* JOSHUA *aside and speaks so as not to be overheard by the girls.*)

DOCTOR. We'd like to study him a little more. You checked him in as a student at the Yeshiva. Therefore, we can assume he is an orthodox Jew. How is it we discover he is not circumcised? (JOSHUA *and* BORUCH *look at one another, shrug their shoulders, and indicate ignorance to the* DOC-TOR). Another thing that has us mystified—he has no umbilicus. (*Again* JOSHUA *and* BORUCH *shrug to indicate ignorance.*) Well, we'll keep him under observation.

BORUCH. When will you let him out, discharge him?

DOCTOR. That depends on the neurologist. Check with me tomorrow around this time. (RACHEL *and* MIL-LIE *approach the* DOCTOR.)

MILLIE. When he is discharged from here, Doctor, should he need any special care?

DOCTOR. Plenty of rest, no excitement for a couple of weeks.

RACHEL. Well, he certainly can't get that while staying in your place, Boruch.

BORUCH. Why not? No one will bother him. It's quiet . . .

RACHEL. Nonsense. He needs taking care of. He can move into our house. Joshua can bring home his assignments. At your place he'd be alone all day. You can't leave an invalid alone.

BORUCH. How about when you're away all day at nursing school?

RACHEL. Our maid is there all day. She'll handle it.

BORUCH. You seem very anxious to get Samson to yourself.

RACHEL. That's a horrid thing to say. And don't you talk to me again until you apologize. Come, Millie. (RACHEL *and* MILLIE *exit.*)

DOCTOR. Did she say she's at nursing school?

JOSHUA. Yes. She is.

DOCTOR. It won't be such a bad idea for her to look in on him, when we let him out.

JOSHUA. What do you mean "when you let him out?"

DOCTOR. No matter what the odds, he should be dead after that accident. Not only is he very much alive, but he shows no physical signs of injury. On top of all this, he has no umbilicus. When did you ever hear of a human being, any animal, without a belly button?

BORUCH. (*Weakly.*) You've got a point there, Doctor.

DOCTOR. Check with me tomorrow around this time. (DOCTOR *exits.* BORUCH *and* JOSHUA *look dumbly at one another.*)

JOSHUA. What happens now? We can't let him come to my house. Rachel will certainly find out what he is.

BORUCH. Don't panic. One thing is certain: we've got to get him out of here.

JOSHUA. How do we do that? Did you see the gleam in that doctor's eye? He's so excited, he thinks he's found the missing link. They'll watch Samson like a hawk. If he blows the whistle that Samson is not your ordinary football player, then we're in trouble. What'll we do?

BORUCH. Stop already with your frantic questions. Now, let's figure this out calmly. That doctor is on during the daytime. He's off at four or six. The nurses change at either four, six, or eight. Visiting hours are until nine. We'll have to get here right after eight and get him out before nine.

JOSHUA. I hope you know what you're doing. How will we get him out?

BORUCH. Let's go. I'll tell you on the way out. (BORUCH *and* JOSHUA *exit.*)

SCENE 4

The same scene. A few minutes after eight that evening. BORUCH *and* JOSHUA *are waiting.*

JOSHUA. They're late.

BORUCH. No, they're not. I told them 8:15, sharp. They've got a minute to go. (*The moment he says it,* MILLIE *and* RACHEL *enter. They are dressed in nurses' uniforms.*)

MILLIE. Well, here we are. What are we supposed to do?

RACHEL. I don't like this.

BORUCH. There comes a time in your life—our lives—when you've got to accept what I say on faith. But for your conscience, I tell you that what we're doing is absolutely correct. Trust us, please.

MILLIE. I'll go along. But if I'm caught, it may ruin my entire medical career.

JOSHUA. Don't worry. We've got every detail worked out. What's more, they can't hold Samson against his will, can they?

BORUCH. And you're a nursing student, Rachel. That's your own uniform.

MILLIE. But if Samson can just walk out, why do you need us?

BORUCH. Samson may have ideas of his own. But he will listen to Rachel. That's the long and the short of it.

RACHEL. Don't sound so bitter. You told me to take him under my wing. You told him to do as I tell him. Just because you're jealous . . .

BORUCH. I'm not jealous.

RACHEL. Ho, ho, not much.

JOSHUA. See here, you two love-birds, we're here to do a job. Later, you may quarrel all you like, but right now let's get down to business.

MILLIE. I agree. What's the prognosis?

BORUCH. Samson is in room 803. You two will go in, see that he's O.K., then signal us out here. Meanwhile, I'll get a wheelchair which I'll give you, when you come out. Then you'll wheel him out, take him down to the main hall, and then through the front door. Meanwhile, Josh and I will be downstairs with a taxi.

MILLIE. What happens to us?

BORUCH. You'll get into the taxi with us. We'll all go to Josh's house where Samson will stay until he feels better.

RACHEL. That will be nice. I'll take care of him . . .

BORUCH. *(Annoyed.)* Let's get going. *(They are about to distribute themselves according to plan, when the* DOCTOR *enters.)*

DOCTOR. Ah, good evening. You really are devoted friends. I suppose you're here, visiting your er . . . er . . . peculiar friend?

BORUCH. These nurses were telling us—

DOCTOR. *(Looking closely at* MILLIE.*)* Are you one of our regulars? Seems I've seen you somewhere before, but not here at the hospital. I know most of the nurses on this floor.

MILLIE. I attended a few lectures you gave at the Einstein College.

DOCTOR. Oh, you're a medical student as well as nurse. That doesn't seem to be . . .

MILLIE. Oh no, I'm a premed. But I simply had to attend your lectures so . . . you see, some of my classmates told me how wonderfully you explain things, and how dynamically you pre-sent the most prosaic detail. I agreed with them, after I heard you, that you make the most obscure and dry fields soooo [romantic.] I just couldn't resist attending your lectures.

DOCTOR. *(Beaming.)* Well, I trust your reaction did not obstruct the substantive information of my lectures . . . *(*MILLIE *takes his arm and leads him off.)*

JOSHUA. Where in hell are they going? I don't like this . . .

BORUCH. Millie is wonderful. You stay here until we get out with Samson. If any complications come up, if the doctor returns, stall him, get him away from the elevator, try to tip us off, Come, Rachel, we've got to hurry. *(*BORUCH *and* RACHEL *exit, toward* SAMSON*'s room.* MILLIE *and the* DOCTOR *soon reappear. She is clinging to him, while he is rhapsodically talking about germs. They move toward direction where* RACHEL *and* BORUCH *had gone;* JOSHUA *frantically signals* MILLIE. *She steers the* DOCTOR *out in the direction away from* SAMSON*'s room. As soon as* MILLIE *and the* DOCTOR *are out of sight,* JOSHUA *rushes to the opposite side and signals frantically.* BORUCH *and* RACHEL *quickly enter; they are pushing* SAMSON.*)*

SAMSON. But I like it here. Everyone is so nice to me. Why can't I stay?

RACHEL. I want to take care of you, have you all to myself.

SAMSON. That's nice. But I should say goodbye to them. Especially to the doctor. He took quite an interest in me.

BORUCH. We've no time. There's a taxi waiting. You can send him a note and tell him how you appreciate his care and interest.

SAMSON. Maybe you're right. Oh—there he is, down the corridor. (SAMSON *tries to rise in his seat and to yell.*) Hey, Doctor . . . . ! (BORUCH *and* RACHEL *quickly wheel him off.* DOCTOR *rushes in followed by* MILLIE.)

DOCTOR. That was my patient. I'm sure he was calling me. What was he doing out of his room? I gave strict instructions . . .

MILLIE. Oh, Doctor, you're too conscientious. You can't be sure the man was Samson, nor can you be sure he was calling for you . . .

DOCTOR. You may be right. But, you as a student should know that in the world of science, especially of medicine, we don't speculate about "you can't be sure"—we make sure. I had better check his room.

MILLIE. But, Doctor, you have time to do that. He'll still be there. You were explaining to me the ambiguity of the difference between forensic medicine and the exact science of all . . .

DOCTOR. Exactly. Now, you take the case of the patient I've been visiting here. This Samson person. I discovered something that is the most extraordinary phenomenon in the entire history of medical science.

MILLIE. (*Eagerly.*) Can you tell me about it? Please?

DOCTOR. It's still very hush hush. I've sent a wire to a colleague who specializes in genetics. He's due here tomorrow morning. I may have to assemble an international conference of specialists. The entire concept makes me dizzy. You've no idea of the import of this amazing find.

MILLIE. (*Innocently but coyly and seductively.*) Please tell me about it.

Here I am embarking upon a career in medicine. I shouldn't really be blocked by secrets. Please?

DOCTOR. (*Responding to* MILLIE's *charm.*) You must understand that this must be kept very confidential. I really don't see how I can tell you. My discovery can lead to an entirely new field of medical research. Who knows . . .

MILLIE. Who knows—you may end up with the Nobel prize.

DOCTOR. Really? You think so? Come to think of it, why not! But see here, that's all the more reason for me to keep it confidential. I can't tell a soul.

MILLIE. But you'll be sharing the secret with your colleagues tomorrow morning; why not tell me. I promise, on my honor . . .

DOCTOR. Well, the fact is, that young man who was hit by a truck, and by all odds should be dead now, shows no signs of injury, internal or external . . .

MILLIE. But that's not so novel. I've read about a child falling off a fire escape and after a four-story fall showed no signs of injury.

DOCTOR. But there's more. (*He agitatedly walks back and forth, debating within himself whether or not to share his secret with* MILLIE.) The real fact is that he is oddly constructed. He does not have a very essential anatomical feature that is common to all men.

MILLIE. He isn't a eunuch?

DOCTOR. No. Nothing to do, partly, with his genitalia. Although I can say this much: he is an orthodox Jew, a Talmudic student, and he is not circumcised.

MILLIE. That's impossible.

DOCTOR. I examined him. I KNOW!

MILLIE. Please don't get excited. I'm trying to be helpful. After all, most of the men on this earth are not circumcised.

DOCTOR. I know that. But the phenomenal physical aberration of this young man is different from all other men. I must correct that; when I say "men" I mean MAN, all mankind. For that matter, all animal life, especially mammals.

MILLIE. *(Really intrigued.)* Now I must know. Doctor, you won't condemn me to sleepless nights until I know, please? Perhaps I can help you. I want nothing except to share in your reflected glory of this great discovery. Please?

DOCTOR. Yes, I'll tell you. This young man, his name is Samson something or other, an orthodox Jew, a Hassid, is not only not circumcised, but—get this now—he has no umbilicus, no sign of a belly button!

MILLIE. Fantastic! It's impossible. Wait till I tell Rachel . . .

DOCTOR. But you promised to keep it a secret.

MILLIE. Don't worry, Doctor. I'll only tell her that he's not circumcised. No belly button—that will be our secret. (MILLIE *turns to go.*)

DOCTOR. Will I see you at my next lecture?

MILLIE. Definitely. I couldn't stay away. *(Smiling with affected shyness,* MILLIE *leaves. The* DOCTOR *exits in direction of* SAMSON's *room. The stage is empty for a moment. Suddenly, the* DOCTOR *comes staggering back.)*

DOCTOR. He's gone! Nurse, Nurse . . . (DOCTOR *runs off in direction which* MILLIE *exited.)*

SCENE 5

The STEIN's *living room again.* JOSHUA *sits unhappily with his head in his hands.* BORUCH *paces about.*

JOSHUA. I can't understand it. Everything was going well. All of a sudden, we're behind the eight ball. Why can't you let the girls in on the act, get them to cooperate, and then . . .

BORUCH. How cooperate?

JOSHUA. Get Rachel to tell Samson he's got to play.

BORUCH. I can't do that. *(Anticipating* JOSHUA's *challenge.)* It's as simple as this: I love Rachel, I want to marry her. But she has become enamoured of this golem. Our love isn't merely physical—it's spiritual, it's cosmic, it transcends everything physical and mundane. We now find her responsive to this physical hulk, Samson. Well, if Rachel and I are to find happiness in a life together, she must get this physical responsiveness out of her system. I will not interfere.

JOSHUA. Meanwhile our team gets all loused up . . . !

BORUCH. I believe my love for Rachel, our future together, is more important than a college football game out of so many thousands played each year. If you'll excuse my cynicism, when you've seen one football game, you've seen them all.

JOSHUA. How can you say that, when our hopes are . . .

BORUCH. Please, let's not discuss America's opiate of the masses at this time. We've got to be pragmatic, figure out what to do. Of first importance to me is the need to be sure that Rachel is in love with me, is devoted to me, and takes seriously the ritual phrase, "forsaking all others." I want her to get this obsession for Samson out of her system.

JOSHUA. And meanwhile, our hopes, our dreams of the Cotton Bowl simply fade away while the great Boruch resolves his love life.

BORUCH. That's not fair. Samson was my creation. Without him, you and the team would be up the creek.

JOSHUA. I'm sorry, Boruch. I believe in you—if it weren't for you, I wouldn't be at the Yeshiva. I am grateful to you for showing me what is important in life rather than what is urgent at the moment.

BORUCH. I'm not looking for appreciation. I simply want the reflective life, and sharing it with someone I love, who loves me.

JOSHUA. So. O.K., we know you love Rachel, you want to marry her, you want to spend your life as the scholar, and all that jazz. But, what do we do now? How can we get Samson to play again, how can we get ready for the big game with Notre Dame?

BORUCH. You've a one-track mind. Doesn't it occur to you that my problem with Rachel is also your problem with Millie?

JOSHUA. I love Millie. I know she loves me. Perhaps it's just as well that we have this difference at this time. Oh, I don't mean that in the long run "love conquers all." I just believe, or maybe just feel that Millie and I will make it, will reconcile her modern, scientific, women's lib outlook on life with the eternal truths of our traditions.

BORUCH. You've been an apt pupil. But you still don't explain how you will reconcile modern dynamics with our orthodox traditions.

JOSHUA. Very simple. The eternal catalyst—Love. For love, we'll each give a little. Millie and I will meet each other half way. You might try it with Rachel.

BORUCH. Rachel and I have a problem that has nothing to do with philosophy, religion, nor any other abstraction. There's a tradition, when it comes to love, of simple, mutual trust, faith, affection. Rachel is going through a phase . . . (RACHEL enters.)

RACHEL. What are you two doing here? Shouldn't you be in class?

JOSHUA. We dropped by to find out how Samson is coming along.

RACHEL. You saw him this morning before you left the house.

JOSHUA. Boruch wanted to see for himself.

RACHEL. Boruch, huh. It seems to me that Boruch is much too interested. Anyhow, I'm taking good care of Samson, and he'll be completely better in a few days. He seems confused. He needs rest.

BORUCH. Will he be well enough to play in Saturday night's game?

JOSHUA. It's important. We're playing Notre Dame, and if we win, we have first crack at the Cotton Bowl.

RACHEL. His health, his peace of mind, and his future are more important than a football game.

JOSHUA. What's happened to you? You used to be so proud of me every time I won a game, when I got my picture in the papers, when . . .

RACHEL. I was an empty-headed kid. There are more important things in life than what's in the sports page. Samson is a dear boy. You, Boruch, seem to have cast some kind of spell over him. You're a regular Svengali. You seem to have that power over people. You convinced Joshua to give up a regular university where he'd fit in perfectly. But no, you had to make him turn religious. Now you have Samson under your spell. You had me for a while . . .

BORUCH. "Had." Apparently past tense. Let me tell you something, before you say something you'll be sorry for. I love you. You told me you love me. Usually, in such cases, two people get married. I had expected you and I to be married. But you seem to have found a new interest, this Samson person. Well, so be it. If you think or believe he's the man for you, then forget about me. I wish you every happiness.

RACHEL. Oh . . . oh . . . Are you laying down the law to me! You are so insufferably arrogant, Mr. Know-it-all . . . I . . . I . . . (RACHEL *runs out*.)

JOSHUA. Now look, Boruch. You may know what you're doing, but you sure have made my sister very unhappy. You know Samson is not a real person, not for Rachel nor for anyone. What are you doing . . . ?

BORUCH. If we have no faith, we may as well succumb to nothingness and become golems like Samson. So far you have found an enriched spiritual life, a purposeful life beyond the transient football segment of your mortality, and meanwhile you are having the best of both worlds—you are flourishing as a Talmudic scholar, and you are succeeding as the football hero . .

JOSHUA. Please, don't call me a football "hero." I'm playing the game because I love it. I want you to know . . .

BORUCH. So I know. Let's not get into an argument. I don't want you to get so excited. I . . .

JOSHUA. I am excited. We have the big game Saturday night, and our one ace in the hole won't play.

BORUCH. I've told you to have faith in yourself. You can do it. I promise you.

JOSHUA. We'll really need a miracle. (SAMSON *enters; he is leaning on* RACHEL'*s arm*.)

RACHEL. I thought you two were gone. Now, remember, you're not to excite Samson in any way.

BORUCH. Hello, Samson. How do you feel?

SAMSON. I think I feel all right.

RACHEL. You see. He is still confused so that he can't even tell how he feels.

BORUCH. There used to be a doctor named Coué. He had a system: if you said each day, "Every day in every way I'm feeling better and better," you'd start feeling wonderful.

SAMSON. (*Looking toward* RACHEL.) Do you think it would work?

RACHEL. Why not try it? It can't hurt.

SAMSON. Every day, in every way, I'm

feeling better and better. (*Pause.*) Hey, you know something—I feel great. I feel wonderful.

RACHEL. Don't hurry it. Don't rush things.

JOSHUA. Mabye, if you feel so good, maybe you'll want to play football on Saturday night?

SAMSON. (*Looking toward* RACHEL.) I don't know. What do you say, Rachel?

RACHEL. We'll see. Let's talk about it tomorrow.

BORUCH. (*Aside to* JOSHUA.) I think he'll come around. (*To* RACHEL *and* SAMSON.) Well, take care of yourselves. See you tomorrow. (JOSHUA *and* BORUCH *exit.*)

RACHEL. I'm glad to hear you say you're feeling much better. In a few days you'll be completely well and you'll be able to leave.

SAMSON. I don't want to leave. I want to stay with you all the time.

RACHEL. But, Samson, you hardly know me.

SAMSON. I know that I have an extraordinary feeling about you. I never felt this way about anybody before. Oh, Rachel . . .

RACHEL. You mustn't get yourself so excited. You must rest. But I will tell you, I like you very much. I, too, have a strange feeling toward you. I never felt this way before.

SAMSON. Even with Boruch?

RACHEL. Even with Boruch. With him, I have a feeling of belonging, of being part of him, of knowing his life is my life, and knowing that he and I are meant to be together for the rest of our lives. Now, all of a sudden, here you are. And I feel toward you as though the life I've led, the life I look forward to, everything I know, all are gone. I can't think when I'm with you. I feel like I'm only a woman with a body that needs you, only you . . . (*Silently,* RACHEL *and* SAMSON *approach each other as though to embrace passionately, when . . . The front doorbell rings.*) I must answer the bell.

SAMSON. You don't have to. Please don't leave me now. Now is the one moment . . .

RACHEL. (*As though coming out of a trance.*) I must . . . (*She exits and soon returns with* MILLIE.)

MILLIE. Hello, Samson. How are you feeling?

SAMSON. (*Mechanically, with a robot-like expression.*) Every day in every way I'm feeling better and better.

RACHEL. (*Flushed and stammering.*) Yes, he's making wonderful progress.

MILLIE. Who's home?

RACHEL. Just Samson and I.

MILLIE. The two of you, alone?

RACHEL. (*Quickly.*) Boruch and Joshua just left. I'm surprised you didn't bump into them.

MILLIE. Does your family know about your accident, Samson?

SAMSON. I don't know. Boruch said he was taking care of everything.

MILLIE. You depend on Boruch for a lot of things, don't you?

SAMSON. Yes.

MILLIE. Before you came here, were you orthodox; did your people behave like Hassids?

SAMSON. I can't answer everything at once. Boruch said if anyone asks me anything, I'm to send them to him for the answers.

MILLIE. But I'm asking simple questions. Why can't you . . .

RACHEL. He's been through a great deal, the poor boy. Please, Millie, don't badger him.

MILLIE. I only want to know . . .

SAMSON. I'm going to find Boruch. (*Despite* RACHEL's *attempt to stop him,* SAMSON *rushes out.* RACHEL *indignantly turns to* MILLIE.)

RACHEL. Now you've done it. He may have a relapse. And I've had him recovering so beautifully. Oh, Millie . . .

MILLIE. (*Smiling at* RACHEL.) You've really flipped over him, haven't you?

RACHEL. (*Paces around the room, most uncomfortably.*) I really don't know. I've never felt this way about anyone before. He's such a great big puppy. I want to take him in my arms and mother him.

MILLIE. He's quite a hunk of man to hold in your arms.

RACHEL. I don't know, I'm all confused. I may have fallen in love with him. I want to have him hold me, kiss me, hold me tightly . . .

MILLIE. And that's what you two were about to do when I interrupted?

RACHEL. Y—y—e—s—s.

MILLIE. Well, my dear almost sister-in-law, it's a damn good thing I came in when I did. There's something queer about our friend Samson. He's different.

RACHEL. Yes, he is different. More different than anyone I ever met.

MILLIE. Well, Rachel, sit down and I'll tell you just how different he is. (RACHEL *sits and fearfully listens.*) Our good friend Samson is an oddball. First, tell me, would you marry a man who is not a Jew?

RACHEL. I don't know. I never thought of it.

MILLIE. Well, think of it now. I don't believe your Samson is a Jew. (*Anticipating* RACHEL's *challenge.*) He is not circumcised. (RACHEL *rises in shock.*) The doctor at the hospital told me. He gave Samson a very thorough examination. But that's not all. (RACHEL *sits.*) Samson is some sort of mutation. He has no umbilical—yes, no belly button.

RACHEL. There must be some reasonable explanation.

MILLIE. Yes, of course. But, he's the first person without a belly button since Adam.

SCENE 6

The locker room the following Saturday evening.

JOSHUA *enters with* BORUCH. JOSHUA *starts to change into his football gear.*

JOSHUA. I've all the faith you've pumped into me. But I'd still feel more confident if Samson were here.

BORUCH. I'm glad the others haven't arrived yet. If they listened to you, they'd simply lie down and let Notre Dame roll over them.

JOSHUA. I've news for you. That's exactly what's going to happen. (*Other members of the team arrive and ad lib greetings, start changing into their uniforms. The* COACH *arrives and goes around to each player; he encourages each one. He then approaches* JOSHUA).

COACH. It depends on you, Josh. This is it.

JOSHUA. You wouldn't exactly be trying to make me nervous, would you?

COACH. Not in a million years. I just want you to go in there and think of nothing else but winning this game. You're taking us all into history. The soldiers who died in thousands of senseless battles are forgotten. But the first Yeshiva team to play in the Cotton Bowl will never be forgotten. (*The* COACH *mounts a bench and begins a pep talk while the lights dim. Pause. Offstage singing.*)

(*Reprise.*)

"Yeshiva Beavers"

(*The lights go on again upon an empty locker room. The loudspeaker blares*)

ANNOUNCER. The Flatbush Yeshiva boys are having a rough time. They've held the line tenaciously, but now, with one minute to go to end the third quarter, it is unlikely they'll overcome Notre Dame's lead of 18 to 0. But this has been a sensational game, perhaps the most exciting I've ever seen. Too bad the Yeshiva lost its star fullback Samson Agronsky. Without him, Joshua Stein can't carry the ball to a first down. The Irish have foiled his aerial attack by intercepting no less than five passes . . . (*During the last half of the announcement, a sad-looking* SAMSON *has dragged himself into the locker room. He wears a long black gabardine. He has heard the dismal news.* RACHEL *enters behind him.*)

RACHEL. Why did you want to come here?

SAMSON. I don't know.

RACHEL. You don't know anything. I keep asking you questions, you refuse to answer. You brush me off by tellling me to ask Boruch. Since I met you, the less I have to do with Boruch the better I like it.

ANNOUNCER. The last quarter is coming up. The best the Yeshiva men can hope for is to hold the line. Only a miracle can save the day for them. I've got to hand it to the Yeshiva team, they put up one brave fight. But it looks like the Irish have the class. Perhaps the sensational past few winning games for Yeshiva were only a freak. In the long haul the Irish are a better team by far . . .

RACHEL. They are not a better team. It's important that the Yeshiva team show them. Samson, can you get out there and play in the last quarter? (*The* ANNOUNCER *keeps droning, filling in time.*)

SAMSON. If you tell me to do it, I will, Rachel.

RACHEL. I'm telling you. Get out there and play as you never have before. (SAMSON *starts changing into his uniform as the lights dim. Pause. Lights come on to an empty stage. We hear the enthusiastic, excited voice of the* ANNOUNCER.)

ANNOUNCER. What a game! What a turn-around. I've never seen anything like it. I don't think anyone has ever seen anything like the centurion phalanx of the Yeshiva team plowing through the Irish. There they go. Samson Agronsky came in during the last quarter and has scored twice. He carried the ball over twice and then Stein kicked a field goal. What a game! It stands now at 18 for Notre

Dame and 17 for Yeshiva, with a minute and a half to go. There's the whistle, Notre Dame is stalling, the Irish are walking in slow motion. A penalty is being called against them. The Irish fall back fifteen yards. What will they do? They're going to kick. There goes the whistle. They're off. I've seen many plays, but this is the dumbest. They think it's the first half when Stein couldn't break away with the ball. What a kick—Stein is in position to receive. He's got it. He's running down the field, Agronsky is plowing through in front of him. Three Irish linesmen are down. Thirty yards, Stein is at the fifty-yard line. Watch him go. He's like a bullet. The Irish backfield are waiting for him on the forty-yard line. Wow! Agronsky spills them, four at once—there they go, clear sailing ahead. Twenty-yard line, ten-yard line, he's over! What a run, what a play, what a game! Ah, there goes the gun. It's over, folks, Yeshiva 23, Notre Dame 18. That cinches it for Yeshiva; they're a shoo-in for the Cotton Bowl. Ladies and gentlemen, this day has seen football history made. Wait, there go the Yeshiva students chasing after their team. They've caught up with them. Listen to it, they're blowing their ram's horn . . . *(Over the microphone we hear the blowing of the Shofar. The* ANNOUNCER'*s voice fades out as the lights dim.)*

SCENE 7

The Stein living room, a few mornings later. Enter RACHEL *and* MILLIE *from outside. They speak while taking off their coats, with* RACHEL *coming and going from the entryway where she disposes of the coats.*

RACHEL. Don't be so nervous. I told you he isn't home. I don't expect him until dinner time.

MILLIE. I don't know how to handle it.

RACHEL. Just keep your mind on the important things: you love him and I know he loves you. That's how I resolved my problem with Boruch.

MILLIE. How romantic can you get! Soooo, "Love conquers all." That old bromide won't help me.

RACHEL. You think Boruch and I are not as sophisticated as you are, or that we are simpletons who are content to compromise.

MILLIE. Oh, Rachel, let's not quarrel. I need help, I need guidance . . .

RACHEL. You need Joshua. And, Joshua needs you. I know. Now, isn't that the most important thing?

MILLIE. You may be content to submerge your individuality, your independence, your . . .

RACHEL. I'm submerging nothing. I'm making sure that I will have a happy and fulfilling life.

MILLIE. And how about this thing you've had for Samson?

RACHEL. I'm grateful to you for waking me up to the facts of life. O.K., so he's a gorgeous hunk of man, I felt romantic about being his mentor, guiding him, helping him, he seemed so helpless . . .

MILLIE. Leave us not get maudlin about it . . .

RACHEL. No, please let me finish. When

you told me about Samson's . . . er . . . er . . . peculiar physical . . .

MILLIE. Yes?

RACHEL. Well, at that point I was forced to face the facts of life. And the most important fact for me is that I love Boruch, and I will be happy to be his wife. Oh yes, I don't exactly accept nor approve all the Biblical injunctions about the woman's place in the life of a man, but women have survived and been reasonably happy in their role. I intend to be happy with Boruch; I intend to make him happy—I love him.

MILLIE. It's not so simple between Joshua and myself. I'm determined to make a career in medicine. He is determined to lead an orthodox Jewish life. Suppose I become a surgeon and have to be on duty during sacred holidays, perform an operation on Yom Kippur—

RACHEL. Human life is sacred. I know this much, you would not only be permitted to perform the operation, you'd be encouraged.

MILLIE. Now, what am I to do? Yes, I love him. Yes, I know he loves me. *(Noise at front door, enter* JOSHUA *and* BORUCH. MILLIE *cringes into a corner.)*

RACHEL. Hey, what are you two doing here? Aren't you supposed to be at the Yeshiva?

JOSHUA. Classes have been called off for the day. We got the official notice—WAHOOO—we're invited to the Cotton Bowl!

RACHEL. That's wonderful.

JOSHUA. C'mon, Boruch, let's take out the vodka, and you, Rachel, bring out some cake. Let's celebrate.

RACHEL. Let's save the celebration for tonight. It's the first night of Hanukah. We'll . . .

MILLIE. How do you expect to be part of the celebration, Rachel? It'll be at the Shul, and women are not permitted to be . . .

JOSHUA. Aw, c'mon, Millie. Knock it off. I'll quote the words of a rather famous Jew: "Render unto Caesar . . ." and so on. You've been sulking enough. Don't you think our love is important enough to find a way in the conflicts between your feminism and our traditions? *(*MILLIE *is embarrassed to have this declaration in front of* RACHEL *and* BORUCH.) Look, Millie, I love you. I believe you love me. I'll be going down to the Cotton Bowl. I want you to come with me . . . as my wife.

MILLIE. But . . .

JOSHUA. This is a yes or no question.

MILLIE. *(Shyly.)* Y—e—s. *(*MILLIE *and* JOSHUA *embrace while* BORUCH *and* RACHEL, *hand in hand, smile approvingly.)*

SCENE 8

On the strand at Brighton Beach. BORUCH *and* SAMSON *stand apart from each other. Silence.* SAMSON *stands like a mummy. He turns to say something, then hopelessly turns away.*

BORUCH. The least you can do is congratulate me—congratulate us, Rachel and me.

SAMSON. Why? Because you are to be married? I want her for myself. I could kill you.

BORUCH. No, you can't. You won't do a thing without me telling you what to do. I can snap my fingers and send you back to the sandpits, you golem. You have no brains, you have no soul . . .

SAMSON. Perhaps no brains, but pain, yes. And you didn't tell me to love Rachel—but I do. Even a golem can love.

BORUCH. Love. That's a miracle not revealed to me in the Kabala. But look at the misery love can bring.

"Who Asked for Love?"

SAMSON.
Whatever your belief
It only brings you grief

SAMSON *and* BORUCH.
Who asked for love?

BORUCH.
It makes your heart quiver and
shiver
It can't possibly be good for your
liver

SAMSON *and* BORUCH.
So who needs this love?

SAMSON.
Whoever wished passion upon us?
What power above could be so low
to con us?

BORUCH.
What cruel God above could so hate
us
To inflict on us this divine afflatus?

SAMSON.
My pleasures were so few
And now I get this witches' brew

SAMSON *and* BORUCH.
Who asked for love?

SAMSON.
In this mis'rable condition
It's time to send for the mortician.

SAMSON *and* BORUCH.
Who asked for love?

(Second chorus).

BORUCH.
It's I who am snared,
And I tell you, brother, I'm scared!

SAMSON *and* BORUCH.
Who asked for love?

SAMSON.
My castles in the air are all rubble,
Falling in love is just asking for
trouble

SAMSON *and* BORUCH.
So who needs this love?

BORUCH.
A person must be masochistic
To make himself a sacrificial lamb

SAMSON.
To be just another statistic,
To take his lumps and say, "Thank
you, Ma'am!"

BORUCH.
What person with even half a brain
Would walk into something so
insane?

SAMSON *and* BORUCH.
Why ask for love?

SAMSON.
I went after the golden fleece,
Now all I want is peace.

SAMSON *and* BORUCH.
Who asked for love,
Who asked for love?

SAMSON. All right, Boruch. What do I do now?

BORUCH. You have a choice. Ashes to ashes, dust to dust—sooner or later, the fate of us all.

SAMSON. Must I go back to where I came from?

BORUCH. I said you have a choice. How would you like to join a whole group of other golems?

SAMSON. You mean other beings without brains, without . . . hearts, without . . .

BORUCH. Exactly. We'll all get together, campaign for you, and get you elected to Congress.

SAMSON. No, thank you. I'd rather go back to my original state.

BORUCH. O.K. If that's what you really want . . . (BORUCH *goes into a trancelike chant, the lights alternate like strobe lights;* SAMSON *slowly falls to the sands on the beach and his form disintegrates. The lights return to normal.* BORUCH *picks up a handful of sand from the spot where* SAMSON *disappeared;* BORUCH *lets the sand sift through his fingers as the lights dim.*)

SCENE 9

At the Yeshiva, a few nights later. It is the Eve of Hanukah. The entire company is assembled to celebrate both the holiday and the triumph of the Yeshiva Football Team. The entire company will start with a rousing reprise of "The Yeshiva Beavers" and conclude with the wild Hassidic dance of scene 1.

"Yeshiva Football Song"

YESHIVA FOOTBALL TEAM.
  We're the Yeshiva Beavers and we'll
    fight to win today.
  We'll hock 'em so hard, fighting for
    ev'ry yard
  They'll schrei "Oy vay! Oy vay!"
    Rah! Rah!

  We're the Yeshiva Beavers, battling
    hard as any Maccabee.
  So all you true believers, pray us on
    to victory.

(Interlude.)

  Down with the Eli bulldog, kill the
    Army mule,
  Schlug the Princeton Tigers, show
    them we're no one's fool.
  We'll tame the Columbia Lions till
    they lie down like lambs.
  Then Harvard and Dartmouth and
    for dessert we'll swallow the
    Fordham Rams. Burp!

  We're the Yeshiva Beavers and we'll
    fight to win today.
  We'll hock 'em so hard, fighting for
    ev'ry yard
  They'll schrei "Oy vay! Oy vay!"
    Rah! Rah!

  We're the Yeshiva Beavers, battling
    hard as any Maccabee.
  So all you true believers, pray us on
    to victory! Rah! Rah! *(Curtain falls.)*

THE END

THE QUEEN'S PHYSICIAN

Ever since it was written, Shakespeare's play, *The Merchant of Venice,* and his treatment of Shylock the Jew have stirred controversy—especially because of the obvious contrast to Christopher Marlowe's vicious portrayal of the Jew in *The Jew of Malta.* Shakespeare did not make a caricature of his Jew; instead, he made him human. Despite this, much dramatic criticism contends that the play is anti-Semitic. At first this assessment seems to be valid, but closer analysis contradicts this view. At the very time that David Lifson was writing his extraordinary play, *The Queen's Physician,* critical research into the true nature of *The Merchant of Venice* was proceeding, notably with some work done by Fredda Brilliant. As a result of her studies she came to the conclusion that the play was in fact anti-Christian, not anti-Semitic. It became apparent that Shakespeare used as a prototype for his Jew a real historical personage, Dr. Roderigo Lopez, physician to Queen Elizabeth I. The cruel fate of this unfortunate Jew who was victimized by a court scandal was not mitigated despite his high standing, the queen's faith in him, and his fine reputation in the entourages of many other aristocrats. None of these advantages saved him from being framed, tortured, hanged, and drawn and quartered by the Christians who surrounded him—including some of the greatest intellects of Elizabeth's court.

In *The Queen's Physician,* David Lifson imaginatively recounts and re-creates the personal tragedy of the great doctor who earned the monarch's trust and favor. The action of the play is propelled by scenes depicting the underhanded plotting that led to the brutal death of an innocent Jew, but Lifson also ironically draws upon the understanding that Lopez was technically not a Jew; he was a Christian, an assimilated Jew from the Marranos, the inheritors of the great flowering of Jewish culture in Spain from Maimonides onward. The play climaxes with the fall of the earl of Essex (the major force behind the intrigue against Lopez), who will himself eventually be executed on a warrant signed by his beloved queen.

It is perhaps poetic justice that although the historical figure of Lopez had generally been forgotten until he was resurrected in Lifson's play, his characterization as Shylock by the master playwright Shakespeare still protests his humanity to the world. But only in Lifson's play do we see the true machinations that enmeshed the original Shylock and at the same time the barbarisms produced by anti-Semitism, atrocities that have been multiplied a millionfold since Shakespeare's day. Such a play is a lesson from history we must never forget, and David Lifson is to be praised for writing it. It is a play that must be seen to understand Shakespeare's Shylock. These two works—*The Merchant of Venice* and *The Queen's Physician*—could be performed in tandem to great advantage.

Herbert Marshall
Professor Emeritus
University of Southern Illinois

Herbert Marshall has been a British theater director in his own London theater. For over a decade he also directed plays in Moscow, translated Russian poetry by Yevtushenko and others, and has published a number of books. In addition to being the director of the Institute for Soviet and Eastern European Culture, he has completed a definitive biography of the great Jewish-Russian actor, Mikhoels, who was murdered by Stalin.

THE QUEEN'S PHYSICIAN

by David S. Lifson

CHARACTERS

ROBERT DEVEREUX, the Earl of Essex
FRANCIS BACON, his amanuensis, friend, and counsel
WILLIAM SHAKESPEARE, a writer of poetry and plays
DR. RODERIGO LOPEZ, physician to Queen Elizabeth I
QUEEN ELIZABETH I
LORD BURGHLEY, Chief Counsel to the Queen
LORD WALSINGHAM, Burghley's colleague
ROBERT CECIL, son of Lord Burghley and cousin to Francis Bacon
DON ("KING") ANTONIO, Pretender to the throne of Portugal
MANUEL LUIS TINOCO, a soldier of fortune
ANDRADA, a double agent for Spain and England
ESTABAN FEREIRA DE GAMA, a Portuguese Marano, friend of Dr. Lopez
LORD COKE, Attorney General of England
LADY IN WAITING to the Queen
A SERVITOR
A COURT CLERK
TOPCLIFFE, torturer in the Tower of London

The action of the play occurs in and around London from late 1593 to early June 1594.

116

SCENE 1

*A room in Essex House: on 16th March
1594. The* EARL OF ESSEX, *Robert Devereux, a commanding figure of twenty-
seven years, makes certain to dominate
all around him. All his thoughts and
actions are egocentric—he is the center
of his universe. He impatiently stalks
about while glowering at his companions. Among them is* FRANCIS BACON,
*an epicene, serious man of thirty-three
years, much respected by* LORD ESSEX
*but fawningly subservient to his patron.
He is a "cold fish" who demonstrates a
marked and tenacious reverence for
facts (should "facts" be elusive, he will
philosophically manufacture them),
from which his judgments and actions
derive.*

ESSEX. That woman!

BACON. Her sacred majesty. . . .

ESSEX. (*Sarcastically bowing to*
BACON.) You still believe that
woman—yes, I said "that woman,"
will she ever make up her mind to
appoint you, my good Francis, to
high office? Bah! We may die of old
age, of the plague, or surely of frus-
tration before she will come to a decision. Something must be done. . .
(*He mockingly bows to an imaginary
Queen Elizabeth.*) to persuade her
majesty to sign the warrant of death
for the traitors. Why does she persist!
The verminous Jew traitor will die, so
why the delay?

BACON. It is her nature to delay. Ah, a
delicious trait.

ESSEX. She is perverse. No one but the
Queen would dare thwart me.

BACON. She did delay for four months

the signing of the death warrant of
Mary of Scotland—also guilty of treasonous plotting.

ESSEX. The two cases are not alike. Our
Queen delayed in order to make certain there'd be no complications with
a Catholic France. But with this Jew
doctor? Why? Does he have a secret
about our virgin Queen that she fears
he will reveal? I cannot believe she
fears the wretch.

BACON. She fears nothing and no one,
as we well know, my Lord. Yet . . . he
may know that which no one else
knows of a possible ailment and the
revelation of which he may have writ
and entrusted to another in the event
of his death.

ESSEX. He knows too much. He betrayed me to my intimates. Yes, he
was my personal physician, too. Why
do you suppose I dispensed with
him? I should have destroyed him
then. While visiting Don Antonio at
Eton, and he'd drunk too much of the
Don's madeira—the Jew cannot hold
his drink—then he blabbered about
my . . . forget it. The Jew is not to be
trusted as a doctor should be.

BACON. Surely he would not betray any
intimate knowledge of our Queen.
That would certainly assure his instant death. He continues to hope for
a reprieve. The detestable poisoner
did confess his hideous crime . . .

ESSEX. Aye, but then he recanted. He
claimed the confession was forced
upon him on the rack. But he never
recanted the villainous gossip he cir-
culated about me.

BACON. Alas, when one places himself

into the confidence of his physician, he must first reflect a million times and then decide against it.

ESSEX. You know me well, good Francis. My life has been exemplary as the most loyal in our Queen's court. Oh yes, a stolen kiss, a fleeting visitation of the clap—but nothing alien to a good, law-abiding Christian. This Jew Dr. Lopez, physician to our blessed Queen no less, while in his cups whispered to King Antonio that I was venereally accursed. It must have reached the Queen's ears, for she sent me hence. Who knows what miserable secret he harbors about her, a secret that only a doctor could know!

BACON. He wouldn't dare speak. Should he betray any secret and sacred trust, he knows well that vengeance would seek out his wife and children.

ESSEX. With him I would execute or banish all of his tribe. That libel he spread about me . . .

BACON. My Lord, you did not say it and I did not hear it. And, is it not possible that Don Antonio lied to you?

ESSEX. Never. He's too stupid to lie, and it would gain him nought. He's become a burden to me and the realm.

BACON. What an impossible figure to be a king! (BACON *swishes in imitation of* DON ANTONIO.) And how he struts about like a peacock! How unlike our English kings!

ESSEX. *(Laughing.)* I thought you fancied his type.

BACON. Not I! I prefer the assertive, manly kind. Antonio would be a more authentic queen than king.

ESSEX. We need him to legitimize our quarrel with King Philip of Spain. He also cements our cause with France.

He served us well at the trial of the conspirators, even though his very intimates are woven into this heinous plot against Her Majesty. Meanwhile, the Jew keeps to his bed under the pretext of a feigned ailment. He may expire of natural causes . . .

BACON. Prisoners may die of various causes in the Tower. Strangulation?

ESSEX. That would not serve our purposes. He must be executed for his treason in accordance with the law. Thus we prove to Philip of Spain and his Catholic world that our Queen is sacred to us.

BACON. A Lopez execution will give pause to all Papists who plot against us.

ESSEX. Come, my good Francis, surely you know how, under the law, we can accommodate our mission.

BACON. Two days ago, on the fourteenth of March, Lord Keeper Puckering wrote to Robert Cecil desiring directions whether to proceed against Fereira and Lopez in the absence of the Lord Chief Justice. Only Lord Tenner, the only judge in commission, is likely to remain in London until Easter, but he is in circuit until Thursday next in Aylesbury. The sergeant elect, Mr. Daniell. . .

ESSEX. Ah, a Daniel come to judgment.

BACON. He may suffice in place of a judge . . .

ESSEX. Yes, he did indeed sit as commissioner in the original proceedings against Lopez.

BACON. My Lord Coke seeks direction concerning the execution of Lopez, for the Jew may die before the execution. They say that if they are to proceed, you, my Lord, and Robert Cecil are to come thither. The Lord Admiral, now in Chelsea, seeks guidance. Lord Buckhurst and the Chancellor of the Exchequer await here in London, although Lord Buckhurst is indisposed with a cold.

ESSEX. Meanwhile, the Jew . . .

BACON. He has not left his bed, for the most part, since his trial. There is suspicion he practices slow poison to prevent his execution.

ESSEX. I doubt it. He is too carefully guarded. Should the execution be deferred, great dishonor and scandal will ensue.

BACON. And should the Lord Chief Justice fail to act, it will be dangerous to Her Majesty and serve dishonorably in the opinion of the world.

ESSEX. Whence comes your information?

BACON. But two days ago from Lincoln's Inn. Mr. Daniell is both learned and wise, and now a sergeant elect. He is acquainted with the state of our cause and doubts not his sufficiency to direct in form of law and manage the proceedings. A judge's name gives countenance, but adds nothing to learning.

ESSEX. All of which signifies . . . ?

BACON. The execution of the traitors need not wait upon Her Majesty signing the death warrant. Be the warrant signed by a proper judge outside the Queen's jurisdiction in London, say in Southampton or other legal jurisdiction, we may proceed to dispose of the traitors at once. (*Pause as* ESSEX *paces and reflects.*) I suggest we proceed and have done with it.

ESSEX. How will it sit with the Queen? Her Majesty likes not being thwarted or compelled. We may gain our ends in disposing of these traitorous conspirators, but we may lose all by antagonizing our good Queen. And, we cannot prod her . . .

BACON. But the populace can.

ESSEX. Explain.

BACON. Her Majesty revels in the devotion and loyalty of her subjects. Not only is she responsive to their will, and thus retains all their support, she actively solicits their good will.

ESSEX. The populace is sufficiently aroused by this hideous crime.

BACON. But not enough to move Her Majesty to sign the warrant.

ESSEX. I know you well, Francis. You have a plan.

BACON. Aye, my Lord.

ESSEX. Must we put you to the rack to draw it from you?

BACON. I will put it simply . . .

ESSEX. And quickly!

BACON. Our gracious Queen continues her uneasiness about the Salic Law, about her legitimate claim to the throne. I understand, from Lord Southampton, that Master Will Shakespeare prepares to write a play on Henry V, that will put the matter to rest. It is much like what he did when the Yorkists were restive and our glorious Queen wished to stop all agitation—Will Shakespeare presented Richard III.

ESSEX. And what potion can Master Will stir to get our queen to be aroused out of her inertia so that we may dispose of the detestable Jew?

BACON. A masque . . .

ESSEX. He will contrive an entertainment that will portray the evil plot, be sufficiently dramatic to inflame the passions of every Englishman, and then . . .

BACON. Then her Majesty will abide by the will of her subjects.

ESSEX. Nay, my friend, it will take too long . . .

BACON. Not so, my Lord. I have Master Will Shakespeare even now waiting for you in my study.

ESSEX. No harm can come of it. Bring him hence. (BACON *hurriedly exits and quickly returns with* WILL SHAKESPEARE, *a young man of thirty years.*) Welcome, Master Will. *(Ad lib exchange of greetings.)* Know you why we asked you to favor us with your presence?

SHAKESPEARE. My Lord Bacon hath suggested you wish me to write a masque for the court.

ESSEX. Does it interest you?

SHAKESPEARE. I must wonder why Francis Bacon does not undertake the chore . . .

BACON. Come, friend Will, you well know I am but a pedant, a stodgy barrister . . .

SHAKESPEARE. But your learning is unequaled in our time.

ESSEX. These pleasantries may be appropriate another time. We have a problem the solving of which may be helped by you and your pen. I will be brief: know you of this matter of the villainous Jew Roderigo Lopez?

SHAKESPEARE. Aye, I know him, alas, but not as a villain.

ESSEX. The knave has been tried most justly, judged, and condemned for his despicable treason. Apparently, the dissembling wretch hath beguiled you amongst others.

SHAKESPEARE. I know him, but not as a Jew.

BACON. Of course he is a Jew. There have been Jews in England with the name of Lopez for more than fifty years.

ESSEX. (*Waving* BACON *to quiet.*) Dr. Lopez is one of the accursed tribe. How then did you know him?

SHAKESPEARE. As Her Majesty's physician. Also, he was at court to attend my plays, often with the Queen. Whether he is or is not a Jew matters not to me.

ESSEX. It matters to me, to Her Majesty, and to England. He is a proven villain.

SHAKESPEARE. I know the doctor as a healer, a doctor devoted to our Queen.

ESSEX. You question the wise judgment of the court?

SHAKESPEARE. If your Lordship concurs with the court's judgment, I defer to a wisdom greater than mine. Dr. Lopez ofttimes observed our troupe whilst we prepared our court masque presentations. He favored me with many astute suggestions based on his vast knowledge of the world beyond our shores.

BACON. Let us to the purpose.

ESSEX. Our purpose is not to debate the virtues, if any, of the treacherous Jew poisoner. What think you of Marlowe's plays?

SHAKESPEARE. Excellent indeed. He knows how to inflame the populace 'gainst his villains.

ESSEX. Can you do likewise?

SHAKESPEARE. I've done likewise—for a noble cause.

ESSEX. And wouldst do likewise for a "noble cause?"

SHAKESPEARE. If I agree that the cause is noble.

ESSEX. It is noble. It is your country, your Queen's sacred life, and the confounding of the Papist rascal Philip of Spain. Now, to the business at hand. My Lord Southampton hath advised you write a play about a treacherous Jew villain.

SHAKESPEARE. What is its import concerning Her Majesty's life? And how doth it relate to your Jew Lopez?

ESSEX. It is to thwart Philip of Spain.

SHAKESPEARE. But Lord Burghley is confident of peace with Spain.

ESSEX. My Lord Burghley is not privy to secret information that concerns the very survival of our England. Philip hath employed his Jew . . .

SHAKESPEARE. But I know not Dr. Lopez as a Jew. He professes himself a true Christian.

ESSEX. Alas, how isolated from real life you denizens of the theater are. But you are not alone. Professing as he doth, he disarms all about him. He is actually the very anti-Christ.

SHAKESPEARE. Dr. Lopez hath been revered: physician to our sacred Queen, to Lord Walsingham, to Lord Leicester, to the Portuguese King Don Antonio, and even to your good self, my Lord.

BACON. Ah, how well did this traitorous spy serve his master, King Philip of Spain!

SHAKESPEARE. I know the doctor as a learned, wise, and just man.

ESSEX. We shall have to discover if Master Will Shakespeare is circumcised.

BACON. *(Drooling.)* What an inspiration! How delicious! *(The others ignore him. At first he grins and then recovers his decorous poise.)* Your new play, Master Will, Lord Southampton advises that it features a Jew much like Dr. Lopez, or shall I say Marlowe's Barabas.

SHAKESPEARE. I am not Marlowe.

ESSEX. Why not rewrite your Richard III and make him a Jew? Babes exchanged in the cradle sort of plot . . .

SHAKESPEARE. There is a story in the latest report from Lord Oxford in Italy. It is a true story. But in it, the Christian is the villain whilst the Jew an innocent victim. Pope Sixtus V himself dispensed justice.

BACON. Who in England would know . . .

SHAKESPEARE. You, my Lord, will have to decide that—and then I may undertake the satisfying of your need. But only if I find it to be true.

ESSEX. Your plot, if you please, Master Will.

SHAKESPEARE. You may recall that Sir Francis Drake raided the Spanish Main. He attacked and sacked the principal town in Hispaniola.

BACON. That was some two years before we destroyed the Spanish Armada.

SHAKESPEARE. True. It seems that two Italian merchants heard of Drake's exploits. A Christian merchant cheered the outcome; a Jew merchant doubted it. Whereupon they wagered: the Christian asserted that Sir Francis had reduced the city of Isabel, whilst the Jew claimed it to be impossible. After the facts were to be verified, the loser of the wager was to sacrifice a pound of his flesh to him who prevailed.

ESSEX. A gory, grotesque tale.

SHAKESPEARE. True, nonetheless.

BACON. And the Jew won and demanded the Christian's life?

SHAKESPEARE. Not so. The Jew lost, and the Christian insisted upon a pound of the Jew's flesh. The Jew refused, and the Christian took him to court. At the trial, Pope Sixtus V decided to preside. He found that the Christian had no right to enter into a contract whereby a human life was placed in jeopardy. Although he punished the Christian by confiscating his property and sending him to the galleys, he also condemned the Jew to a like sentence for having entered into such a contract. They both protested it had all been a jest. Yet withal, the Christian had insisted upon his pound of flesh and has resorted to the courts. Of course, the Pope prevailed.

ESSEX. How does this serve our purpose? The Jew is the victim and not the villain.

BACON. A simple solution. Perhaps Master Will would reverse the roles.

ESSEX. Eh? What means that?

BACON. Have the evil Jew maliciously demand the pound of Christian flesh. No one will ever know the true facts.

SHAKESPEARE. There is a possibility there. But there is more to the tale . . .

ESSEX. No matter. The principal thing is to show the Jew as a villain. How soon may we present your play at court?

SHAKESPEARE. I must know this Jew. My characters do not spring like Venus from the brow of Zeus.

BACON. What more must you know? In your plays you've revealed identifiable villains whom you've never met . . .

SHAKESPEARE. I've met their like. But a Jew? If Jew he be. I must talk with him.

ESSEX. We shall arrange it. You shall visit him in the Tower—unless Her Royal Mightiness decides beforehand to sign his death warrant. (ESSEX *turns to* BACON.) Arrange for Master Shakespeare to have private audience in the Tower with the condemned Jew.

BACON. At once.

SHAKESPEARE. What if, after Dr. Lopez is executed, it is discovered he was indeed innocent?

BACON. Better that ten innocent men should suffer than one guilty man escape.

SCENE 2

A Cell in the Tower of London. Its lone occupant is the wretched, despairing figure of DR. RODERIGO LOPEZ. *He is seventy years old. Despite an anticipation of his horrible fate, he conducts himself with dignity, allowing an occasional mournful sigh.*

The door to the cell clanks open. WILLIAM SHAKESPEARE *enters.*

LOPEZ. (*Squinting in the dim light.*) I know you . . . ?

SHAKESPEARE. I'd scarce know you.

LOPEZ. I scarce know myself. Bring you news of my wife, of my children?

SHAKESPEARE. Alas, not directly. I know they are well and pray for your deliverance . . . as do I.

LOPEZ. I do know you. You are the poet William Shakespeare, writer of plays.

SHAKESPEARE. That I am.

LOPEZ. Why are you here? What mission . . . ?

SHAKESPEARE. You have ofttimes appeared at my plays at court. Not only have you been a loyal patron, but you have helped me when I sought information about the world beyond England.

LOPEZ. I no longer know a thing . . . except that I am innocent of the hideous accusations that have condemned me.

SHAKESPEARE. How can you prove your innocence?

LOPEZ. Ah, here lies the dog buried. Lord Essex wants no proof of innocence. He hath used me for some vile scheme of court intrigue. Proof of my innocence is the last thing he needs to further his plans. Know ye not that to be merely accused of treason is inevitable death!

SHAKESPEARE. What plans? He is loyal to our Queen. Yes, he seeks war with Philip of Spain. But that is because Philip constantly plans to undo Her Majesty.

LOPEZ. At times I am comforted to be out of court politics, of groveling for favors, of . . . But why are you here? Yet, I should not ask, for it is indeed a blessing that you have come.

SHAKESPEARE. I will come to the point. I've been asked by my Lord of Southampton to write a play to present at court and then at the Globe. The piece must have a Jew in it.

LOPEZ. I am not a Jew.

SHAKESPEARE. Yes, we know. But since the beginning of this century, there have been crypto Jews at court; they, too, were physicians. Two of them were named Lopez.

LOPEZ. I believe in Jesus Christ.

SHAKESPEARE. Your good wife Sarah is indeed a Jewess and related to known Jews of Antwerp . . .

LOPEZ. What difference does all this make? Jew or Christian, I am to die of purported treason. Why do you thus torment me with your questions?

SHAKESPEARE. Perhaps the Queen will pardon you.

LOPEZ. Thus have I, too, deluded myself.

SHAKESPEARE. I've not deluded myself in you. I remember you as a kindly and learned man—a healer of the afflicted. I seek more of your history for my writing. The Jew I write about must be an understandable, authentic human being, and not a caricature. Please help me.

LOPEZ. Shall I tell you I have no time for it? I have more time than can be measured by all the sands of the Arabian desert. What else have I to do but brood and despair. It may prove a diversion. What would you know? At what stage in my life shall I begin?

SHAKESPEARE. When you first appeared in court and met our Queen.

LOPEZ. Some thirty years ago I was attached, as physician, to the household of the late Lord Leicester. Ah, there indeed was a man! Through him I consorted with his company of players, among whom was your fellow actor James Burbage, and your current friend, his son Richard.

SHAKESPEARE. How came you privy to the affairs of the Queen's Council?

LOPEZ. I enjoyed the friendship and good wishes of many at court. The Lord Treasurer Lord Burghley and his son Sir Robert Cecil assisted me in obtaining passports for various relatives of mine in various European cities. Thus, when I was asked to work in divers ways for my Lord Walsingham, I gratefully consented.

SHAKESPEARE. What nature of work?

LOPEZ. My Lord Walsingham requested information from the Continent. My relatives brought valuable information from Europe. Lord Walsingham was deeply grateful for the intelligences. Through him, my skill as a physician reached Her Majesty's ears. Queen Elizabeth appointed me her physician—that was some ten years ago.

SHAKESPEARE. Was not elevation to Queen's physician honor enough? Why did you become involved with court intrigue?

LOPEZ. Four years ago, at the request of Lord Walsingham and Lord Essex, her Majesty enrolled me as interpreter and liaison between Don Antonio, the would-be King of Portugal and the court.

SHAKESPEARE. Why you? You are a physician. Whence came you to interfere in affairs of state?

LOPEZ. I am of Portuguese ancestry, and I speak the tongue as well as those of Spain, Italy, and France. I neither sought nor liked my charge. Lord Essex persuaded me.

SHAKESPEARE. Robert Devereux was your friend as well as patient . . . ?

LOPEZ. And now he is my mortal enemy. I know not why. He hath manufactured this spurious charge of treason and venomously pursued my conviction and certain death. The trial was a theatrical charade, for none escapes once accused of treason. What would it gain me had I effected the death of my benefactress and beloved Queen? Some wretched pittance from the cretinous King Philip of Spain? Think you for that I would forfeit my income, my position, the security of my family, all of which depends upon Her Majesty's gracious favor? And the constant fear of detection, no less my conscience—the very hint of such a course would have been madness.

SHAKESPEARE. Have you petitioned the Queen?

LOPEZ. Aye, indeed. She graciously replied that not a hair of my head should perish, and that I should have but a short imprisonment, a little loss of practice in my profession, which cannot countervail the credit of the state—which Her Majesty doth so much respect.

SHAKESPEARE. With the Queen's faith in you why do you yet languish in this pass?

LOPEZ. There is a spider who doth weave his web—Francis Bacon. He will piss in Lord Essex's ear and declare it rains and my Lord Essex will believe him. But my travail started when I could not deny the request of my benefactor, Lord Walsingham . . . (*Lights fade and then rise on next scene.*)

SCENE 3

The throne room at Windsor Castle, 1590. QUEEN ELIZABETH, *in her regal splendor, is attended by Lords* ESSEX, BURGHLEY, SIR ROBERT CECIL, *and* SIR FRANCIS WALSINGHAM. *The* QUEEN, *in her fifty-seventh year, is vigorous, alert, dominates all with her sharp and wily mind whilst her quicksilver behavior fluctuates from haughtiness to ribald coquettry as she blatantly flirts with all the men in her retinue, and they all defer to her—except* ESSEX, *who is always the gallant.*

ELIZABETH. Are we not further provoking the troublesome Philip of Spain by harboring the Pretender to the Portuguese throne? *(The courtiers try to speak at once, but* ESSEX *boldly asserts himself.)*

ESSEX. Doth not the Papist Philip provoke us? He relentlessly, ruthlessly wars upon us. Contrary to the wishes of Henry of France and Your Majesty, he grasps Portugal within his fist. Sooner or later there will be a confrontation between Philip and us.

BURGHLEY. Surely he learned a lesson in the defeat of his armada.

ESSEX. Apparently not. He continues to harrass our ships and to send his spies and assassins to corrupt our England.

WALSINGHAM. My intelligencers bring reports of his preparations for another armada to invade us.

ELIZABETH. What solid evidence have we for a national policy? What legitimate claim has Don Antonio to the throne of Portugal to warrant our support?

WALSINGHAM. Don Antonio is the natural son of the Infante Luis who was the son of King John III. Don Antonio's mother was a beautiful Jewess, I'm advised, whose name was Violante Gomez. Strictly speaking, our Don Antonio has no claim whatsoever upon the Portuguese throne. Yet, his father was extremely popular while the Don hath some history as a valiant soldier. The populace responds to his facile charm and infectious ebullience, most desirable in a monarch of a Latin land.

ELIZABETH. Are there no other legitimate claimants to the throne?

WALSINGHAM. Yes, your Majesty. The Duke of Braganza, whose wife is the only daughter of John III's younger son, the Infante Duarte. But the Duke has no popularity, hence no support within his native land. When King Cardinal Henry died, Philip's army crossed over from Spain. While the Duke of Braganza held aloof, Don Antonio rallied his countrymen to resist the Spanish invasion.

ESSEX. *(Interrupting.)* And despite the valiant stand by Don Antonio near Lisbon and farther north, he was forced to flee. But, he was unequivocally recognized as king, and the rump of the Cortez in Lisbon in effect crowned Don Antonio the Portuguese King.

ELIZABETH. It pleases me that Philip of Spain have a neighbor king who is the son of a Jewess.

WALSINGHAM. King Antonio then fled to France with considerable treasure.

ELIZABETH. *(More keenly interested at*

the word "treasure.") Hath he much of this treasure?

WALSINGHAM. I fear he hath left much in the court of France. Much went toward his attempt to seize the Azores some eight years ago, and . . .

ESSEX. Why resurrect melancholy history! He is little burden to us. France favors him with a small pension. We help some by maintaining him nearby at Eton.

CECIL. My information is that the Jew Mendes, who traffics for us when need be in France and Italy, urged this Portuguese "king" to hasten to the Portuguese Indies, seize them, and thus have a base. Apparently Don Antonio is more content with the blandishments of the French court and our English hospitality. He does not stir in his own behalf.

ELIZABETH. Catherine de Medici at the French court is a shrewd person. She respects Mendes. He actually conducts great affairs 'twixt France and our England. And Mendes approves of this Antonio.

ESSEX. Your Majesty should have more direct contact with King Antonio.

ELIZABETH. But he speaks no English, whilst my currency of Portuguese is bankrupt. Would that he spoke Latin or Greek, but alas, I'm told he's unschooled.

WALSINGHAM. Dr. Roderigo Lopez, Your Majesty's physician is a Portuguese and fluent in its language. He doth serve as our liaison with Don Antonio.

ELIZABETH. We are aware. That makes me uneasy. I'd rather our physician devoted his time and thoughts to our person.

WALSINGHAM. His nostrums may serve our body politic as well as Your royal personage. He awaits without should we wish to consult him concerning "king" Antonio.

ESSEX. Your "good" doctor is a knave. I trust him not. He harbors in his home disreputable and discredited foreigners, undoubtedly crypto-papists, who constantly plot to undo Your Majesty. Philip seeks to assassinate you.

ELIZABETH. My lord, we must judge by facts . . .

ESSEX. And the facts are that this Jew doctor is more concerned with intrigue than with his professed "noble" calling.

ELIZABETH. "Professed?" Dr. Lopez is not only a most noble soul but also a devoted friend who has eased and comforted Your Queen no matter the indisposition that afflicted her. Take care what you say, Robert.

ESSEX. I know what I know. I will never be convinced that your "good" Doctor did not conspire with his creature Andrada to deliver the Portuguese king to the Spaniards at Dunkirk.

CECIL. We arrested this Andrada . . .

ESSEX. Only to seek to have him released by the intervention of this intriguing doctor with whom he may reside in Holborn.

ELIZABETH. Your Queen has every confidence in Dr. Lopez. Our kingdom is safe from all plots, whilst our physician guards our person.

ESSEX. We have discóvered some dozen plots to destroy Your Majesty. The Catholics, aided and abetted by the monstrous Philip of Spain, will never cease their heinous attempts upon your sacred life.

BURGHLEY. All the more reason to treat with the Spaniard and arrive at a lasting peace.

ESSEX. Peace! With the anti-Christ Philip!

BURGHLEY. (*Draws a prayer book from his garment, points to a passage, and hands it to* ESSEX.) My Lord, read you the fifty-fifth psalm.

ESSEX. (*Reading aloud.*) "Bloodthirsty and deceitful men will not live out half their days." (*Angrily, he flings the book back at* BURGHLEY.) Were you a younger man, My Lord, I would challenge you to a duel—you are most insulting. I pray Your Majesty reprove . . .

ELIZABETH. I will have none of this. Our people seek peace. I seek peace. How can we achieve this peace when we viciously quarrel amongst ourselves!

BURGHLEY, ESSEX, *and* WALSINGHAM

We quarrel not with Your Majesty . . .
We defer to your wisdom . . .
Our devotion is to Your Majesty's peace of mind . . .

ELIZABETH. All these words go round and round. Knew I not of your petty intrigues, I'd need a host of doctors to clear my head. My Lord Walsingham, bring in my physician and good friend Dr. Lopez. (WALSINGHAM *exits and quickly returns, accompanied by* DR. LOPEZ, *who is well attired, diffident, and decorous yet dignified, but with extra humility to the* QUEEN. *Upon* LOPEZ's *entrance, the* QUEEN *waves off all the others, and they exit.*) My Lords, we will be alone with our doctor. (*The* QUEEN *and* LOPEZ *are alone.*) We learn you are much concerned with matters not medical.

LOPEZ. My sole interest is Your Majesty's welfare.

ELIZABETH. Your remedies and medications take many forms.

LOPEZ. Madam . . .

ELIZABETH. There is much gossip that you served the late Lord Leicester as his poisoner.

LOPEZ. I protest, Your Majesty. You recall the late Lord as a most compassionate and gentle friend. He would have given his life, as would I, for Your Majesty's welfare.

ELIZABETH. Aye, he was my comfort. How unlike was he to these spiders who constantly weave their webs about me. What choice have I but to depend upon them? They have in truth discovered a number of Catholic plots to undo me.

LOPEZ. Your people love you—perhaps even the Catholics. As for those found guilty, "I fear (they) speak upon the rack, where men enforced do speak anything."

ELIZABETH. There is much suspicion in our court that Your Queen is about to be the victim of a poisoner's plot.

LOPEZ. All monarchs are potential victims of contending factions. But not you, Madam. You are surrounded by loyal, devoted people who revere you. Their love protects you.

ELIZABETH. Then what of this spy Andrada? Is he not King Philip's creature?

LOPEZ. I know that he is paid by Lord Walsingham to spy upon the Spaniards.

ELIZABETH. How know you this?

LOPEZ. From both Lord Walsingham himself and Andrada. This spy hath been of great service to your realm.

His mission has been to explore the possibility of a lasting peace between Your Majesty and Philip.

ELIZABETH. And what instrument do you play in this proposed harmony of peace?

LOPEZ. This Andrada is not of a courtly appearance sufficient to represent England. My Lord Walsingham instructed him to advise the Spanish monarch that Dr. Lopez, personal physician to Your Majesty, will intercede to discuss a basis for peace.

ELIZABETH. We would think that your concern for the health of our person, your work in the hospital, your domestic obligations, would all occupy you and leave no time for you to meddle in affairs of state.

LOPEZ. Your Majesty is always correct. As a doctor, my mission is to heal the afflicted and to maintain the vigor of the healthy. Should not my dedication to the health of individuals also try to improve the health of nations?

ELIZABETH. Nobly said. But you are not the rara avis free from man's acquisitive nature. How will you personally benefit from your efforts?

LOPEZ. His Majesty of Spain has pledged me 50,000 gold crowns should I succeed in effecting a peace treaty.

ELIZABETH. We suspected you sought some personal recompense. And should you fail?

LOPEZ. Then I shall have cozened your enemy out of his money.

ELIZABETH. That pleases us not. We will not consent to have any of our people to be deceitful in behalf of our England. We are much vexed with you. (*Pause.*) Hath the Catholic king responded to these overtures?

LOPEZ. He hath indeed. And as a token of his serious intent, he sends you this precious ring. (LOPEZ *brings forth a ring of precious stones which he offers to the* QUEEN. *She waves it away.*)

ELIZABETH. We need no earnest of his intent. We want it not. We cannot and shall not be bought. Now for this business at hand. Your Andrada had been arrested and then released in your custody . . .

LOPEZ. His release awaits your approval.

ELIZABETH. My Lord Essex advises he is a despicable intriguer, and much too close to our Catholic enemies.

LOPEZ. Only to sustain our cause. I will vouch for him whilst he be in my custody.

ELIZABETH. If we may not trust our personal physician, whom may we trust? So be it. Lord Burghley will be so instructed. Mark you, Doctor, guard your trust.

LOPEZ. My only trust is my Queen's welfare.

ELIZABETH. How fares your good wife?

LOPEZ. Tolerably well, Your Majesty.

ELIZABETH. And your son?

LOPEZ. He succeeds excellent well at Winchester.

ELIZABETH. Would I had a son . . .

LOPEZ. Alas, dear Lady, 'tis too late.

ELIZABETH. In the Old Testament, Sarah gave birth at ninety.

LOPEZ. Those were the day of miracles.

ELIZABETH. I weary.

LOPEZ. May I hear your divine heart?

ELIZABETH. Aye, do so. (*The* QUEEN *offers her bosom.* LOPEZ *professionally applies his ear.*)

LOPEZ. It beats in harmony with the heavenly bodies.

ELIZABETH. You are a dear friend. I trust you above all others.

LOPEZ. I revere you above all the world. I urge Your Majesty to bathe at least once each month, whether you need it or not.

ELIZABETH. I do and shall. You may go now. (LOPEZ *prepares to leave. She stops him.*)

Oh, do let me see that bauble. (LOPEZ *presents the ring. She holds it and looks at it longingly, then reluctantly returns it.*) Do bring your wife and daughter to visit me. (LOPEZ *exits as the lights dim. When the lights rise again, the scene is the same;* ESSEX *is on one knee before the* QUEEN.)

ELIZABETH. You have been most neglectful of me, Robert.

ESSEX. I, Your Majesty . . . ?

ELIZABETH. Exactly. We are alone, why address me so formally?

ESSEX. You are my love beyond all these trappings of majesty.

ELIZABETH. Indeed. And do you love me as a woman?

ESSEX. I do . . . more than all . . . more than ever.

ELIZABETH. Alas, I grow old.

ESSEX. You were never more ravishing, my Bess.

ELIZABETH. Always the supreme courtier.

ESSEX. I never dissemble to you, my only love.

ELIZABETH. Show me, tonight in my bedchamber. Come as you did before. *(He embraces her passionately.)* Save your manhood for tonight.

SCENE 4

The quarters of DON ANTONIO, *Pretender to the Portuguese throne. The* DON, *a foppish poseur, stands with a tankard of madeira from which he has copiously imbibed. He is about forty-five years old. Seated at a table with drinks before each, are* ANDRADA, *a swarthy intriguer;* ESTABAN FEREIRA, *in his fifties, who conducts himself with businesslike efficiency despite his apparent impoverishment, having fallen from his high estate in Portugal—he is a crypto-Jew; and* LUIS TINOCO, *thirtyish, with a pleasing appearance, very much the soldier of fortune.*

ANTONIO. *(Drinking and with a swagger.)* Ah, nothing can equal our Portuguese madeira.

TINOCO. I fancy good dry sack.

ANTONIO. You have not developed a Portuguese palate. We've wasted our efforts and wine on you.

FEREIRA. *(To* ANTONIO.) Now that you are fortified with your precious spirits . . .

ANTONIO. Do not sneer at it. This valuable madeira grows scarcer and scarcer each day. Like my fortune, it quickly evaporates.

FEREIRA. You still have your jewels and your very valuable equestrian equipage.

ANTONIO. I must find a good Jew who will advance me a healthy purse on its pledge. Ugh, these indispensable Jews . . .

TINOCO. There are no Jews in England. But why Your Majesty's contempt? Your sainted mother was Jewish.

ANTONIO. *(Furious.)* You know too much and talk too much. Had my father married within the Faith . . . *(He crosses himself.)* I'd be on the Lusitanian throne today. And Philip would be courting me. Courting! Courtiers! They are vermin scurrying around for crumbs of cheese.

ANDRADA. Your Majesty must not be bitter. We carry the banner of Christian civilization.

FEREIRA. Woe to civilization.

TINOCO. Woe to Christianity. What say you, Your Majesty?

ANTONIO. I leave these matters to my advisors. They're best suited to create and then grapple with puzzlements.

TINOCO. I believe that Lord Essex is the man of destiny to resolve all our problems.

ANTONIO. Well said, my good Tinoco. But where is he when we need him? He is more enraptured with his own glory, with defeating Philip than he is with my legitimate claim to the throne of my beloved Portugal.

TINOCO. The mills of the English gods grind slowly. Simply because you are a threat to his enemy Philip, you may depend on his devotion to your cause.

ANTONIO. When will these Englishmen act! I should have remained at the French court. Catherine de Medici is Catholic, and we have common cause.

FEREIRA. Respectfully, Sire, it is unwise to speak of religious matters in England.

ANTONIO. True. Especially if it should be overheard by the Queen's physician.

FEREIRA. He is loyal to you, Your Majesty, and a fellow Portuguese.

ANTONIO. I trust him only as long as I dangle the bait of the 50,000 crowns I promised him.

ANDRADA. He grows impatient. What if Philip match your bond—but with immediate, hard cash?

ANTONIO. He would not dare. The royal courts of England would have him hanged. Essex already suspects him of traffic with Spain.

FEREIRA. The Earl of Essex may seek to undo the doctor, but Lord Burghley is chancellor, and he is dedicated to accommodating a peace with Spain. He will use Dr. Lopez in these negotiations if he can.

ANTONIO. No negotiations unless there is a pre-condition that the crown of Portugal be restored to me!

LOPEZ. *(Entering. He has overheard the last burst of braggadocio.)* And so it should be, Your Majesty.

ANTONIO. And what brings you here?

LOPEZ. To attend upon your Majesty, to receive your wishes or commands. (LOPEZ *hesitates to continue.*)

ANTONIO. And perhaps an earnest upon our bond.

LOPEZ. My faith in your destiny is sustained in my faith in your bond.

ANTONIO. You know my wishes, my commands. Can't you get these laggard Englishmen to respond! Essex makes empty promises. Catherine of France is ready to attack in the Lowlands. Now is the time for England to seize Lisbon. But nothing happens . . . nothing!

LOPEZ and ANDRADA. We try, indeed we try to stir them.

ANTONIO. *(Sarcastically.)* "Indeed you try." Bah, you try to cozen me. These months of idleness have beggared me.

All that interests you, Dr. Lopez, is your miserable money. (*In temper,* ANTONIO *gulps down his drink and flings himself out of the room.*)

LOPEZ. (*Pouring himself some madeira and reflectively drinking.*) King Antonio could do well with a sedative. Well, gentlemen, what good can we do for England today . . . ?

ANDRADA. Or for ourselves.

TINOCO. I must leave for Calais at dawn.

LOPEZ. Your visit here has been too brief. Why leave so soon?

TINOCO. Urgent business.

ANDRADA. (*Sneering.*) What "urgent business?"

LOPEZ. (*To* TINOCO.) Nay, answer not while I am present. I'd rather not know.

ANDRADA. You should know. All four of us should know.

LOPEZ. Not so. We are involved with portentous intrigue. Princes vie with one another; kingdoms are in bondage to foreign tyrants, while religions are too willing tools to serve whomsoever pays most. Alas, I see no happy outcome. This Portuguese clown struts like a popinjay and demands obeisance and does nought in his own interest. The lowliest cotter earns a millionfold more respect.

TINOCO. Such lofty talk, tsk, tsk, tsk. Yet you serve him.

LOPEZ. I serve my Queen. It is her wish. Her ministers deputized me to attend upon this Iberian peacock. (*Disgustedly,* LOPEZ *takes a long drink of wine, walks away from the others, and stands brooding at the window.*)

TINOCO. It grows late and I must away.

ANDRADA. Perhaps Don Antonio hath more to relate to you.

TINOCO. I've had enough of him to last. Tonight I must ride to Dover. I sail with the morning tide. (*He ad libs his farewell to* FEREIRA *and* ANDRADA. *En route to exit, he offers his hand to* LOPEZ.) I must go.

LOPEZ. What compels you to these dangerous missions? Expose yourself to no danger. (TINOCO *and* LOPEZ *walk out of the others' earshot.*)

TINOCO. You may trust me. My reward is a good purse. Actually, I've been given a substantial advance purse. I serve none other than the Lord closest to the Queen—Lord Essex.

LOPEZ. I'd rather you had not told me. Be warned, my friend. Essex seeks power. He is vainglorious, rash. He will sacrifice anyone to gain power.

TINOCO. I am but one of his many agents. They roam the continent and send him reports.

LOPEZ. I, too, have my sources—and I venture to say they are more dependable.

TINOCO. His establishment is more extensive and widespread than Walsingham ever dreamed possible or my Lord Burghley ever effected. I am merely a gatherer of information useful to England. Although I send it to the Earl of Essex for his use, I know I serve England and our Queen.

LOPEZ. You travel alone?

TINOCO. Always alone. "Down to Ghenna or up to the throne / he travels the fastest who travels alone."

LOPEZ. God speed you. (TINOCO *ad libs exit.*)

FEREIRA. (*Hastening out with* TINOCO.) I'll see you to your mount. (FEREIRA *exits with* TINOCO.)

ANDRADA. (*To* LOPEZ.) You are much too melancholy, my friend.

LOPEZ. With sufficient cause. This dreary England wearies me. When I think of a warm residence with my close kin in either Antwerp or Constantinople . . .

ANDRADA. Why not go to them?

LOPEZ. I have not the wherewithal. Would that Don Antonio would honor at least half the 50,000 crowns due me. There appears no prospect.

ANDRADA. I know from whence the 50,000 may come. (*They sit at the table like huddled conspirators.*) I have been in direct contact with the Spanish ambassador in Brussels. He brought me to King Philip of Spain. The king discussed a plan with me. He was much delighted with it, proof of which he offered me a token, which I will soon reveal to you.

LOPEZ. What plan?

ANDRADA. King Philip will undertake to pay you the 50,000 crowns due you but which you'll never obtain from Don Antonio. The king was so pleased that he embraced me.

LOPEZ. And wherefore was the king so moved?

ANDRADA. We propose that you, Dr. Lopez, bring about peace negotiations between Spain and Her Majesty's ministers.

LOPEZ. How sweet are the very thoughts of peace! I may try, but France and England will not desert Antonio.

ANDRADA. Our plan solves that problem.

LOPEZ. How?

ANDRADA. As one would a flea under a monk's shirt—eliminate him.

LOPEZ. Eliminate . . . ?

ANDRADA. Precisely. In your attendance upon this Portuguese Pretender, you do administer specifics for his frequent ailments?

LOPEZ. Yes . . . ?

ANDRADA. When he is next indisposed, you must administer to him a deadly poison which will finish him off. Then the 50,000 is yours. (LOPEZ *rises, in deep thought.*) You do well to consider the matter. King Philip hath sent you a token of his esteem as a pledge—this most precious ring. (ANDRADA *hands* LOPEZ *a dazzling ring;* LOPEZ *takes it.*)

LOPEZ. We'll speak more of this. (FEREIRA *returns.* LOPEZ *hides the ring in his cloak.*) Ah, dear Andrada, I must wait upon Don Antonio—when he deigns to appear. Favor me with a message to my wife when you return to Holborn. Simply tell her I am detained here at Eton and may not return home till tomorrow. (ANDRADA *indicates agreement.*) Estaban, would you not wish to return with Andrada to my home?

FEREIRA. Not yet. I must a word with you and divers other matters to attend. (ANDRADA *ad libs his exit.*)

LOPEZ. This involvement with Don Antonio becomes irksome and burdensome. It keeps me from the hospital.

FEREIRA. We can easily extricate ourselves whilst we line our purse.

LOPEZ. (*With a sardonic look toward door where* ANDRADA *exited.*) You have, I suppose, a plan. How readily we succumb to intrigue.

FEREIRA. How secure are you in Don Antonio's pledge of 50,000?

LOPEZ. As certain I am that the Messiah comes tonight.

FEREIRA. Would you welcome a guarantee?

LOPEZ. Continue—I am listening. But before you speak, know you that I will not engage in any plots of murder.

FEREIRA. Nor would I.

LOPEZ. Come, your plan. (LOPEZ *sits at the table whilst* FEREIRA *agitatedly walks about, hovering over* LOPEZ.)

FEREIRA. Were it not for you, dear Roderigo, I'd be a beggar on the highways. You've taken me in and comforted my family.

LOPEZ. Enough. We are fellow exiles. Our survival depends upon . . .

FEREIRA. Yes, depends upon our mutual trust. My trust in you . . .

LOPEZ. Enough of this sentimentality. We do what we must. Your plan?

FEREIRA. I've become impoverished since Philip seized my estates in Portugal. Were I to regain them, I would no longer impose on your bounty nor grovel to that empty-headed poseur of a king, nor suffer daily the uncertain tolerance of the perfidious English.

LOPEZ. So?

FEREIRA. Don Antonio's son, Dom Manuel and a number of our fellow Portuguese nobles here in England have delegated me to treat with Philip. We would pledge loyalty to Spain, acknowledge Philip our legal sovereign, and . . .

LOPEZ. "And," yes and . . . and what of Don Antonio?

FEREIRA. He'd no longer be an obstacle to peace, according to the Spaniards, especially since his son and heir hath agreed to the plan.

LOPEZ. And your reward . . . or stake in this?

FEREIRA. Philip will restore my estates, my family and I will live in peace, dignity, and tranquility.

LOPEZ. There is more to this?

FEREIRA. Philip wishes you, with me, to initiate peace negotiations between Spain and England. Philip believes that you have both access and influence in Elizabeth's court.

LOPEZ. How far hath this plan progressed?

FEREIRA. I have discussed it with Philip's agents who . . .

LOPEZ. I do not wish to know who they are.

FEREIRA. We've exchanged letters by which we've established mutual trust. And, mark this, I have forwarded to the Spanish Ambassador Dom Manuel's complete agreement.

LOPEZ. The prospect of peace is most persuasive. For peace I would do whate'er must be done. But never forget, dear friend, we must not become dupes between Burghley and Cecil's peace party and Lord Essex's bellicosity. We'd be crushed between them.

FEREIRA. Then you agree?

LOPEZ. For the Queen, yes. For England, yes. I will work for peace. But always remember: nought is to be in writing, no hint of our purpose, else we be undone.

FEREIRA. Have no fear. Should correspondence become inevitable, it will be in innocent code.

LOPEZ. If that be all, and it be enough . . .

FEREIRA. *(Extending his hand.)* You approve? Your word . . .

LOPEZ. *(Grasping the hand.)* I like it—agreed. Now hurry off before it grows too dark. I shall dine here with the erstwhile king. (ANTONIO *enters, speaks with his customary arrogance.)*

ANTONIO. I am hungry.

LOPEZ. That is a healthy symptom. *(To* FEREIRA.*)* Godspeed. (FEREIRA *exits while the petulant* ANTONIO *pours himself more wine).*

ANTONIO. Where are the servants?

LOPEZ. *(Bowing.)* Your Majesty.

SCENE 5

BACON's *study in Essex House.* BACON *is seated at his escritoire.* WILLIAM SHAKESPEARE *enters.*

BACON. Welcome, Master Will.

SHAKESPEARE. Greetings. Lord Southampton sent me to you.

BACON. Do sit. (SHAKESPEARE *complies.)* I speak for my Lord Essex. He grows impatient, this play about the Jew . . .

SHAKESPEARE. I make prodigious progress. A play portrays divers people. I must explore and develop each one's life.

BACON. 'Twould not be amiss should you portray a few of us here at Essex House, you know . . . so that we appear manly and heroic.

SHAKESPEARE. An idea worthy to explore . . . yes, why not . . . ?

BACON. Should it please you, I see myself in a role. I am not merely my Lord's amanuensis. My life has a destiny.

SHAKESPEARE. There is a destiny that shapes our ends.

BACON. Indeed, how true. But I do not wait upon Dame Fortune. Carpe diem!

SHAKESPEARE. Your wit doth serve your enthusiasm.

BACON. Destiny needs encouragement. My Lord Essex furthers my cause.

SHAKESPEARE. Your cause? And pray . . . that is . . . ?

BACON. To serve our England, as judge, as a state minister, wherever it pleases Her Majesty to assign me. My father was Keeper of the Great Seal of England. A peerage would recognize my services to the state. I would guide the destinies of our glorious England. It is not the emoluments of office I seek. I would use my place and power for the spreading of learning, for the creation of a new and mighty knowledge, for a vast beneficence, spreading in ever wider circles through all humanity . . . ah, the glory I foresee!

SHAKESPEARE. Capital! But the interpolation of political fancies would distract from the main plot and drama of my play.

BACON. And the main plot or drama is . . . ?

SHAKESPEARE. Lord Essex and I—all of England—would have the profanations of the sanctimonious Jew a self-condemnation . . .

BACON. Yet it doth appear that you seek to vindicate the villainous wretch.

SHAKESPEARE. My play is a comedy, with an obligatory love story. This I have resolved, but for the ending. I seek a device. My lovers quarrel, but the device must reconcile them.

BACON. Use the acquisitive instinct of all mortals. They descend like vultures upon loot from the Jew.

SHAKESPEARE. Yes, that may work. But what kind of loot?

BACON. The Jew hath much gold and jewels. There was one bauble most significant and damning in the evidence at the trial: a precious ring. 'Twas given the poisoner by the King of Spain. A motive to damn the doctor.

SHAKESPEARE. Where is the ring now?

BACON. The estate, wealth and goods of a condemned and to be executed traitor goes to the crown. The Queen now possesses the precious ring.

SHAKESPEARE. If the Queen doth have it, it needs must serve a happy purpose. An idea I must explore.

BACON. But when? Lord Essex, not to say myself, grows most impatient. Her Majesty remains unresolved. You must prod her.

SHAKESPEARE. I make progress.

BACON. Wherefore has thou not consulted with us? You seek a well-rounded character in the Jew. And from him you expect to deduce the truth? Nay, Master Will, you needs must induce a point of view.

SHAKESPEARE. A writer of plays need not succumb to a deductive nor inductive philosophy. He must only to himself be true and not be shackled to arbitrary limitations.

BACON. As you will. Therefore, you must be fully acquaint with the details of the indictment, the accusations, the prosecution, and the inevitable judgment.

SHAKESPEARE. "Inevitable . . . ?"

BACON. Conclusively. The villain was most fairly tried and judged by the noblest minds in England. The trial was conducted with careful interrogations of the wretched Jew's fellow conspirators. *(While* BACON *speaks the lights dim then rise upon the Guildhall in London, January, 1594.)* Come, I will a tale unfold that will congeal thy blood. Learn you of this detestable treason. *(At a large table are seated Lord* BURGHLEY, *Attorney General* COKE, *the Earl of* ESSEX, ROBERT CECIL, *and* FRANCIS BACON. *They are interrogating* ESTABAN FEREIRA DE GAMA.)*

COKE. Your name is Estaban Fereira de Gama?

FEREIRA. Aye, my Lord.

COKE. Where do you lodge?

FEREIRA. High Holborn.

BACON. Do you not dwell with the Jew Lopez?

FEREIRA. With Dr. Lopez, yes.

COKE. You are a native of . . .?

FEREIRA. Portugal.

COKE. What brought you to England?

FEREIRA. My estates were seized by King Philip of Spain. I then supported the cause of Don Antonio and came here in his train. Now that King Antonio despairs of his claim to his throne, I am lost and my family is penniless.

ESSEX. Therefore, to repair your fortunes, you conspired with your host and friend, this "doctor" Lopez?

BURGHLEY. *(To* ESSEX.*)* Gently, dear Robert. We will uncover motives in proper time. Presently, we seek facts.

COKE. The accused will answer.

FEREIRA. I perceived a method to repair my fortunes, recover my estates, and secure my family.

ESSEX. And that method . . . ?

FEREIRA. To make an accommodation

with Spain. Others have done so and were thereby enabled to return to Portugal and enjoy the bounty of their restored estates. A half year ago, I wrote to the Spanish Ambassador in France, Don Cristoforo de Moro, whereby I offered my submission to the Spanish king. My proposal included a like offer by Don Antonio's son and heir, Dom Manuel and other Portuguese nobles to do likewise. They invited me to act in their behalf.

BURGHLEY. And Dr. Lopez?

FEREIRA. I took him into my confidence.

ESSEX. Did you approach "Dr." Lopez or did he you?

FEREIRA. I do not recall.

ESSEX. You must.

FEREIRA. I protest that I speak the truth.

ESSEX. (*Signals by nodding toward off-stage.* TOPCLIFFE, *official torturer in the Tower, enters.*

ESSEX *again speaks to* FEREIRA.) Know you this man?

FEREIRA. No, my Lord.

ESSEX. He is the chief interrogator at the Tower of London. His ways of extracting and discovering the truth are always successful.

FEREIRA. (*Trembling.*) I speak the truth.

ESSEX. There has been mention of poison.

FEREIRA. True.

ESSEX. Yes? Go on . . .

FEREIRA. When I spoke with Dr. Lopez concerning my negotiations with Don Moro, I first showed him the writing of Dom Manuel, son of King Antonio.

COKE. When and where was this conversation?

FEREIRA. Some months ago, in Dr.

Lopez's dwelling. Manuel Andrada was present. We did all three agree I should write to Don Cristoforo de Moro, the Spanish Ambassador in France, how, beside myself who sought to accommodate myself, I did hold Dom Manuel sure and that the said Andrada should procure answer in Calais, whither he went.

ESSEX. What said the Doctor?

FEREIRA. He agreed to give me the promission of the 50,000 crusadoes which he had of King Antonio . . . to present it to the King of Castile, and that I might allege to him how I had won the doctor and left him doing the King's service in persuading the Lords of England that they should not help the said Don Antonio in anything. Wherefore I gave him my word on behalf of his Catholic Majesty to see him recompensed the said amount in such sort as it should seem good to him.

BURGHLEY. And wherefore should the Spanish King pay out 50,000 crowns to your Dr. Lopez?

FEREIRA. To effect peace between the two nations.

ESSEX. (*Motions to* TOPCLIFFE, *who hovers ominously over* FEREIRA, *who is terrified as* ESSEX *continues his interrogation.*) You are withholding the truth. One way or another, we will have the truth from you.

FEREIRA. B-b-b-but I tell only the truth.

ESSEX. The poison?

FEREIRA. I know not of poison.

COKE. (*Perusing a letter in his hand.*) This letter from a certain Francisco Torres in Brussels or Antwerp, that we intercepted, addressed to a certain Diego Hernandes in London.

Who is Francisco Torres?

FEREIRA. (*Squirms, but is too aware of the hovering* TOPCLIFFE.) The letter for "Diego Hernandes" was intended for me.

BURGHLEY. And this "Francisco Torres?"

FEREIRA. Manuel Luis Tinoco. (BACON *and* ESSEX *confer away from the others.*)

BACON. 'Tis the same Tinoco who is our agent.

ESSEX. I never . . .

BACON. We commissioned him to approach the Duke of Braganza in Portugal to lead an uprising.

ESSEX. It was merely talk. Nothing came of it.

BACON. He may disclose that he worked in your behalf.

ESSEX. And how many others doth he serve? I shall personally interrogate this adventurer Tinoco. No connection with me will be proved. (BACON *and* ESSEX *resume their places at the table.*)

COKE. Who is this Tinoco?

ESSEX. Yet another of "King" Antonio's entourage.

COKE. This intercepted letter is suspiciously innocuous. (COKE *reads the letter.*) "The bearer hereof will tell your worship the price in which your pearls are held; and will advise your worship presently of the uttermost penny that will be given for them; and will receive what order you will set down for the conveyance of the money and wherein you would have it employed. Also, this bearer will tell you in what resolution we rested about a little musk and amber, which I am determined to buy; but before I resolve myself, I will be advised of the price thereof. And if it please your worship to be my partner I am persuaded we shall make good profit."

BURGHLEY. It appears innocent unto itself. Merely commerce.

ESSEX. There must be more enfolded and hidden therein. Bide a while and we shall decipher it. This wretch before us fears some disclosure. What is it?

FEREIRA. Nay, in truth, my Lord.

ESSEX. You have communicated with your friend, compatriot, and host, the good doctor?

FEREIRA. No, my Lord.

ESSEX. I suggest you were in communication. We have your secret note— yes, we apprehended it two days ago; whilst you were in custody at Eton, you smuggled out a note to Dr. Lopez. Apparently you knew not of our arrest of D'Avila upon whom we found this enigmatic letter read by Lord Coke. You did say, and I quote from your note which you attempted to smuggle, you implore Dr. Lopez "in any wise to prevent the coming over of Gomez d'Avila, for if he should be taken, the Doctor were utterly undone without all remedy."

BACON. And Lopez did reply that he did send once or twice to keep d'Avila away and that he would spare no expense, though it cost him £300.

ESSEX. (*To* COKE *and* BURGHLEY.) We intercepted both these notes. (*To a shattered* FEREIRA.) In addition, you, Estaban Fereira, attempted to subvert and suborn your young warder at Eton, Pedro, with an enormous amount of money. (ESSEX *reads.*) According to the sworn statement of said Pedro, "to go to the Spanish Secretary of Wars in the Netherlands and procure with him to see the dispatch or anything else he hath for me. And as soon as thou hast seen it, thou shalt put a word or two of thine own hand on a small piece of paper, which thou shalt send unto me through the conveyance of Antonio Fallerio, which is in Flanders. And if Manuel Luis Tinoco is there, he will do anything for thee; and if not, the Secretary will grant that thou shalt bestow that letter as in this I have requested thee." The remainder of the statement concerns Pedro's proposed journey with detailed instructions, means of communication, etc.

FEREIRA. I spoke not so with warder Pedro.

COKE. Your Gomez d'Avila, who is now in our custody, attempted to send a message to your friend, Dr. Lopez.

ESSEX. Again, Dr. Lopez. He appeareth both the base and fulcrum of a heinous plot. Know you not, Estaban Fereira, that the doctor hath betrayed you?

FEREIRA. I am much confused. I know only my loyalty to Her Divine Majesty and to you, good sirs, who have favored me with the security of English hospitality.

ESSEX. And you, you ingrate, repay us with treacherous plots!

FEREIRA. Never. I am sadly misunderstood. Lord Burghley knows of my loyalty and devotion to peace for this kingdom.

BURGHLEY. I know of these letters wherein lie the melancholy evidence of your betrayal.

FEREIRA. (*Frantic, hysterical.*) Not I! Look to Dr. Lopez. Perhaps he knows of betrayals. He hath been in the pay of Spain for a number of years. He formulated the arrangement to bring Don Antonio's son over to the interests of Philip of Spain. Did not Lopez secure the release from prison of the known spy Andrada, specially to have Andrada journey to Spain to arrange the doctor's poisoning of King Antonio!

ESSEX. Poison? (*Lights dim, then rise to focus on a corner downstage upon* WILL SHAKESPEARE *and* DR. LOPEZ.)

SHAKESPEARE. Did you indeed plot to poison Don Antonio?

LOPEZ. Nay! Never! Hast not ever been so angry with one that you compulsively exclaim, "I could kill him." So it was with King Antonio and me. His promises came to nought, whilst he continued to beguile his followers with vain blandishments of impossible glories. It came to pass that he outraged my patience. I may have, without serious intent, threatened to poison him. (*Lights dim on* LOPEZ *and* SHAKESPEARE; *then they rise again on the scene in Guildhall.*)

BURGHLEY. Did not this Tinoco come to England precisely to confer with you and Dr. Lopez and remained no longer than overnight? Why did he flee England in such haste? What guilt pursued him hence?

FEREIRA. Lopez was out of London at the time. Tinoco hastened away lest he be discovered as an illicit visitor. Above all, his sole mission was to advise Dr. Lopez through me that peace negotiations were progressing favorably.

ESSEX. I urge that we arrest this Jew Doctor Lopez and proceed to a trial . . .

FEREIRA. Of the doctor?

BACON. Not entirely. A trial of the doctor, of you Estaban Fereira, and of Tinoco.

ESSEX. Remove this prisoner and keep him from any and all contact with his fellows. (FEREIRA *is removed.*)

COKE. And now . . .

ESSEX. We arrest this Jew Dr. Lopez.

CECIL. The Queen's physician! On what grounds? On the gossip of frightened mice!

ESSEX. Lopez will be interrogated and sufficient evidence elicited to condemn the traitor.

COKE. Legal procedures must be observed.

ESSEX. Definitely, for I will attend to that matter myself.

SCENE 6

Windsor Castle. An evening during Christmas week, 1593. Music and dancing. ELIZABETH *dances with a courtier. The dance ends.* ELIZABETH *comes forward and encounters* DR. LOPEZ. *He bows to her.*

LOPEZ. There are matters of great import I must convey to Your Majesty.

ELIZABETH. What? In this holiday season? We celebrate the Prince of Peace.

LOPEZ. I speak of peace. The late Lord Walsingham appointed me to approach Spain to explore a basis for peace.

ELIZABETH. We know of that. And we cherish your devotion to your queen. Dear Walsingham so informed me. I pray you succeed. Nothing would be dearer to my heart. Let Philip lead a Catholic Europe provided he acknowledges me the leader of a Protestant Europe. And he must accept the sovereignty of Holland.

LOPEZ. Alas, the alternative is needless, absurd war.

ELIZABETH. But might not the struggle be for the good, the destruction of Catholicism and the transfer of the Spanish Empire to benign English rule. Yet I would not sacrifice one English life in such a war. By the accident of birth I am a Protestant leader. I sought it not—a destiny thrust it upon me. I'd much rather lead a Renaissance than a Reformation. How I hate, abhor the wastefulness of war!

LOPEZ. You have blessed this heavenly isle with at least thirty years of serene peace, in your time.

ELIZABETH. Only because I delay precipitate action with quick, impulsive decisions. Amazing how many urgencies inevitably disappear by simply being ignored. Time resolves all, whilst mine enemies are confounded by being put off and off and off, to their utter confusion. But, dear Dr. Lopez, we philosophize, we pontificate, we have all solutions to man's afflictions, yet I remain without an heir of mine own body. 'Tis sad.

LOPEZ. It is physiologically impossible. You remain a virgin.

ELIZABETH. *(Laughing)*. Meanwhile, I dissemble to the world. A prince of France, the dread Czar of the Russias, they all seek my hand. Virgin, you say—at my age 'tis not a state of which to be proud. How tedious grows the charade. And so I must pretend, keep my secret for reasons I would not divulge to a soul except you, dear Dr. Lopez, for I know you and trust you above all others. You come not to me with petitions and harrassments for preferments, for . . .

LOPEZ. I wish only to serve you, dear Lady. Yet, one small favor . . .

ELIZABETH. Yes?

LOPEZ. My friend and compatriot, Estaban Fereira de Gama, hath been arrested. I will vouch for him should Your Majesty have him released in my custody. I will be fully answerable.

ELIZABETH. We will not intefere until we are fully acquainted with the details.

LOPEZ. May I hear your heart ere I leave?

ELIZABETH. (LOPEZ *affixes his ear to her bosom. He then lifts his head.*) Yes?

LOPEZ. Your divine heart beats in placid and gentle rhythm of the universe. Eat moderately, sleep and rest, and continue your riding.

ELIZABETH. (*She waves her hand in dismissal.* LOPEZ *exits. A* NOBLEWOMAN *approaches the* QUEEN.) Thank you.

LADY IN WAITING. Madam, Sir Robert Cecil awaits your pleasure. He says 'tis urgent.

ELIZABETH. Bring him to us. (NOBLEWOMAN *retires, but she quickly returns with* ROBERT CECIL. *He is puny, has a distorted body, and his movements are awkward.*)

ELIZABETH. Welcome, dear Robert. Come you to dance?

CECIL. If it would please Your Majesty. My preference is no.

ELIZABETH. You appear distraught. Such melancholy state ill suits our festivities.

CECIL. A most delicate matter, Your Majesty. I come from Guildhall. My cousin Robert Devereux is determined to uncover a malignant plot 'gainst your royal person. He is determined to destroy Dr. Lopez.

ELIZABETH. Our royal physician and most trusted friend?

CECIL. I've hurried to you ere more mischief be done.

ELIZABETH. Wherefore doth Essex seek to undo the Queen's physician?

CECIL. The Earl of Essex perceives Dr. Lopez as an intriguing instrument of those who seek peace with Spain. Among such, my father Lord Burghley, who is dedicated to your gracious Majesty's pacific reign, while Robert Devereux seeks a most brutal and unnecessary war 'twixt your England and Spain. Thus, Lord Essex uses Dr. Lopez as a pawn in his intrigues. He claims, and doth produce evidence in substantiation, that Dr. Lopez deals with Spain.

ELIZABETH. What think you on it, Robert?

CECIL. Lord Essex hath uncovered a mare's nest. His accusations have no merit and should not be encouraged. Nonetheless, he hath ordered the arrest of Dr. Lopez.

ELIZABETH. What think you, Robert?

CECIL. There is nothing to any plot, so-called, involving your doctor. We did search Dr. Lopez's home. We found no papers, no documents, nothing incriminating. Yet Lord Essex insists such evidence hath been burned or destroyed in anticipation of our investigation.

ELIZABETH. What profiteth Lord Essex to hound our Doctor?

CECIL. Your Majesty's servants are highly diligent and efficient in seeking out the various plots of thine enemies. My Lord Essex believes he can demonstrate that his secret spies are more efficient in protecting your Majesty and foiling the Jesuits' plan to advance the Infanta of Spain to the sceptre of our England—your England, by the sword if need be, and with murderers to dispose of your sacred self.

ELIZABETH. But—my own, my devoted physician? How comes he into these devious plots?

CECIL. We thoroughly searched his house. We found nothing—absolutely nothing of malice to incriminate or involve Dr. Lopez in any plot.

ELIZABETH. Know you this, Robert: Dr. Lopez informed me that he was approached in behalf of the king of Spain, of being offered a goodly sum to intercede in behalf of peace 'twixt our kingdoms. We like not this scheming and so informed the doctor. That ended the matter. Now what sayeth Lord Burghley.

CECIL. We are of one mind.

ELIZABETH. Aye, father and son.

CECIL. Nay, dear Lady. Only your welfare concerns us. And for such we seek to preserve peace in your realm, and we work for your peace of mind. Robert Devereux is restive, constantly stirring alarums, so fears he imminent rebellion and war to overthrow your commonwealth. In his rivalry with your appointed and legal officials, he seeks means to enlarge his foreign intelligence, to surpass Lord Burghley who, in your interests, is devoted to maintain peace. Meanwhile, the Earl of Essex seeks open war with Spain and constantly tries to prove Spanish perfidy. We much doubt that Dr. Lopez seeks and plots harm to you and England.

ELIZABETH. Alas, our good doctor is a mite too greedy. He sought to deceive King Philip and cozen him of his money. We would have no part of anything so unseemly to our crown. Dr. Lopez was told as much.

CECIL. The Earl of Essex will certainly arrive any moment. He seeks your approval for a warrant to arrest your Majesty's physician.

ELIZABETH. We will see him. You will await the outcome in an adjoining chamber. There will be further instructions in this matter.

CECIL. There was talk of the rack—but the royal consent is needed.

ELIZABETH. The English common law forbids torture. Torture is contrary to the very nature of Englishmen. Torment practiced in other lands is not used in England—it is taken as servile! The nature of our nation is free, stout, hauld, perhaps prodigal of life and blood. But contumelies, beatings, servitude, and servile torment and punishment we will not abide.

CECIL. Are we then to infer that you . . .

ELIZABETH. We will have no torture of that poor old doctor. Meanwhile, perhaps our astrologer, Dr. Dee, may help to illuminate this farrago. Go now, good Robert, but await our call. (CECIL *exits. A* LADY IN WAITING *enters.*)

LADY. The Earl of Essex hath arrived and implores audience.

ELIZABETH. Bring him hence. (ESSEX *enters, bows low, and is about to speak. The* QUEEN *waves him to slience.*) You have much displeased and distressed us, Lord Essex.

ESSEX. 'Tis not possible, for I seek only your goodwill, for only that sustains me. Nay, my Lady, someone must have conveyed misinformation to your royal ear.

ELIZABETH. Can you deny that you seek to arrest our good friend and personal physician? He is most capable, honest, and most devoted to our royal person and to England. Why do you hound this old man?

ESSEX. He is the center of a plot with Philip of Spain to undo us.

ELIZABETH. You have proof of this?

ESSEX. Indeed, yes. We have letters we have intercepted, letters carried by his creatures between this Jew doctor and your enemies.

ELIZABETH. It has been reported that you searched his house. Were these letters discovered there?

ESSEX. No, your Majesty. We found nothing of malice nor incriminating. Undoubtedly he burned all that might betray him.

ELIZABETH. We are informed 'tis all a mare's nest—and we suspect a web woven by your spider friend Bacon.

Hah, you petition the crown to appoint him our attorney general! Know you that our physician and dear friend is highly thought of at St. Bartholomew's Hospital. They and we, yes we—your Queen, have found him skillful in his counsel on correct dieting—see my own figure—and on purging and bleeding. He lectures on anatomy at the college of physicians. Your step-father Leicester, as did Lord Walsingham, delivered their lives into his capable hands—as does your Queen. He is both honest and zealous. Even your toady Bacon did praise him as observant, with a pleasing and pliable behavior. You, yes you, Lord Essex, failed to corrupt him to become one of your Spanish intelligencers. You dare to arrest this loyal servant of your Queen merely on the word or scribblings of your wretched spies!

ESSEX. Not so, Your Majesty. We discovered a ring of considerable value which he received of Philip of Spain.

ELIZABETH. We know of the ring. The good Doctor offered it to your Queen. We refused to accept it, for we seek nought from our enemies nor accede to devious plots.

ESSEX. Yet, under interrogation your "good" Doctor denied all knowledge of the ring.

ELIZABETH. Interrogation? You dared employ the rack . . .

ESSEX. No, never without Your Majesty's approval and authority.

ELIZABETH. As though that would deter you. Who else was present at the interrogation?

ESSEX. My Lord Burghley, Robert Cecil, myself, and Lopez. Lopez, like a dissembling Jew, did utterly with greater oaths and execrations deny all the points, articles, and particularities of the accusations. His denials could not stand against much evidence against him.

ELIZABETH. And your colleagues, did they concur with your conclusions?

ESSEX. *(He hesitates and falters but for a moment.)* Lord Burghley believed your doctor, in part, for my Lord Burghley is much aware that Dr. Lopez in consort with the devilish machinations of one Andrada had been negotiating a possibiity of peace with Spain.

ELIZABETH. And we seek peace! Our people seek peace! Our minister Lord Burleghy is so instructed by us. Yet you thwart it in all you contrive! Your Queen's very life is entrusted to Dr. Lopez, and you dare allege monstrous motives to him. First you foist this Pretender to the Portuguese throne, this fancy Don Antonio, upon us and employ Dr. Lopez to be his mentor, his interpreter, his sponsor. Now for reasons to which we are not privy, you discard all that previously you championed. Why? What do you seek and covet? Being your Queen's trusted friend seemeth insufficient for your floundering, restless soul. We like it not.

ESSEX. Your sacred Majesty knows not that . . .

ELIZABETH. The affairs of state are safely in the hands of Lord Burghley. You attempt new fields of conquest and conduct a state other than our own. You meddle, sir, and made a muddle of our affairs. Your obstinancy refuses to accept the truth even when your Queen tells it you. Your anti-Spanish obsession confuses everyone, mostly yourself. You are a rash and temerarious youth! We charge you to meddle no more! Our honor is concerned herein.

ESSEX. *(In a rage.)* Youth! Yes, youth indeed! Mine honor is at stake. Come what may, I will prove the Cecils utterly mistaken, and I will bring your Dr. Lopez to justice! *(In a rage, ESSEX flings himself out.)*

ELIZABETH. *(Walks to opposite door and beckons CECIL to enter.)* We must discover the truth or falsity of these accusations, rash though they appear. You will hie to Lord Burghley and arrange for a trial of our physician. We will allow Lord Essex to present his rather tenuous case. Oh yes, and have our Solicitor General Coke conduct the trial. We must and shall be fair to all concerned. The Earl of Essex, Lord Burghley, and you, Robert, will be judges. *(CECIL bows and exits as the lights dim.)*

SCENE 7

Essex House. Outside the chamber of LORD ESSEX, FRANCIS BACON *converses with a* SERVITOR *who carries a tray of food.*

SERVITOR. Thus it hath been for over two days. He will not respond to my knocking and pleas. Not a morsel of food hath passed this door. He may be . . .

BACON. Don't say it. Our Lord Essex may sulk and deny the world, but he shall live to greater glory. (*Pause.* BACON *paces thoughtfully.* SERVITOR *places tray on a bench, then he exits. Finally,* BACON *raps loudly on the door.*) My Lord, are you well?

ESSEX. (*His voice from beyond the door.*) Don't plague me! Go away.

BACON. You haven't eaten in over two days.

ESSEX. My thoughts are my food.

BACON. Exactly my dish. I would share them with you.

ESSEX. Don't cozen me.

BACON. We have a confession from the Jew Doctor. (ESSEX *eagerly opens the door.*)

ESSEX. What did he confess?

BACON. Wellllll, it's not strictly speaking a confession . . .

ESSEX. You'll make no fool of me! (*Exits back into his room as he slams door.*)

BACON. (*Baffled, but tries to speak through the door.*) There's to be a trial. You are one of the judges. We must prepare the indictment and proofs.

ESSEX. (*As he suspiciously opens the door.*) Another trick?

BACON. No, my Lord. 'Tis the truth. Her Majesty hath consented to a trial of the Jew Doctor.

ESSEX. (*Pouncing upon the food; ravenously eats; paces.*) You have restored my appetite. Now I will repay him for thwarting me, maligning me with his gossip. He tried to corrupt Her Majesty's mind against me—me, the Earl of Essex. I, too, have royal blood in me! Yet I am Her Majesty's most loyal and devoted subject. (*He mimics* LOPEZ.) "Yes, your Majesty, only I, Dr. Lopez am devoted to you. The Earl of Essex is setting up a rival government, the Earl of Essex has his own secret spies who rival those of Your Majesty's Privy Council. The Earl of Essex hath squandered your royal exchequer on this quondam King of Portugal. The Earl of Es . . .

BACON. Her Royal Majesty denies she is of such mind.

ESSEX. How know you?

BACON. I sought audience with our Queen. She graciously admitted me.

ESSEX. And . . . ?

BACON. I assured Her Majesty of your undying devotion. If you erred, it was because of your enthusiasm to secure her welfare and that of England.

ESSEX. I need no champion, my good Francis. Yet, I see no harm.

BACON. I confess my mission was in part self-interested. I sought to seek out her sentiment concerning my possible appointment as Lord Solicitor. I offered her a precious jewel got from my mother. Her Majesty rejected it.

ESSEX. There you erred dismally. Her Majesty may procrastinate like the eternal female, and she will be of no constant mind. But she cannot be bought.

BACON. So I discovered. And Coke hath the appointment.

ESSEX. I tried, my friend. But in time you will be rewarded, I promise. Who was with our Queen?

BACON. Lord Burghley and your cousin Robert Cecil entered ere I departed. She recounted to them your asseverations about the scheming Jew Doctor. Robert Cecil protested there was nothing to it. I countered with your loyalty and good judgment. Then Her Majesty consulted with Lord Burghley and both concluded that only a trial would uncover the truth. Thus, we are to present our case in court.

ESSEX. Yours is not the only jewel Her Majesty rejected. She also returned one offered her by Lopez—a precious ring. 'Tis unlike her. Perhaps, in your case, she sought not to be bought. But why reject a friendly offering from her physician?

BACON. She may have feared some secret, hidden poison in the Jew's ring that might have killed her.

ESSEX. *(Excited.)* There we have it! Poison! A most dangerous and desperate treason. The point of conspiracy was Her Majesty's death. The executer—Dr. Lopez! The manner—poison! I will pursue this and make it appear as clear as noonday. Ah, my good Francis, your fat cousin Robert Cecil will either see it our way or confess he, too, leans toward Rome.

BACON. He would not dare.

ESSEX. Now tell me of the Jew's confession.

BACON. When he was confronted by both Fereira's and Tinoco's confessions, he completely crumbled.

ESSEX. Was the rack employed?

BACON. No, my Lord. We had not Her Majesty's consent, nor dared we petition her.

ESSEX. *(Smiling knowingly.)* Nor any suggestion of its employment?

BACON. None. But by happenstance, there appeared Richard Topcliffe, official "persuader" of the Tower. At the sight of him, the Jew became hysterical and rattled on. Between frantic asseverations of utter ignorance and wild revelations of complicated and impossible plots, he completely betrayed himself.

ESSEX. You must fully understand, Francis, that upon the life of our beloved Queen hangs the entire structure of our state. Her lamentable demise would foist upon us a Catholic sovereign, a complete revolution in our system of government—all of us would be eliminated, your precious cousins the Cecils with the rest of us. Philip and his Catholics have murdered William of Orange and Henry III of France. We must thank the Almighty that Mary Stuart is no longer a threat.

BACON. Her Majesty dwells unhappily upon the episode.

ESSEX. Beheading is a benign execution for treason. The Jew will not fare so pleasantly. We will vindicate our Queen, soothe her conscience, if such it needs. Let us now prepare for the trial. I have proven myself her hero on the field of battle. Now indeed, I will win my spurs and saddle as a statesman worthy to lead our country.

SCENE 8

Guildhall, London, January 1594.

Present, seated at raised table, are LORD BURGHLEY, ROBERT CECIL, *Solicitor General Designate* COKE, FRANCIS BACON, *a* COURT CLERK, *and the* EARL OF ESSEX. BURGHLEY *peruses a letter.*

BURGHLEY. How came you by this letter, my Lord Essex?

ESSEX. Being aware of the wicked plotting and devious devices of the conspirators, we arrested and interrogated Estaban Fereira de Gama, if you recall. He is now in the custody of King Antonio at Eton. Because of information obtained from the prisoner, we alerted customs at Rye, Dover, and Sandwich to intercept, detain, and read all correspondence 'twixt Portugal and England. We then extended the order to cover all correspondence in a foreign tongue arriving at these ports from the continent. Much mischief is being plotted at the Escurial, Brussels, Calais, and Lisbon.

CECIL. What mean you "mischief?"

ESSEX. To undo our kingdom, destroy our beloved Queen, and foist the Bishop of Rome upon us.

BURGHLEY. Our intelligencers from the continent are certain King Philip of Spain seeks to negotiate peace. Our dear Queen seeks this peace as well.

ESSEX. If peace she seeks, wherefore do we support and aid the French king whilst Philip pursues a defensive war upon the Low countries? Speak up, Francis.

BACON. The supports and aids of Her Majesty to the French king are a principal impediment and retardation to Philip prevailing according to his ends. Should he succeed in troubling the waters here, he might divert our succours from France.

BURGHLEY. Philip learned his lesson in '88. Likewise he was confounded in his plots to cause friction 'twixt us and Scotland.

ESSEX. Philip and his counselors and ministers have descended to a course against all honor, all society and humanity, odious to God and man, detested by the heathen themselves, which is to take away the life of Her Majesty, which God have in His precious custody, by violence or poison. This vile matter might be proved to be against all Christianity and religion, as well as against nature, the law of nations, the honor of arms, the civil law, the rules of morality and policy—the most condemned, barbarous and ferine act that can be imagined . . .

CECIL. Her Royal Majesty . . .

ESSEX. Yes, Her Majesty! She did, upon the advice of Francis Bacon, write to the Archduke to complain of the designs against her life by the Count de Fuentes and Don Diego Ibarra, as well as other Spanish ministers in the Lowlands together with English Catholic fugitives there. Our Queen desired him to signify to these facts to the king of Spain, enabling the king to vindicate his own character by punishing these ministers and delivering up to her such fugitives as were parties to such designs.

COKE. And did the Archduke respond?

BACON. Alas, our blessed Queen hath been ignored. Divers persons, English and Irish, corrupted by money and promises, resolved and conjured by priests in confessionals, were sent into our land to execute the wretched and horrible deed. When some of them were taken, they have with great sorrow confessed these attempts.

BURGHLEY. Hath not the Spanish king entered Paris and is reconciling his opponents?

BACON. Not so, my Lord. 'Tis much confusion there. Therefore the Spaniards seek no disturbance from hence, where they make account that were Her Majesty removed, upon whose person God continue His extraordinary watch and providence, here in our England would be nought but confusion which would further their intended ruin of this state according to their ancient malice.

ESSEX. Amongst the number of these execrable undertakers, there was none so much built and relied upon by the great ones of the other side as was this physician Lopez; nor indeed none so dangerous. Consider, my Lords, the aptness of the instrument, or the subtlety and secrecy of those that practiced with him, or the shift and evasion which he had provided for a color of his doings, if they should come into question. Whereas others would encounter infinite difficulties in the very obtaining of an opportunity to execute ths horrible act, this man, in regard to his faculty, and his private access to Her Majesty, had both means to perpetrate and to conceal, whereby he might reap the fruit of his wicked treason without evident peril.

COKE. And the others: Tinoco, Andrada, and Fereira?

BACON. (ESSEX *signals* BACON *to speak.*) As accomplices of Lopez, they being Portuguese and of the retinue of King Antonio, the king of Spain's mortal enemy, they were men thereby freed and discharged from suspicion and might send and receive letters out of Spain without jealousy, for they were thought to entertain intelligences for the good of their master. And for the evasion and mask that Lopez prepared, it seemed he intended but to cozen the king of Spain without seeming ill meaning.

COKE. Therefore, by the great goodness of God, this matter fell into the hands of good, honorable, and sufficient persons who disclosed this foul and monstrous treason. How came you to detect this villainy?

ESSEX. Members of Her Majesty's council considered that some of the retinue of King Antonio were not unlike to hatch these kinds of treason, in regard they were needy strangers, entered into despair of their master's fortune, and like enough to make their peace at home, by some such wicked services as these. Hence, we grew to have an extraordinary vigilant eye upon them. This Lopez, of nation a Portuguese, and suspected to be in sect secretly a Jew, professed physic in this land, being withal a man most observant and officious, and of a pleasing and appliable behavior; thus rather than for any great learning in his faculty, he grew known and favored at court and then sworn physician of Her Majesty and grew to good estate and wealth. Insinuating himself greatly, and being of the same nation as King Antonio, he pretended to solicit the king's causes at court, for which he was to gain 50,000 crowns.

BURGHLEY. His intrigues, history, and machinations at court are not treasonous.

ESSEX. As a wholly corrupt and mercenary nature, he wished to secure payment and cast his eye upon a more able paymaster—hence his secret pact with the king of Spain.

CECIL. Lopez asserts he was designated by the late Lord Walsingham to negotiate with Spain.

ESSEX. And Lord Walsingham is dead. The crafty Jew offers a dead witness.

BACON. There are live witnesses—his fellow conspirators. One Manuel Andrada, formerly of King Antonio's entourage, confessed he had plotted with Lopez the poisoning of King Antonio. This man, coming hither, was, for the same his practice, appearing by letters intercepted, apprehended, and committed to prison. Other letters intercepted by good diligence revealed that Andrada advertised he had won Dr. Lopez to King Philip's service. But Lopez, having understanding thereof, contrived a secret conference with Andrada and persuaded him to take the matter upon himself, and that he had invented the advertisement touching Lopez only to secure credence with Spain. Lopez convinced Andrada that if he remained free, he would achieve Andrada's release. Lopez's subtle persuasion and direction and lessoning resulted in Andrada's answering to absolve Lopez. Upon his release, Andrada was suffered to leave the realm and hasten to Spain, in pretence to do some service for Don Antonio, but in truth to continue Lopez's negotiations and intelligence with King Philip. Andrada returned to Lopez with assurances and encouragements from King Philip with a token of a very precious jewel for Lopez, as an earnest of their understanding. The cunning Jew offered the jewel to Her Majesty, knowing in advance she would refuse it.

CECIL. Your information, credible as it may be, does not establish guilt of treason upon Dr. Lopez.

BACON. Lopez did indeed contrive to get Andrade out of England into Calais. There he was near to both England and Flanders, thus in an expeditious position to communicate to and fro between Lopez and the Spanish ministers. But the Spaniards looked with disfavor upon Andrada and delegated Manuel Luis Tinoco as their emissary to Dr. Lopez. Of this Tinoco they first received a corporal oath, with solemn ceremony, taking his hands between their hands, that he should keep secret that which should be imparted to him and never reveal the same, though he should be apprehended and questioned here. They acquaint him with the letters of Andrada which he was to pass to Lopez through Estaban Fereira de Gama who had secretly passed to the service of the King of Spain.

BURGHLEY. This Tinoco had expressed a desire to come to England provided we guaranteed him safe conduct. We so complied, but made safe conduct only into England, but not out of England. *(General laughter.)*

ESSEX. Lopez cautiously refrained from writing to Tinoco or through him to the Spaniards. Instead, he did convey all communications through Fereira. Meanwhile Lopez did subtly continue to ingratiate himself with her Majesty whilst conducting his liaison with the Spanish ministers. Lopez did bind himself closer and closer to Fereira, even suggesting to Fereira that the administering the poison to the Queen was in syrup, knowing that Her Majesty never useth syrup. Thus Lopez thought it would be a high point for his own justification if things would come to any question.

BURGHLEY. The letter. The prisoner should be brought hence and interrogated about its seeming innocence . . .

ESSEX. 'Tis in cipher, my Lord.

BURGHLEY. Have the prisoner brought in. *(He signals to* TOPCLIFFE *who exits and quickly returns with* LOPEZ *between himself and a warder.* LOPEZ *still conducts himself with dignity, albeit he shows signs of suffering and bewilderment.)* Because of your constant attendance at Court as our good Queen's physician, you are known to us.

COKE. *(Takes letter from* BURGHLEY.*)* This letter which appeareth innocent of any great moment, seems to convey a meaning other from the language as written.

LOPEZ. I know of no letter.

COKE. This letter was apprehended upon the person of one Gomez d' Avila, known to you . . . (LOPEZ *shakes his head.*) It is from one Francisco de Thores. Manuel Luis Tinoco hath confessed he is the writer of this letter. *(Throughout the entire proceedings,* LOPEZ *is baffled, frightened, and confused. He shakes his head upon each assertion and tries to deny the accusations.)* The letter sayeth, "This bearer will tell you the price in which your pearls are esteemed, and in what resolution we rest about a little musk and amber, which I am determined to buy." Are you prepared to decipher these words?

LOPEZ. I know not a Francisco de Thores. I know of no amber or musk. I am a doctor, a healer of the afflicted. I deal not in pearls.

ESSEX. My Lords, Manuel Luis Tinoco did voluntarily confess the words should be deciphered in this sort: By the allowance of the pearls he meant that the Count de Fuentes and the secretary did gladly accept the offer of Lopez to poison our Queen, signified by Ferera's letter; and for the provision of amber and musk, it was meant that the Count looked shortly for a resolution from the king of Spain concerning a matter of importance, which was for burning the Queen's ships; and another point tending to the satisfaction of their vindictive humor.

CECIL. Wherefore is this interpretation of the letter so validated?

ESSEX. All roads lead to Dr. Lopez. Manuel Luis Tinoco made no haste to reveal anything, but thought to dally and abuse in some other sort . . .

CECIL. He doth assert you interrogated him in French, a language alien to himself; that you did confuse and befuddle him to a confounding of all issues at hand.

ESSEX. This Tinoco was fairly interrogated, without torture, and he constantly referred to Dr. Lopez as his liaison in London and at Court.

CECIL. It is not responsive, your Lordships. We refer to the deciphering of the "ambiguous" letter.

BACON. Estaban Fereira supplied the true meaning and did also advise Dr. Lopez was to be the ultimate recipient of the letter. We have won from Tinoco his letters from Count de Fuentes and the secretary, in both of which mention is made of the Queen's death. The letters from the Count affirm the terms of the Commission, and that of the secretary of that great service whereof should arise an universal benefit to the whole world. The letters from the fictitious Thores were to Pedro de Garrera and one to Juan Pallacio designating the taking up of large sums of money and to be shown to Lopez for his assurance. Tinoco, who managed the matter abroad, and Fereira who resided here to maintain contact with Lopez, were severally examined without torture or theatening, did in the end volunteer and clearly confess the matters mentioned. Their confessions fully consent and concur, not only in substance but in all points, particulars, and circumstances. Their confessions are expressed in their own natural language, testified and subscribed with their own hands, and in open assembly at the arraignment of Lopez in Guildhall, were by them confirmed and avouched to Lopez to his face, together with all letters and pertinent documents thereto.

COKE. (*To* LOPEZ.) When you were asked if these accusations were proved against you, what would you say? The record indicates you answered that you would yield yourself guilty of the fact intended. To which you did attest with your confession in writing . . .

LOPEZ. No! Not so. When I was confronted by Fereira, I did say and write that I did indeed communicate through him for peace 'twixt Philip and our glorious Queen. You do but twist my words.

COKE. You agreed that Philip pay you?

LOPEZ. I meant only to cozen the king of Spain of his money. I did so inform Her Majesty. But treason? Never!

BACON. Are you retracting your con-

fession because you well know that a conviction for treason means all your goods and estate are confiscate by the crown? Is your avariciousness urging your retraction?

LOPEZ. No! I revere the sacred holiness of Her Majesty's person. She hath befriended me and my family. She would not allow you thus to abuse her friend and physician . . .

COKE. Your excuses are manifestly false. You opened this matter neither to Her Majesty nor to any councilor of state, to toil on and enveigle these parties with whom you did treat . . .

LOPEZ. Under direct instructions from Lord Walsingham . . .

BACON. Who, unfortunately for you, is dead and cannot testify in your behalf.

COKE. You came too late to this shift, after betraying your guilty conscience, in denying those treaties and conferences until they were evidently and manifestly proved to your face.

LOPEZ. (*Despairingly.*) I only confess to negotiating for peace . . .

COKE. You further conferred with Fereira about the manner of his assurance of your Judas money, that it should be placed in the hands of such merchants as he should name in Antwerp rather than in England. You declared the purpose to be, after the horrible fact done, you will immediately fly to Antwerp where you would tarry a while and then convey yourself to Constantinople where, it is affirmed, the Jew Don Salomon, your near kinsman, would await you. Thus you had cast your reckonings upon the supposition of the facts done.

LOPEZ. I am honored in England. I am

Her Majesty's own physician and friend. I have saved her precious life when she was afflicted with a pernicious, foul ucler. By accusing me of these heinous designs, you accuse the judgment of my closest, most revered friend, our sacred Queen.

BURGHLEY. Take the accused hence whilst the court deliberates its design. *(Lights dim to indicate pause. Lights up,* LOPEZ *absent.)* Bring forth the accused. (LOPEZ *is brought in.)* The decision of this court, now justly determined, may securely be universally published. It reveals how, by God's marvelous goodness, Her Majesty hath been preserved. It is hard to say whether God hath done greater things by Her Majesty or for her: if you observe on the one side how God hath ordained her government to break and cross the unjust ambition of two mighty potentates, the king of Spain and the Bishop of Rome, never so straitly between themselves combined; and on the other side how God hath protected her, both against foreign invasion and inward troubles, and singularly against many secret conspiracies made against her life; thereby declarng to the world that He will indeed preserve that instrument which He hath magnified. But the corruption of these times are wonderful, when the wars which are the highest trials of right between princes, that acknowledge no superior jurisdiction, and ought to be prosecuted with all honor, shall be stained and infamed with such foul and inhuman practices. Wherein if such great a king hath been named, the rule of the civil law, which is the rule of common reason, must be remembered: *"Frustra legis auxilium implorat, qui in legem committit."* Who hath sought to violate the Majesty Royal, in the highest degree, cannot claim the preeminence thereof to be exempted from just imputation. It is the final judgment of this court that this Lopez is condemned for the highest treason that can be imagined. Her Most Sacred Majesty will be petitioned to sign the death warrant.

SCENE 9

Essex House. Late May 1594. BACON *and* ESSEX *are discovered. In this scene,* BACON *appears more epicene than usual.*

ESSEX. What say you, my golden boy, to our being becalmed, frustrated and in despair of Her Majesty moving in this matter?

BACON. 'Tis indeed as though we labored like Hercules and end as a Tantalus.

ESSEX. Master Will Shakespeare hath failed us.

BACON. Nay, not entirely. I have read his masque about Lopez.

ESSEX. And . . . ?

BACON. 'Tis most poetic, highly romantic . . .

ESSEX. And the Jew?

BACON. I must confess he doth not appear as villainous as would suit our plans.

ESSEX. I would haul Master Will together with Lopez to Tyburn Hill!

BACON. Thereby you would indeed make history. Shakespeare's star riseth each hour.

ESSEX. You, good Francis, should have writ the drama. But your poetry is too labored, and you are inclined to see into the mind of mortals rather than into their hearts and souls. Your exquisite intelligence riseth not to view heaven.

BACON. And heaven . . . ?

ESSEX. 'Twere for Her Majesty to sign the Jew's death warrant.

BACON. Surely Her Majesty's affection for you would crush all scruples she holds against it.

ESSEX. Her scuples and her feminine sensitivity delay her decision. Not until Lord Walsingham assured her that legally Mary of Scotland may be beheaded rather than suffer the extreme penalty of disembowelment whilst still alive, would she sign the death warrant.

BACON. It may well be that she cannot allow herself to abide the castration and disembowelment of her "dear friend" Dr. Lopez. Can you, will you assure her of his quick dispatch?

ESSEX. No! This Jew will undergo all the extremities of the law.

BACON. Then you must woo the Queen. Her affection for you must be exploited.

ESSEX. To the point, Francis.

BACON. She is a woman. Virgin or no, she yearns for the warmth of physical fondling.

ESSEX. Not of late, as far as I'm concerned. I cannot bring myself . . . Have you seen how blackened her teeth have become? Ugh! And her coquettishness as she gets older embarrasses me.

BACON. King Philip bedded the monstrous Mary.

ESSEX. Would you?

BACON. The wrong sex. (*He giggles.*)

ESSEX. I will consider your suggestion. As for your boys, I'd not like the Queen to be acquaint with your predelictions. She takes not kindly to the vagaries of men. That is why, since your brother Anthony came home in disgrace from France, I've kept him from Court.

BACON. Our whims and titillations differ.

ESSEX. (*Brooding, then suddenly alert.*) Woo the Queen, you say? Yes, a capital idea. But she wantonly teases my cock to no avail.

BACON. How exquisite!

ESSEX. But for our purpose . . . why not? I shall close my eyes and conquer her. Then . . .

BACON. Then . . . ?

ESSEX. Then, at the proper moment, she'll sign!

BACON. And Master Will's labors? His play?

ESSEX. We'll need it not. Dismiss him gently. For if the play continue to keep aflame the outcry against the Jew's villainy, we may assist this Shakespeare person to present it eventually. Keep him content somehow . . . we may need a writer of his talent one day. (ESSEX *exits. Lights dim to indicate a short passage of time. When lights rise again,* BACON *and* SHAKESPEARE *are discovered.* BACON *peruses a manuscript which he soon hands to* SHAKESPEARE.)

SHAKESPEARE. Why didst solicit me to

write the play? Surely you could write a proper masque.

BACON. I view the cosmic, the universal involvements of man.

SHAKESPEARE. Hmmmn . . .

BACON. What?

SHAKESPEARE. I did not speak.

BACON. First, a play must appeal to and strike at the emotional involvement of each character. But I objectively see man as a puppet, or chessman in a universal game.

SHAKESPEARE. How see you Lopez?

BACON. A pawn in a game of politics.

SHAKESPEARE. And this pawn, hath he not eyes, hands, organs, dimensions, senses, affections, passions? Fed with the same food, hurt with the same weapons, subject to the same diseases, healed by the same means, warmed and cooled by the same winter and summer, as a Christian is?

BACON. No, not in the affairs of state.

SHAKESPEARE. Do you really believe Lopez guilty of the detestable treason to poison our Queen.

BACON. My belief is not relevant. My Lord Essex must prevail over the pusillanimity of those who fear Spain and would seek peace. What matters then the testicles of one Jew.

SHAKESPEARE. The fall of one sparrow . . .

BACON. I like the friendship of your Antonio and Bassanio. You should give them more scenes together, more emphasis upon that.

SHAKESPEARE. But Antonio offers his life for his friend . . .

BACON. True, but there would be a closer physical affinity in their relationship.

SHAKESPEARE. I have done much work . . .

BACON. A writer is never judged by the time or effort he applies.

SHAKESPEARE. The play is ready.

BACON. Have you ever experienced the frivolity, the holiday spirit among the hordes who view a hanging on Tyburn Hill? Those hordes will flock to your play should you show the Jew indeed a villain of the vilest kind. But a sympathetic Jew? Nay, Master Will, he must be the devil incarnate.

SHAKESPEARE. I do not write for a transient moment . . . the audience may despise him, but also understand him. No man is a disembodied spirit of evil. Tamburlain, too, was a person.

BACON. You've made your Shylock a persecuted martyr and avenger. It won't do. And, cannot you make the wise Duke of Venice a duchess? 'Twould please Her Majesty.

SHAKESPEARE. Venice never had a . . .

BACON. Come, you are not that much of a purist. Didst give the other merchant the name Antonio for polishing the image of the quondam "king" of Portugal?

SHAKESPEARE. Merely another name common to a Latin country. He, too, is an identifiable person. I do not build a character as does a stone mason a house out of rock. I confess to you, I've had a devil of a time with the Jew.

BACON. You should have dispatched him early on. Your play leaves him alive.

SHAKESPEARE. The play is a comedy.

BACON. Present your play as it is and you'll undoubtedly be laughed out of the theater. Your play will go down in defeat and never be heard of again.

SHAKESPEARE. What of Lopez? The play was to have . . .

BACON. My Lord Essex hath plans. The matter will be resolved and the Jew will pay the penalty on Tyburn Hill.

SCENE 10

ELIZABETH's *Chamber in Windsor Castle, 1 June 1594.* ELIZABETH *is being helped to dress by a* LADY IN WAITING.

LADY. Shall I tighten the bodice and bring it up . . . ?

ELIZABETH. Indeed not. No, not this one. I shall wear the black Italian taffeta with the broad gold bands and crimson lined sleeves. (ELIZABETH *stands in her drawers and her breasts exposed. The* LADY IN WAITING *briefly exits and quickly returns with the dress.* ELIZABETH *is helped to dress; the dress is left open to the waist.*)

LADY. You have never appeared more beautiful, Your Majesty. No wonder your people love you.

ELIZABETH. And I love them. I'd rather die than diminish by one iota our mutual affection. Yet, how much longer . . . I'm on the brink of the grave.

LADY. *(Horrified.)* Oh no, Madam. How can you . . .

ELIZABETH. No, I don't think I shall die as soon as all that. I'm not as old as some suppose. (*The* QUEEN *is now dressed; she primps and dons a red wig.*) See if the Earl of Essex has arrived. If he has, bring him to me at once. (LADY IN WAITING *exits.* ELIZABETH *continues her primping.* LADY IN WAITING *appears at the door.*)

LADY. The Earl of Essex. (ESSEX *enters, bends and rests on one knee before the* QUEEN, *who waves off the* LADY IN WAITING *who exits.*)

ELIZABETH. Robert, at last. You have been most naughty—absenting yourself from us.

ESSEX. There are many of Your Majesty's affairs that command my attention.

ELIZABETH. Lord Burghley assures me our affairs are well in hand. Oh, I suppose the Irish are troublesome. When aren't they.

ESSEX. I would Your Majesty sent me to Ireland. They'd trouble you no more.

ELIZABETH. And so ye shall go. I would I had more loyal followers as you, dear Robert. (*She is obviously flirting with him.*) Were there no difference in religion between us and the Irish, we would be one people devoted to each other.

ESSEX. Philip of Spain instigates and arouses the Irish to harass us, even to plot against your precious life.

ELIZABETH. King Philip hath tried to have me murdered fifteen times. How the man must love me. Alas, these fatal differences in religion turn upon bagatelles. Horace wrote, *"quidquid delirant reges, plectuntur Achivi."* Just before you entered, I was talking about the mutual love between your Queen and the people. That should be the basis of all religion.

ESSEX. And it is the basis of my life: my love for you, my Queen.

ELIZABETH. Careful, Robert. First, you

are married; second, we are blood cousins, and . . .

ESSEX. And I love none but you.

ELIZABETH. Yet you indulge in an ambiguous, inexplicable, self-imposed exile from our court.

ESSEX. A man's life needs must be dedicated to his sovereign's and his nation's glory. Condemn it as mine obsession, but no other goal guides my days and nights. All directed by my true love of you, my dearest Queen.

ELIZABETH. As your Queen or as a woman?

ESSEX. As both, specially as a woman! Your loveliness arouses . . .

ELIZABETH. Careful, or you'll burst your codpiece.

ESSEX. Taunt me, laugh at me if you will, but all I've ever dreamed of in a woman is you, my Queen, my love, my life . . . (*He approaches* ELIZABETH *and takes her hand. She is responsive as he caresses her; he fondles her breasts. She finds a bulge in his breast-pocket as she tries to bring her hand under his vest.*)

ELIZABETH. What have you hidden there that obstructs my desire?

ESSEX. Something you can dispose of forthwith. Here . . . (*He presents a document to her.*) It needs but your signature.

ELIZABETH. And would I thus sign away my realm to you, dear Robert?

ESSEX. No. I but wish you to sign away your heart to me as I have given my heart to you.

ELIZABETH. (*As she passionately embraces him.*) And what am I to sign?

ESSEX. You need not sign. I want only you. Let us to your bedchamber . . .

ELIZABETH. Tell me . . .

ESSEX. Simply the death warrant for that Jew.

ELIZABETH. (*Only slightly drawing back.*) You are devious, my beloved.

ESSEX. Only devoted to my Queen, my monarch, my love . . . Here, sign . . . (ELIZABETH *is in a dreamy, lustful mood. She takes the document and signs it.*) Come with me, my beloved. You may be Queen of England, but more important to me is that you are Queen of my heart. (*He lifts her in his arms and carries her out to her bedchamber.*)

ELIZABETH. (*Frivolously taunting him.*) Careful, my love, don't injure your manhood.

CURTAIN

EPILOGUE

Outside the Tower of London, the night of 25 February 1601. The scene is eerily lighted by torches of pitch.

WILLIAM SHAKESPEARE, *seven years older than last we saw him, with a slightly bald pate, on his way to appear-* ing like portraits of him made familiar in later centuries, walks onto the scene.

SHAKESPEARE. This is Tower Hill where I witnessed a most historic sight early this morning. Robert Devereux, first knight of our glorious Queen

Elizabeth's kingdom, the Earl of Essex and his war party triumphed, in a drama that ended this morning. They triumphed over a woebegone, lonely, old Portuguese Jew. Like other mornings, the glorious sun rose with one purpose—to shine on Robert Devereux, for all universal forces existed but to serve and be subservient to the Earl of Essex, his Queen's favorite. Some six years ago, Lopez's former friends who benefited from his generous hospitality implicated the doctor in the spurious plot. They were also condemned, as accomplices, to an unspeakable death for treason. The frenzied populace revived its waning hatred of Spain. Pamphlets and playlets inflamed the masses against the iniquitous Jew. I delayed my play for a year, for my Jew Shylock is unlike the popular portrait of Dr. Lopez. They share one characteristic in common—their humanity. The Queen's delay helped not the doctor. If she perceived him to be innocent, her own preoccupations allowed for no action to be taken in his behalf.

The three wretched men, bound to hurdles, were dragged through Holborn—what thoughts the sight of his house stirred within the doctor's breast. Then up to Tyburn Hill. A vast multitude in holiday spirit awaited them, waited to enjoy the gory spectacle. When the doctor attempted to make a dying speech, the derisive mob shrieked with laughter. The pathetic old Jew was strung up on the gallows, then cut down and revived, followed by castration, revived again, disembowelled, and the quivering flesh cut up into quarters. Immediately thereafter, Fereira suffered a similar fate. Tinoco saw the horror that faced him—the shrieks and moans of his dying companions maddened him. When he was cut down from the gallows, he quickly recovered. Then, with courage and power fed by his desperation, he attacked his executioner. The mob responded to this turn of events by cheering on his bravery. But his doom was inevitable against uneven odds, for the executioner was aided by two burly spectators who felled young Tinoco with a blow upon his head. Thus, this young, adventurous foreigner was also castrated, disemboweled, and quartered whilst the populace enjoyed the grisly quivering contortions of the hacked flesh and the scaffold drenched with blood.

Our gentle, tender Queen treated the doctor's widow with mercy by restoring to her the deceased doctor's goods and chattels. However, our virgin Queen Elizabeth kept King Philip's ring which she still wears on her finger.

It is now little more than six years since that gory episode. The magnificent, heroic Robert Devereux was this morning beheaded for his self-confessed treason to Her Majesty. *Requiescat en pace.*

THE END

APPOINTMENT IN MINSK

Appointment in Minsk is first of all theater about the theater. Reality and illusion merge in its cast of characters where actual and fictional personae intermingle. In pace and plot, the action of the play proceeds briskly with the purposeful vigor that has endowed the maxim "the show must go on" with the force of a commandment. In the opening moments of the work, we witness a rite of passage in the Vilna Troupe where a major role is passed from a dying veteran of the repertory company to an untrained but ambitious newcomer who will go on stage that very night. In the last scene, thirty-four years later, that novice—now a star himself—has just made *aliyah* and is already involved in the nascent theater of the brand-new state of Israel.

For all that it represents the traditions of the theatrical world generally, *Appointment in Minsk* focuses precisely and lovingly on the Jewish stage. It celebrates the legendary excellence of the famous East European and Russian Yiddish troupes and their loyalty to the great Yiddish dramatists and their plays. It demonstrates the stubborn endurance of these producing companies in the face of poverty, war, pogroms, and pressures to join the Communist Party and renounce Judaism.

Added to the challenges from the frequently hostile world outside, there are internal perturbations. Inevitably—what else might we expect from actors, and Jewish actors at that?—jealousies, rivalries, and differences of artistic opinion divide the players. There is dissent between the champions of the traditional repertory as a mirror of a specifically Jewish world and those who believe that the Yiddish stage should assimilate and reflect contemporary social and political currents. There is even disagreement about what it means to be a Jew in a country—and that means almost any country—where professing allegiance to Judaism exclusively is at best tolerated and, more typically, perilous.

The last issue is dramatized in the pointed contrast between the play's fictional protagonist, Jacob Gold, and Shloyme (Solomon) Mikhoels, a virtuoso Russian actor of outstanding distinction who was made head of the Moscow State Jewish Theater in 1928. Invited to join that theater, Jacob does not quarrel with the

157

master's aesthetic judgment. Quite the contrary, in act 2, scene 1, the young actor and the artistic director spiritedly reach agreement that the Yiddish stage ought to mount not only Jewish plays, but Yiddish translations of the masterpieces of world drama as well as the innovative new works that were revolutionizing theater.

However, Jacob rejects the stage as a forum for politics. Not even the illustrious Stanislavsky's offer of work in the Moscow Art Theater can persuade him to join the Party. Jacob has learned his lesson. Something of an activist in his early youth, he now suffers the consequences: he is persona non grata in countries where he would like to immigrate. Hence he has become resolutely apolitical. he proclaims a single loyalty: "I'm a Jew, born a Jew and I'll die a Jew."

By contrast, Mikhoels finds art and politics compatible bedfellows. What is more, he is firmly committed to Marxist principles and absolutely convinced that after World War II, Jews and *yiddishkayt* will enjoy an unprecedented golden age in Soviet Russia. Equally dire in its misjudgment is Mikhoel's unswerving belief in Josef Stalin. Today we know how cunningly that premier cultivated the famous actor's trust and exploited his talent and reputation among Jews; for example, sending him to the West in 1943 as chairman of the Jewish Anti-Fascist Committee whose charge it was to build support for the war effort of the USSR. Act 2, scene 6 is carefully drawn from this mission. And so, sadly, is the radio bulletin at the play's climax. Mikhoels indeed met his death in Minsk in what was made to look like a car accident. Not only did the Russian press later reveal that his murder had been ordered by the secret police, Stalin's daughter divulged her father's complicity in the assassination and the subsequent cover-up. As to what Mikhoels was doing in Minsk, he had, as the play's title states, an appointment there. He was on official government business, representing the State Theater Prize Committee that only two years earlier had honored him!

It is entirely appropriate that Jacob Gold be in Israel when Mikhoel's death is announced. Pain resonates in the cry which ends the play, "Long live Israel," but triumph too, for in that country, Jews and Jewish theater are free to be as political or as disaffiliated as they choose. The achievements of Solomon Mikhoels and countless other talented Old World artists and intellectuals who lived their lives in and for the Yiddish theater have significantly enriched the contemporary Israeli stage. Nor does their legacy end there. That the dynamic traditions and inspiring history of the Yiddish theater have also stirred the American dramatic imagination is abundantly manifest in *Appointment in Minsk*.

Ellen Schiff

Ellen Schiff is Professor of French and Comparative Literature at North Adams State College, Adams, Massachusetts. She has published widely on modern theater. Her monumental work, *From Stereotype to Metaphor*, depicts the Jews and minorities in contemporary drama.

APPOINTMENT IN MINSK

by David S. Lifson

CHARACTERS

PINCUS SHLANSKY, an old actor
BRAINA, his wife, an actress
MARSHALOV, Artistic Director of the troupe
ARNOLD ZWEIG, a German officer
A GERMAN OFFICER
SOPHIE FINKEL, a young actress
MICHAEL FINKEL, her husband, an actor
JACOB GOLD, a young man
LEV SHEININ, special investigator for the Soviet KGB
AN OLD ACTOR
STANISLAVSKY
THREE POLISH SOLDIERS
ZUSKIND
MIKHOELS
HOTEL PORTER
HERMAN YABLAKOFF
THREE ISRAELI SOLDIERS

ACT I

SCENE 1

Vilna, 1915, a winter afternoon. The stage of an old theater. Anxious, worried actors, stage manager, and director MARSHALOV *cluster around an emaciated,* SICK OLD ACTOR, PINCUS SHLANSKY. HE IS *the character actor who plays "Todras" in the play under rehearsal,* Farvorfen Vinkle, *by Hirschbein. His wife,* BRAINA, *cradles him in her arms.*

PINCUS. *(Gasping for breath.)* I can't . . . it's no use . . .

MARSHALOV. But you must. The entire future of our troupe, the future of the Yiddish theater depends on you. You must go on.

BRAINA. Leave him alone. You want he should die on you!

MARSHALOV. But what should we do? Without him there's no play. We'll have to close down.

BRAINA. So close down. His life is more important than all this play acting nonsense . . . *(With a derisive gesture.)* "The show must go on . . ." Tfui on all my enemies!

MARSHALOV. You don't know what you're talking about. Our main support—and just because, and only because we are Jews are we able to hold our Jews together and win respect for the Jews—not just because we are actors, but because we are Jews . . .

BRAINA. Fancy speeches won't help if Pincus dies on the stage. Then, how will that help the Jews?

MARSHALOV. I don't know. But what can we do? *(Two* GERMAN OFFICERS *enter; one is* ARNOLD ZWEIG.)

ZWEIG. Good afternoon.

MARSHALOV. You're early. It's a few hours yet to curtain time.

OFFICER. We simply came by to make sure that everything is in order. We have reserved seats for two dozen of our Imperial German Army Staff. Our Herr General expects a perfect performance. We assured him.

MARSHALOV. You shall have it. *(While* GERMAN OFFICERS *talk between themselves,* MARSHALOV *and the actors remain in a group.)* So take him home, Braina. But come right back. If necessary, I'll play Todras. I don't know how I'll manage to be prompter, stage manager, and every black year knows what else.

BRAINA. So where is it written you have to play tonight?

MARSHALOV. You heard what the German officers said . . .

BRAINA. Today they're your friend. But watch out for tomorrow.

MARSHALOV. How can you talk that way! Colonel Arnold Zweig is a Jew.

BRAINA. Jew or not, a German is a German. Remember! And the Russians are no different.

MARSHALOV. So what should we do? Lay down and die, maybe . . .

SOPHIE. Not for me. Once this war is over, I'm going to America.

MICHAEL. If I say so. *(The* GERMAN OFFICERS *are conversing between themselves.)*

ZWEIG. It's orders from the general staff. All minority national groups must be encouraged to assert their culture, identity, proclaim their nationality. In that way we pry them away from the Czar's Russia.

OFFICER. Our guns will do that.

ZWEIG. We have to think after the war, after we've beaten the mujiks. (*They are interrupted by the entrance of a youth,* JACOB GOLD, *who enters with packages of food. He wears an ill-fitting Russian army uniform. Upon seeing the* GERMAN OFFICERS, *he turns to flee.*)

OFFICER. Stop or I'll shoot.

JACOB. I didn't do anything. I'm just bringing some food for these starving actors.

OFFICER. (*To Director* MARSHALOV.) Is that true? (MARSHALOV, *confused, shrugs his shoulders.*) You're a Russian soldier. What are you doing here? Do you know we can shoot you as a spy?

JACOB. Who me? I'm not a Russian soldier. I'm not any kind of a soldier. I was cold . . . I needed clothes . . . so I . . .

OFFICER. I could swear I saw you in our German mess hall last week. Yes, I remember, you were wearing a German uniform then.

JACOB. Yes. Of course I remember you. You helped me to an extra portion of beef stew. That's why I was there. Last week, the German soldiers had beef stew, so I became a German soldier. The week before, the Polish army had potato pudding—real potatoes—so . . .

OFFICER. So you became a Polish soldier.

JACOB. Say, that's right.

ZWEIG. And this week . . . ? ((ZWEIG *pokes in the food package carried by* JACOB.)

JACOB. This week the Russians have stuffed cabbage, so . . .

OFFICER. So this week you're a Russian soldier.

JACOB. But I'm not a soldier. The only way I could get to an army kitchen is in uniform. Otherwise my brothers and sisters, my mother, and these actors would starve to death.

OFFICER. (*To* ZWEIG). What'll we do with him?

MARSHALOV. You must let him be. You gentlemen have supported us, given us hope—and that's a wonderful thing, whatever your reasons. But we couldn't have survived without the food Jacob brought us.

ZWEIG. Hmmm, Jacob fed you. If we let him go, he'll be shot in that uniform.

MARSHALOV. We have plenty costumes. We'll give him proper clothes.

ZWEIG. We'll see you tonight at the play. (*Both* GERMANS *exit. Actors forage among* JACOB's *food packages.*)

MARSHALOV. Here, Pincus, we have food. Jacob, give him first.

BRAINA. (*Trying to feed* PINCUS.) Here, it'll give you strength. (PINCUS *cannot eat.* BRAINA *helplessly turns to* MARSHALOV.) It's no use. I don't think he'll last till tonight.

MARSHALOV. (*Tries to comfort* BRAINA *while he shrewdly appraises* JACOB). Jacob, you've been coming to the theater every night. Why?

JACOB. Because of the war, there's no circus around here. I love the circus, and this is the next thing to it. And all of you have been good to me. I have no family and . . .

MARSHALOV. But you told the German officers about your mother, your brothers and sisters . . .

JACOB. I hoped even a German officer might have a heart. The truth is, I'm all alone, and you have been like my family.

MICHAEL. What maudlin nonsense. Soon he'll have us in tears.

MARSHALOV. Leave him alone, Michael. Even the German officers had more heart than you. (*He turns to* JACOB.) From now on, you're an actor. Tonight you make your debut. You'll play the grandfather Todras in Hirschbein's *Farvorfen Vinkle.*

JACOB. Wait, how can I . . . He's such an ooooIllddd man. I'm only seventeen, so how can I . . . ?

MARSHALOV. Leave it to me. Come, I'll add at least sixty years to your life. (MARSHALOV *leads* JACOB *out of the stage.*)

BRAINA. Pincus, Pincus, Pincus, what'll we do with you now?

PINCUS. (*Weak and barely audible.*) Go your way. Just leave me to die.

BRAINA. Jews don't walk out just because someone thinks he's dying—or even really dying, which you're not. Come, I'll take you home.

MICHAEL. Does our big wind of a director expect us to sit around until he's ready!

BRAINA. Don't be such a loudmouth. Pincus has to get home.

MICHAEL. Home? Since when is he a special character to be excused from a rehearsal. I want you to know . . .

BRAINA. (*Aside to* MICHAEL.) For God's sake, haven't you any humanity at all! He's dying.

SOPHIE. (*overhearing.*) Oh, my God. The poor man. What can we do?

BRAINA. Nothing. Just help me put his coat on. I'll ask the porter to help me get him home.

(MICHAEL *has turned to the food and is wolfing it.* SOPHIE *helps* BRAINA *with* PINCUS *as they lead him between them to the exit.*)

SOPHIE. I'll come by after the rehearsal. Do you need anything?

BRAINA. No. And thank you. Once we're home it'll be all right. (BRAINA *and* PINCUS *exit.*)

MICHAEL. Come, this stuffed cabbage isn't bad. That Jacob is an angel. Have some.

SOPHIE. How can you stuff yourself! That poor old Pincus is dying.

MICHAEL. Life goes on. We've seen enough dying in this war to get used to it. If I stopped to mourn for only those I've known, I'd need a thousand years to live.

SOPHIE. You're a brute.

MICHAEL. You didn't have to marry me. Ha, some married life!

SOPHIE. It was the only way my mother and father would let me go on the stage—as a married woman. You knew it, and we made an agreement.

MICHAEL. Sooo, we're married. You may be, but I'm not. You might at least show some appreciation to me for rescuing you from that pigsty shtetl where you shared your life with mangy, scrawny goats alongside a cemetery. Don't you think you owe me some affection! (SOPHIE *remains silent.*) You're waiting to be raped by the soldiers in a pogrom. You have three armies to choose from for your deflowering. One of these days I'll make you know I'm your husband. (*He stalks about.*) I ought to drag you by your hair to my bed.

SOPHIE. (*She cowers in fear, then she stands up to him.*) You wouldn't dare.

MICHAEL. Why did I ever get involved with this life, this impoverished, arty theater—and with you. Our wonderful director promised we'd be playing in the European capitals, Bucharest, Vienna, Prague, Paris. We'd even get to America. Phooey. That's why I married you—his promises, and he said he needed you for the company.

Some decrepit company! Everyone is frightened, so nobody comes to the theater. We eat on the leavings from the armies.

SOPHIE. Some day the war will be over. Then you'll get to your European capitals.

MICHAEL. And you?

SOPHIE. No matter what happens, I'm going to America.

MICHAEL. You'll go where I say you'll go. No matter the reason we married, you are my wife and you'll go where I go.

SOPHIE. I'll go to America, and without you. (MICHAEL, *threateningly, advances on her when* MARSHALOV *and* JACOB *enter.* JACOB's *appearance has been completely transformed into an old man; when he speaks it is the voice of a very old man.*)

MARSHALOV. Don't be so spry. You're an old man, so walk like one.

JACOB. Yes. Is this the way you mean?

MARSHALOV. Perfect. I couldn't do it better myself.

MICHAEL. (*To* JACOB.) Hey, don't I know you? I remember seeing you in the Hirschbein Troup in Warsaw.

JACOB. It could be. I was much, much younger then.

SOPHIE. Then you must have been a child actor—the Hirschbein Troupe played in Warsaw almost ten years ago.

MICHAEL. How do you know so much? This fine old man, this veteran schaushpieler doesn't need you . . .

SOPHIE. My husband knows about the theater only when its spotlight is on him. At least, I know its history, and I know you. You're Jacob the angel who has been feeding us this past month.

JACOB. (*Still the old man.*) No, no.

Jacob is my grandson.

SOPHIE. (*Making a grab for* JACOB's beard.) You—you're Jacob and I'll prove it.

JACOB. (*In his normal voice.*) Watch out, you'll ruin my makeup!

MARSHALOV. Watch out! He's playing Todras tonight.

MICHAEL. (*With a forced laugh of disgust.*) This kid, this nothing is going to play Todras? I know that in wartime we have to use all kinds of ersatz—but in a troupe where I play, I don't appear with amateurs, war or no war.

MARSHALOV. The theater is always a war. And you'll play, all right. The German Army ordered us to play, we'll play, and so will you. If you can stop stuffing that big mouth of yours for a while, you'll come help me with the lights. (MARSHALOV *and* MICHAEL *exit.* SOPHIE *and* JACOB *remain alone.*)

SOPHIE. So, you're becoming an actor. You don't know what you're letting yourself in for.

JACOB. I have an idea.

SOPHIE. You might as well join up with some wandering gypsies.

JACOB. How about you?

SOPHIE. I'm going to be a star, a prima donna. In the theater I'm a mentsch, a personality, and not buried alive in a muddy, miserable little shtetl. Yes, a star!

JACOB. Are you a star?

SOPHIE. No, not yet. But you can be sure I will be. And I'll travel all over Europe, all over the world—America!

JACOB. Do all actors have dreams like that?

SOPHIE. Don't you?

JACOB. I don't think so. Not yet, anyway. I read plays. I plan how they should be done. But to travel all over the world? Not for me. I'm staying in RUSSIA, there's a new world coming to Russia after this awful war. The people will get rid of the Czar who enslaves the Jews. You'll see, the Jews will walk with their heads in the air, proudly like the best of the citizens. We Jews will be like everyone else . . .

SOPHIE. You mean like the ignorant mujiks who will kill the Jews the first chance they have at a pogrom? Really, you're such a child.

JACOB. I'm as old as you are. And age never made anyone smarter. You must believe in the future. There's a new Russia coming—after the war.

SOPHIE. And how are you going to get rid of the Germans?

JACOB. The same way Russia got rid of Napoleon. And with them, Russia gets rid of the Czar and all the anti-Semitic aristocracy. You'll see.

SOPHIE. No, I won't see. I'll be in America. I'll act not only on the Yiddish stage, but on the Engllish stage, too. And then the cinema. People from all over the world will cheer me.

JACOB. I think I'd settle just to have you cheer me.

SOPHIE. If you're a good actor, of course I'll applaud you.

JACOB. I don't want to be just an actor. I want to stage the plays, pick them, design them, cast them, direct them . . .

SOPHIE. A real artist. Don't you want to write them, too?

JACOB. Maybe some day . . .

SOPHIE. Dream on.

MARSHALOV. (*Enters.*) Ready, everybody. We'll give it a quick runthrough. Places, everybody . . . (*Actors assemble, take their places as lights dim.*)

SCENE 2

That night. Applause is heard. The rear of the stage is presumed to be the audience. The actors take their bows facing the rear of the stage. The imaginary curtain falls. The actors relax. An agitated JACOB *confronts* MICHAEL.

JACOB. Listen, you bastard . . .

MARSHALOV. (*Seeing* ZWEIG *enter.*) Quiet, everybody.

ZWEIG. (*Beams at* MARSHALOV; *they shake hands in mutual congratulations.*) Superb! I've seen nothing better in Berlin. (*To entire company.*) Congratulations. Our commandant has nothing but praise for you. You've made me proud to be a Jew and proud of you. (*Murmured pleasure.*) You must come to Berlin.

MARSHALOV. We're ready.

ZWEIG. So is Berlin, but, alas, we're at war. When the war is over, we'll see. (*General felicitations as* ZWEIG *ad libs his exit.*)

JACOB. (*Resuming his quarrel with* MICHAEL.) You're a dirty scoundrel. I've a good mind to . . . (MARSHALOV *and* SOPHIE *try to keep the two actors apart.*)

MICHAEL. Listen, you clown, you belong in a circus, picking up after the animals. You're still wet behind the ears. Go get yourself diapered. Just look at him. By accident, he falls into a role and right away he's a big-shot trying to tell me how to act.

JACOB. You mean an actor can't behave like a decent human being! In the middle of my speech, you start to dance and ruin my entire scene.

MICHAEL. So what! Tonight I topped you, so tomorrow you'll top me. I top you, then you top me . . .

JACOB. That's not right. It's not good theater, it's not decent, it's not . . .

MICHAEL. You little pisher, don't you tell me about the theater. Soon you'll try to teach me acting! You've got a lot to learn about the theater, and acting, and respect for your fellow artistes.

JACOB. (*Infuriated. He shakes a fist in* MICHAEL'*s face.*) You see this fist— the next time you mug and try to "top" me and to ruin my scene, I'll break your damned jaw.

SOPHIE. (*Succeeding in parting the two.*) Both of you, stop it! You're like children.

MICHAEL. He comes on stage for the first time in his life, without training, without experience, and already he's taking over and telling experienced actors what to do.

JACOB. I'm not telling you anything— anymore. Just watch your step.

MICHAEL. Big shot, so what will you do?

JACOB. (*Raising his fist.*) You'll find out quick enough.

MICHAEL. I'll teach you to threaten me, you . . . you . . .

SOPHIE. (*to* MICHAEL.) Go, go, take off your makeup and change your costume. (*She succeeds in getting* MICHAEL *to leave. Then she turns on* JACOB.) So, that's how it's going to be! You're going to be a troublemaker?

JACOB. Don't you understand? The scene was serious, I was trying to make peace between the two families, then, in the middle of everything he starts to whistle and dance. No one paid attention to what I was saying——no one . . .

SOPHIE. Michael is a great actor, an artist, one in a million.

JACOB. You're not fooling me. I've watched the two of you these past few weeks. Why do you put up with him?

SOPHIE. How dare you! He's my husband.

JACOB. I heard about that, too. How your parents wouldn't let you go on the stage unless you were married. Oh, I know.

SOPHIE. You know too much. If you're going to be a troublemaker, you'll only be making trouble for yourself.

JACOB. But Sophie, I want to tell you . . .

SOPHIE. I am Mrs. Finkel. Don't you dare ever call me Sophie. I'm Mrs. Finkel, the wife of the great Michael Finkel. (*Angrily, she stalks out. A disconsolate* JACOB *is left forlorn.*)

SCENE 3

Odessa, after the war and after the Russian Revolution. Scene is in the green room of the theater. MARSHALOV *impatiently paces about.* LEV SHEININ, *a young man with an authoritative air, enters. Despite being preoccupied.* MARSHALOV *welcomes the newcomer.*

MARSHALOV. Hello again.

LEV SHEININ. Did you read my play?

MARSHALOV. Yes, but this is not the time to discuss it.

LEV SHEININ. Why not now?

MARSHALOV. Mr. Sheinin, look, it's late, I'm waiting for the final curtain. I'm running a theater, I have a million things on my mind. Maybe tomorrow . . .

LEV SHEININ. Tomorrow I have to go to Moscow. It's important that we talk now.

MARSHALOV. Why? I'll still be here tomorrow and, I hope, many more tomorrows.

LEV SHEININ. In less than half an hour, you'll see why. I arranged for a famous visitor to see you after the play is over.

MARSHALOV. So go have your famous unknown produce your play.

LEV SHEININ. My play is a Yiddish play and must be produced by a Yiddish troupe. By a Jew and for Jews.

MARSHALOV. I'm glad you told me it's Jewish. Otherwise I'd think it was written by Chmielnitzki.

LEV SHEININ. You don't understand. If I didn't have to go to Moscow . . .

MARSHALOV. So go already to Moscow. You sound like a character in Chekhov's play, "I must go to Moscow." What's so important for a Jew in Moscow?

LEV SHEININ. I'm with the government. I'm a special investigator.

MARSHALOV. But you want to be a writer.

LEV SHEININ. Yes. I want to get out of government.

MARSHALOV. I'll tell you this much about your play: I can't believe it. According to you, the Russian mujiks must get together, it doesn't matter what the cause is—as long as it brings them together, unites them in a common cause?

LEV SHEININ. Yes, exactly.

MARSHALOV. Even if their cause is pogroms, to kill Jews?

LEV SHEININ. If that is the way for the peasants to unite and together with the proletariat in a common cause . . .

MARSHALOV. And you claim to be a Jew! Get out, you bastard . . . (MARSHALOV, *infuriated, shoves* LEV SHEININ *out of the theater.* MARSHALOV *beside himself in rage, fumes about the room.* MARSHALOV *takes out his watch from vest pocket, then eagerly approaches corridor to the stage.*

Loud and prolonged sound of applause. Actors come into room, from the stage.

MARSHALOV. The audience loved you.

MICHAEL. Maybe they loved the play, not us.

MARSHALOV. Don't be so modest. Our theater is a happy, wonderful combination that reaches out and arouses the audience.

MICHAEL. You too! You've been infected, diseased by Jacob. Everything must have a life force, a great social meaning . . . a . . .

MARSHALOV. Why not? If not, we are clowns, we might as well do juggling acts.

MICHAEL. So we juggle words and situations and chaaracters. What do those numbskulls out there know or sense what a playwright has to say? This production of *Uriel Acosta* is a . . .

JACOB. *(Entering.)* It's a reaffirmation of their Jewishness, their identification with their heritage . . .

MICHAEL. Aha! The philosophe of the theater is going to teach us about theater, once again and again and again.

SOPHIE. *(She has entered and heard the last few remarks.)* I must admit that the role of Judith that I play is very wishy-washy. I just feed lines.

JACOB. The great English poet said, "They also serve who stand and wait."

MICHAEL. My Sophie waits for no one. We should go back to the wonderful Goldfadden operettas. Then she will star, excite everyone in roles like Shulamith.

JACOB. But the great folk drama of . . .

MICHAEL. If you want to lecture about the Yiddish theater, go become a professor in a college.

MARSHALOV. You know, Jacob, Michael has a good point. We have to give the public what it wants.

MICHAEL. I hope I never have to play *Uriel Acosta* again.

SOPHIE. Maybe you're right. But it has wonderful roles for each one of us.

JACOB. For once I must agree with Michael. How much longer will the public be so stupid and applaud this sentimental, maudlin nonsense.

MARSHALOV. It's good theater. As actors, you can sink your teeth into every role, into each character, savor each word.

JACOB. But I think . . .

MICHAEL. Let's listen to the great brain. For him a great classic is maudlin and sentimental. Soooo, now he's also a critic as well as an "actor." Soon he'll be a playwright, maybe the director. Who knows what else.

SOPHIE. Enough already. Why must you both fight all the time! You give me a headache. Stop it right away!

OLD ACTOR. (*Much excited, enters, stutters in his excitement.*) We have a visitor, a distinguished guest, a . . . You'll never guess . . .

MARSHALOV. So tell already.

OLD ACTOR. I still can't believe it. When they told me at the box office that he had reserved two seats, I told them they should have given him a box, and without any charge. Just imagine, that HE should come to see our Yiddish theater, our . . .

SOPHIE. So, will you tell us already, you long-winded idiot . . .

OLD ACTOR. (*To others.*) You'll never believe it in a million years. (*Turns to* SOPHIE.) That's no way to talk to your professional colleague. I'll have you know . . .

JACOB. Look here, unless you tell us, we'll all get dressed and leave the theater. Then you can entertain your distinguished guest by yourself. Let's go, everybody.

OLD ACTOR. But, he's . . .

MICHAEL. We don't care anymore. Come, Sophie . . .

OLD ACTOR. You must wait. He particularly came to see you actors. He said . . .

MICHAEL. We don't care what "he" said. I don't care if "he" is the Graf Pototsky, the Czar himself, or even Lenin. The theater can survive with or without the Czar or Lenin.

OLD ACTOR. But not without our great directors. (*He goes to the door and peers out, then he triumphantly announces—*) I have the great pleasure and honor of introducing the distinguished régisseur, Constantine Stanislavsky. (*All are very impressed.* STANISLAVSKY *enters. Ad lib greetings among all.* STANISLAVSKY *kisses* SOPHIE's *hand.*)

MICHAEL and MARSHALOV. We are honored.

STANISLAVSKY. No, it is I who am honored. I've spent a lifetime in the theater, and never have I seen such sublime, inspired acting. (*He turns to* JACOB.) And where were you trained?

JACOB. I've had no training.

STANISLAVSKY. Impossible. You're joking. Such sensitivity, such timing, and the voice . . . Ah, the voice! Members of my Moscow Art Theater study for years and never reach your heights, your understanding, your . . .

JACOB. Actors who have no talent have to study for years.

STANISLAVSKY. (*Amused and skeptical.*) Oh, I see. You have a God-given talent. You are above studying, developing, perfecting your art?

JACOB. I didn't say that.

STANISLAVSKY. Then how do you approach a role? Don't you study the character's background, his psychological makeup? His . . .?

JACOB. Yes, I suppose that's all part of it. But first I simply try to remember something in my own life, in my past that I may have in common with the character, and relate that to him and the situation he's in.

STANISLAVSKY. I see. And young as you are, you can relate to King Lear or Boris Gudonov in terms of your own life.

JACOB. If I can't, then I have no right to undertake the role.

MARSHALOV. (*Interrupting and edging between* JACOB *and* STANISLAVSKY.) Herr Stanislavsky, we are all greatly honored. You must meet our ingenue, Sophie Finkel . . . (STANISLAVSKY *and* SOPHIE *exchange gracious acknowledgments.*) and our leading man, our esteemed and distinguished Michael Finkel. (MICHAEL *and*

STANISLAVSKY *bow to each other and shake hands.*)

MICHAEL. I must say I entirely agree with you, Gospodin Stanislavsky. How else can a true artist interpret and perfect a role unless he studies the character, even for a year if necessary.

STANISLAVSKY. (*With a significant and amused look at* JACOB.) My method exactly. However, not only did I come backstage to submit my humble respect and admiration for your great talents, but also to make you an offer. At the Moscow Art Theater, we're always looking for new talent, new faces. You have talent beyond anything I've ever encountered on our Russian stage. I would like you to come to Peters . . . I mean, to Leningrad and join our company for a year, then come to Moscow and become part of our principal company. (*Excitement among all.*)

MARSHALOV. Even though it meant the break-up of our troupe which I've built . . . ?

STANISLAVSKY. I'd want you, too. We can use, we need your talent. Sooooo, what do you say?

MICHAEL. We are honored. Of course we'll go.

STANISLAVSKY. (*To* SOPHIE.) And you?

SOPHIE. I go with my husband.

STANISLAVSKY. (*To* JACOB.) And you?

JACOB. At once. I'll go even right now! Who wouldn't want to be in the great Moscow Art Theater! Are you sure you want me?

STANISLAVSKY. More than anyone else. So, it's agreed. We'll meet at my hotel tomorrow morning, say eleven o'clock, and make all arrangements.

(STANISLAVSKY *turns to leave; when he reaches the door, he turns to the others.*) Oh, by the way. There's one small detail. As artists, it should not trouble you, and I hope you will understand that it is merely a formality. I hope you will all be realistic about the facts of life. In the Moscow Art Theatre, no one in the company is a Jew. Naturally, you will be expected to change your religion. No problem. (STANISLAVSKY *benignly smiles and quickly exits before anyone from the stunned company can respond.*)

MICHAEL. (*With an awkward laugh after an uneasy silence.*) So, my friends and fellow Jews, when do we leave to join the Moscow Art Theater?

JACOB. You can go. No one's stopping you. I'm a Jew, born a Jew and I'll die a Jew.

MICHAEL. Stanislavsky said we should be realistic . . .

MARSHALOV. I don't understand it. Lenin said that each nationality must and should be encouraged to strengthen its individual race, or religion, or nationhood.

SOPHIE. Maybe the new regime wants to be like America, a melting pot.

JACOB. We can be a culture within a culture. They can keep the Moscow Art Theater. What do you say, my director?

MARSHALOV. They'll have to kill me before I'll deny I'm a Jew. (MARSHALOV *polls the other actors. They resolutely affirm their Jewishness. Finally, he turns to* MICHAEL *and* SOPHIE.) So, Michael, how will it be?

MICHAEL. (*Demurs. He uncomfortably looks about, then helplessly glances toward* SOPHIE *whose face betrays nothing.*) I've got to think . . .

MARSHALOV. What's there to think? You are a Jew or you're not.

JACOB. (*Taunting* MICHAEL.) What can you expect from the "great" artist? We might have expected . . .

SOPHIE. (*Ferociously turning to* JACOB.) Don't you dare be the law and conscience of your betters! My Michael knows what's right and you can all depend on him to do what's right. (*She goes to* MICHAEL's *side while the others exit. When they are alone, she resolutely confronts* MICHAEL.) What will it be?

MICHAEL. Thank you for standing up for me . . .

SOPHIE. You're my husband. (*Awkward pause.*)

MICHAEL. I'll do what you say I should.

SOPHIE. We must try to get away to America. Czar or Bolsheviks, the Russians will destroy us one way or another.

MICHAEL. Yes, America.

SCENE 4

A few years later; a large hotel suite in a provincial Russian city near the Polish border. Actors furtively look through curtained windows through which is heard noise of screams, *gunshots, a mob out of control. The worried, cringing group are frightened and they caution one another away from the windows. yet now and then, one or another cannot resist peering through a curtain fold at the specially loud and horrifying scream that follows intense shooting.*

MARSHALOV. *(Sits at piano in order to calm his small troupe.)* It's happened before. It will happen again. Come, children, it will pass over. It happened before and it will happen again. Meanwhile, we are actors and we must rehearse.

JACOB. I'm ready.

MICHAEL. What kind of idiocy is this? Oh, I see, that nonsense about "the show must go on." You're out of your mind. First the Russians, then the Polish hooligans. They don't like each other, so they kill the Jews. And this is a full scale pogrom. Just listen to what's going on . . .

SOPHIE. What will we do?

MARSHALOV. What can we do but wait till it blows over. Maybe, please God, they'll pass us by.

MICHAEL. *(Hysterically.)* But if they don't . . . we'll be slaughtered here like rats!

MARSHALOV. Stop it! Your hysteria is no help to anyone—not even to yourself.

SOPHIE. *(At window.)* Oh, my God! They've just bayoneted an old Jew.

MICHAEL. *(At window.)* The soldiers are coming here; they're coming in . . .

JACOB. *(To MARSHALOV.)* Shut him up. The soldiers will hear him and come here. *(Turns to SOPHIE.)* Get him to shut up or I'll strangle him.

MARSHALOV. I have a Romanian passport. Maybe they'll respect it and leave us alone.

MICHAEL. But you're not sure . . .

JACOB. Maybe . . .

MICHAEL. I'm not staying in this hole to be slaughtered. I'll hide behind the wall in the courtyard. They'll never find me. Come, Sophie . . .

SOPHIE. No. I'll stay with the others. Please stay; you'll never get down in time . . .

MICHAEL. I always said you're crazy . . . *(MICHAEL rushes out. Noises are much louder.)*

OLD ACTOR. *(At the window.)* The soldiers have come into the front door.

SOPHIE. Can you see Michael?

OLD ACTOR. No. If he's going to hide in the courtyard, that's behind the hotel. He must have gone down the back; I can only see the front.

MARSHALOV. Maybe they'll pass us by. But if they come in here, let me do the talking.

JACOB. If they'll let you talk.

MARSHALOV. Such remarks don't help. Now everybody, pretend we're rehearsing *Shulamith*. Places for the second act. *(While actors arrange themselves, MARSHALOV plays the lullaby theme. Above the music is heard the tramp and shuffling of soldiers passing in the corridor. The soldiers pass. The actors sigh with relief. Suddenly a loud banging on the door. Actors are petrified in fright. The door is hurled open. A DRUNKEN SOLDIER grins at them, then calls out to his mates down the hall.)*

1ST SOLDIER. Ho, ho. A whole nest of Zhids. Hey, look what I found . . . *(He and two more SOLDIERS crowd into the room. They carry guns and naked swords.)*

MARSHALOV. *(With quiet authority.)* You're intruding on a rehearsal.

2ND SOLDIER. Who are you?

MARSHALOV. We're actors.

1ST SOLDIER. They're Zhids.

MARSHALOV. We're Romanian actors.

3RD SOLDIER. Romanian? Prove it.

MARSHALOV. *(Producing his Romanian passport.)* Here, my Romanian passport.

1ST SOLDIER. *(Examining the document.)* That's right. It's Romanian. They're Romanian actors all right.

2ND SOLDIER. They're Zhids.

3RD SOLDIER. Have them sing something for us.

1ST SOLDIER. *(To* MARSHALOV.*)* You heard him! Play a song. *(*MARSHALOV *returns to sit at piano.* 2ND SOLDIER *leers at* SOPHIE; 1ST SOLDIER *observes and almost falls over in his drunkenness as he makes a mock bow to her.)* You, sing. *(*SOPHIE *sings to* MARSHALOV'*s accompaniment;* 2ND SOLDIER *starts to paw her.* JACOB *stirs to interfere; the other actors restrain him,* 1ST SOLDIER *has seen* JACOB'*s attempt.)* Sing a Romanian song—you—sing. *(*JACOB *sings with* SOPHIE.*)* Now, dance. Both of you! *(*JACOB *and* SOPHIE *dance while* MARSHALOV *plays. Noise of guns outside, then loud screams. Voice of* MICHAEL—"*No! no!" then wailing, shots,* MICHAEL *screams.* SOPHIE *falters;* JACOB *takes up the song and forces her to sing and dance with him.)*

2ND SOLDIER. *(Coming between* JACOB *and* SOPHIE.*)* I can dance better than you. *(*JACOB *and* SOPHIE *cling to each other.* 2ND SOLDIER *raises his sword and is about to slash at* JACOB, *when a loud whistle is heard.)*

1ST SOLDIER. That's our signal. We have to hurry. Let him go. *(*SOLDIERS *quickly collect themselves and rush out.)*

SOPHIE. *(Frantic.)* That was Michael's scream. They found him. *(She rushes to door but is stopped by* MARSHALOV.*)*

MARSHALOV. You wait here. I'll find him. *(Stops* JACOB.*)*

JACOB. I'll go with you. *(*MARSHALOV *exits. The actors remain in tense quiet;* JACOB *tries to calm* SOPHIE.*)*

OLD ACTOR. *(Plays single notes on the piano.)* So, children, we made our debut to the heroes of the glorious people's Revolution.

JACOB. They are not the Revolution.

SOPHIE. We should have run away to America. What were we waiting for . . . ? *(*JACOB *runs out to join* MARSHALOV.*)*

OLD ACTOR. *(To* SOPHIE.*)* To America. You talk like a child. With armies and fighting on every side, how would you get out of the country?

SOPHIE. We'd walk, that's how. Michael and I—we'd get there. *(*OLD ACTOR *keeps tinkling at the piano,* SOPHIE *nervously paces, others huddle and whisper. Noise at door.* MARSHALOV *and* JACOB *enter, carrying a dead* MICHAEL *between them.* SOPHIE *screams and rushes at them. She then pounds* JACOB *with her fists.)* You—you—you monster! He wanted to go to Moscow with Stanislavsky. But you shamed him out of it. You with your damned pious holiness. Not the pogromists, but you, you killed him . . .

CURTAIN

ACT II

SCENE 1

Moscow, early 1930s. On stage of Gossett, the Soviet State Yiddish Theater. MIKHOELS *is concluding the morning rehearsal of* Travels of Benjamin III *by Moche Sforim.* JACOB *is sitting on the side of stage. Ad lib close of the scene by the actors.* MIKHOELS *nods to* ZUSKIND.

ZUSKIND. We'll all take lunch now. Be back exactly one hour from now. (*Actors disperse and exit.* ZUSKIND *nods to* JACOB *and speaks with* MIKHOELS.) You and your guest joining us?

MIKHOELS. Not now. We have much to talk about. Here we'll have more privacy.

ZUSKIND. Aren't you eating today?

MIKHOELS. Maybe Benjamin in the play lives on air and dreams, but not I. Bring me back something (*He turns to* JACOB.) And you, my friend, we'll talk now. But first, what would you like to eat?

JACOB. Nothing, thank you.

ZUSKIND. A real actor. At least he has one talent, not to eat.

MIKHOELS. In the state theater we all eat.

ZUSKIND. You're right. In the state theater you eat—you eat out your guts.

MIKHOELS. Enough. The hour will be over before you go. Bring an extra container of tea for our guest. (ZUSKIND *exits.* MIKHOELS *invites* JACOB *to sit.*) Zuskind is one of our greatest actors. Everyone loves him.

JACOB. I know. I've seen him.

MIKHOELS. I hope he stays with the Yiddish theater. You see, our theater is Yiddish. He is more cosmopolitan. He claims our audiences are made up of all kinds, Jews and gentiles. Yet he'll go to the Jewish restaurant. Now, let's talk theater. You want to join our company?

JACOB. If I can fit in, it's my cherished dream.

MIKHOELS. Assuming you have the talent, why shouldn't you fit in?

JACOB. The first thing I should tell you is that I'm not a member of the Communist Party.

MIKHOELS. Yes, that could be a problem. But let's take one thing at a time. I've looked over your papers, the history of your acting career. It's very impressive. I like the roles you've played, the dramas you've been in. But you should know we have a different idea about Yiddish plays.

JACOB. I know. That's one of the reasons I want to be in your company.

MICHOELS. (*Riffling through papers, obviously* JACOB's *dossier.*) You traveled with the Vilna Troupe . . .

JACOB. Until they went kaput. But even so, I would have left.

MIKHOELS. Why?

JACOB. A difference of opinion about their repertoire of plays. Always the same ghetto life, with superstition and beggary—like always the DYBBUK.

MIKHOELS. Don't you think that is the true drama of the Jewish past?

JACOB. I didn't expect you to be a champion of the Yiddish bourgeoise theater.

MIKHOELS. You are right. I am not. I

only want to learn about your ideas. There's a new wind sweeping from the East, from Russia. Did you find any signs of it in Europe, in America?

JACOB. No. All of it a voyage into nostalgia for the Jews who have fled from the shtetls. They go to the theater only to relive the past they left in Romania, Poland, and Russia. They keep asking for "laughter and tears."

MIKHOELS. *(Smiling.)* And what's wrong with that? Even though I may agree with you, can't you see the old plays being done with an interpretation of the class struggle?

JACOB. They weren't written as polemics, for politics.

MIKHOELS. So what plays would you do?

JACOB. I would do, in addition to the great classics, like your proposed production of *King Lear,* plays by some of our Jewish poets. There is great lyricism among our Jewish writers. They illuminate our lives and how we can point to a better world.

MIKHOELS. And you say you're not a member of the Party.

JACOB. No.

MIKHOELS. How about plays, contemporary, not by Jewish writers but translated into Yiddish?

JACOB. Why not, if they're good.

MIKHOELS. *(Again riffling through the papers in his hand.)* How is it that you did not ever get to the United States?

JACOB. First, I had contracts in other countries, specially in the Argentine. I did apply to get a visa to the United States, but they had restrictions, quotas. Oh, I had some of my former colleagues sign papers for me, but in my day I also signed papers—too

many. You see, I had to leave the Argentine because I appeared at protest meetings against the regime that was fighting the unions. Marshalov wrote me from New York that the United States government has me on a list of undesirable socialists.

MIKHOELS. I see where you'll become a member of the Party yet. You'll find out that the only hope for the Jews is here, in Russia. You'll have to hear what Stalin says.

JACOB. I used to think that way about Germany, when Arnold Zweig and the German Army helped us establish a Yiddish theater in Vilna. Look at Germany now.

MIKHOELS. This too shall pass. The workers will destroy this new lunatic. He's like a loud-mouthed braggart in a beer saloon, disturbing everyone else. He'll go too far and then someone will beat him up and throw him into the gutter.

JACOB. I hope you're right. The more I travel, the more I believe that the whole world is Hitler.

MIKHOELS. *(Laughing.)* You must not despair. I heard you're a good actor. Even if you are mediocre, I want you in the company.

JACOB. Why? If I'm not good, why should you take me?

MIKHOELS. I want you to learn that Russia is the hope of the world, especially for Jews. You'll find out that our leader Stalin is like a father to us. Now, before the others come, I want you to give me a scene or a song. It isn't really necessary, but in honesty, I must report that I did give you an audition. What shall it be?

JACOB. I always liked this piece from Leivick's *Golem.*

MIKHOELS. Good. Do that. (JACOB *does a selection from the* Golem. *At its conclusion,* MIKHOELS *nods in approval.*) Splendid! Now a song.

JACOB. A capella?

MIKHOELS. What else? (JACOB *sings the rousing* "Romania, Romania, Romania." MIKHOELS *applauds together with a few of the actors who have drifted back from lunch. Among them is* ZUSKIND *who offers* MIKHOELS *his food and to* JACOB *a cup of tea.* MIKHOELS *speaks to* ZUSKIND.) Did you go to the Jewish restaurant or to your cosmopolitan one?

ZUSKIND. They're all cosmopolitan. There are no longer any strictly Jewish restaurants. You'll find gentiles or Jews in all of them.

MIKHOELS. So how many gentiles were in the restaurant?

ZUSKIND. Today he wasn't there.

SCENE 2

A few years later.

SOPHIE's *suite in a New York hotel. Phone rings.* SOPHIE, *now more mature than when we last saw her, hurries in from bedroom, picks up the phone.*

SOPHIE. Hello . . . yes . . . ah, Marshalov. Come right up. (*She replaces phone, primps, then phones room service.*) Please send up set-ups . . . for two. No . . . just set-ups. (*She replaces phone, then takes out two bottles of brandy from a cabinet and places them on the table. She then waits at the door. A knock. She opens the door. An older, more urbane and sophisticated* MARSHALOV *enters. They embrace—as friends. He offers her a bunch of flowers.*) Oh, my friend—this is wonderful. And how sweet of you to bring me flowers. (*She places flowers in a vase and pours some water from a decanter which she prepared for the drinks, into the vase. She bubbles with delight as she busies herself.*) Such a dear, dear friend! These flowers are divine. How are you? I can't tell you how good it is to see you.

MARSHALOV. Wonderful? Good? So how can I describe what I now see? You look radiant, lovely, beautiful!

SOPHIE. And I can act, too . . .

MARSHALOV. You're telling me!

SOPHIE. So why can't I get a job?

MARSHALOV. It's the times, it's talking pictures, it's the depression, it's everything . . .

SOPHIE. So tell me about yourself. There's so much to catch up on. Our lives were so close to one another, then—phtt! I can't tell you how happy I was when you phoned. I want to know everything . . . but EVERYTHING . . . since we last saw each other in Europe . . .

MARSHALOV. Oh, Sophie, so long ago . . .

SOPHIE. Too long. And you said you *had* to see me. What's it about? (*A knock on the door.* SOPHIE *opens the door to a waiter who wheels in a cart with set-ups. She signs for it. The* WAITER *exits.* SOPHIE *busies herself at the cart with the brandy.*)

SOPHIE. What would you like?

MARSHALOV. Whatever you're having.

SOPHIE. Mine's scotch on the rocks.

MARSHALOV. As Sholem Aleichem

would say, what harm can it do? I'll have the same. (SOPHIE *dispenses the drinks;* MARSHALOV *takes his, and walks about.*) Ah, Sophie, Sophie. America. Here we are with nothing and no one to hurt us.

SOPHIE. Except our memories.

MARSHALOV. So, drink, to good memories for the future. (*While* MARSHALOV *tosses his off,* SOPHIE *sips hers.*)

SOPHIE. Sit down. You're walking around like you're directing a play.

MARSHALOV. I wish I was. There's just nothing. The Yiddish stage is as good as dead. Except for Maurice Schwartz and his *Yoshe Kalb.* Oh yes, and the Artef.

SOPHIE. Don't I know it.

MARSHALOV. I saw Schwartz. He's like on a merry-go-round, trying to stay alive. He wants me to be in his *Shylock's Daughter.*

SOPHIE. Soooo?

MARSHALOV. The way he's doing it, it should be called *Shylock's Daughter's Father.* Oh, he's good, he's devoted to Yiddishkayt, and if not for him, who knows if there would be a Yiddish theater in New York—or America. But everyone in his company must be in his shadow.

SOPHIE. But it's a job. It's better than these tootsie roles I have to play in night clubs. I would take a job with Schwartz or anybody, as long as it was in the theater.

MARSHALOV. So now let me talk from the bottom of my heart, from my soul to you, Sophie, as a woman and as an artist. (SOPHIE *smiles, raises her glass in acknowledgment.*)

SOPHIE. You are too gallant.

MARSHALOV. You know me from the beginning of your career. Did I ever lie to you? Of course not, it's not my style. I have no time to waste on being gallant. You don't need cheap night club dates. You are a great actress.

SOPHIE. Who has to eat, regularly.

MARSHALOV. I know how talented you are. You played in my company—comedy, tragedy, ingenues or character roles like "Mirele Efros," a mature woman. If I were Schwartz, I'd grab you for the title role in *Shylock's Daughter.*

SOPHIE. Soooo, go tell Schwartz. Go tell the world. Go . . .

MARSHALOV. I don't have to tell anyone as long as I know. (*He puts down his drink, sits, and turns to her.*) Now, listen carefully. MGM, the movie producers have given me a contract . . .

SOPHIE. Wonderful! You'll be a Hollywood star.

MARSHALOV. Not as an actor, God forbid. Now that they're going to produce only talking pictures, they want me as a coach for their actors.

SOPHIE. But with your accent? For talking pictures . . .

MARSHALOV. Ah, Sophie, Sophie. You, of all people to ask such a question. It's not the accent—it's the meaning and feeling the actor must project. It's a good contract for five years . . .

SOPHIE. Congratulations. I'm very happy for you.

MARSHALOV. I'm not. Yes, it's a good, a wonderful chance. But two things are missing.

SOPHIE. And they are . . . ?

MARSHALOV. The stage, the theater . . . and more important, you.

SOPHIE. Me?

MARSHALOV. Yes. You. I want you to come with me.

SOPHIE. But . . .

MARSHALOV. As my wife. Please say yes. I love you. I've loved you from the first moment . . .

SOPHIE. Since Michael was murdered?

MARSHALOV. Before that. From the moment I first saw you. I didn't dare tell you.

SOPHIE. Oh, Boris. How can I tell you.

MARSHALOV. There's someone else?

SOPHIE. Not exactly. But I do like you . . .

MARSHALOV. Love?

SOPHIE. Even that. But . . .

MARSHALOV. Not enough to marry me?

SOPHIE. I don't want to hurt you. Yes, not enough to marry you.

MARSHALOV. I've directed many plays with brilliant dialogue in exactly such situations. Now, I don't know what to say . . . yes, I do. I can get you a contract with MGM, as sort of one of my assistants. Then we'll see what happens. There's a wonderful English word: propinquity. We'll see what happens, like letting nature take its course.

SOPHIE. Boris, sit down. I want to read you part of a letter I received yesterday from Jacob.

MARSHALOV. Our Jacob?

SOPHIE. Yes.

MARSHALOV. How did he know where to write you?

SOPHIE. Didn't you once tell me that the Yiddish theater is like a little shtetl? What happens in Buenos Aires is known right away in Warsaw or on Second Avenue. He knows I'm in New York, so his first letter was to our Hebrew Actors Union address. I answered it, and maybe every other month I get a letter from him.

MARSHALOV. Is he the reason you turned me down?

SOPHIE. I don't know. Let me read parts of his letter. (*She fetches the letter from her purse and selects passages which she reads.*) "You asked what plays we are now rehearsing. Our monumental project is a new version of *King Lear* with Mikhoels in the title role and Zuskind as the Fool. Our discussions at rehearsal are very exciting. Mikhoels is not emphasizing the influence of family traditions, the patriarchal figurehead; instead he shows how bourgeois sentimentality is out of joint with the future. According to Mikhoels, Shakespeare was the voice of the proletariat . . ."

MARSHALOV. What nonsense! He was the poet for all mankind . . .

SOPHIE. This is not a lecture hall, nor is it a debate. Do you want to hear what Jacob . . .

MARSHALOV. Please go on.

SOPHIE. I'll skip all that. Except that it explains why, according to him, the Soviet theater is the best in the world . . .

MARSHALOV. Where has he been! What has he seen! Does he know anything about the Japanese theater? What does he know about the Spanish theater, or for that matter about the Greek, ancient or modern? All these arrogant newcomers know everything overnight—phooey!

SOPHIE. I'm only reading what he says, I'm not arguing with you. Should I . . . ?

MARSHALOV. I'm sorry, please go on.

SOPHIE. "Maybe, when this season is finished, I'll try again to come to America. Even though I'm not a member of the Communist Party, last year the Americans refused to give me a visa. I'll try again and ask you to sign papers for me. I'll need someone else. Maybe you can locate Boris

Marshalov. After all, he knows me, knows how I'm only interested in the theater and not in politics. Please let me know if you can reach him. Now, more about myself. I work hard at the theater but it's worth it. I believe my capabilities have developed more than I ever believed possible. All of this, thanks to Mikhoels' teaching and faith in me. I would tell you more about him, but I'd have to use Aesop's fables, if you know what I mean. Ah, Sophie, if you only knew how much I . . ." Oh well, the rest is personal and not really important.

MARSHALOV. Not important? I see, all right. The rest is the most important, to me. So that's why you won't come with me to Hollywood? (SOPHIE *remains silent.*)

MARSHALOV. Why did you leave Russia? For just a chance like this one. Ah, Sophie, here in America all doors are open to you . . .

SOPHIE. You don't know what you're saying. I tried out for a part with the Artef. They wouldn't even let me audition because I wasn't a member of the Communist Party. I told them I would think about joining. But when they asked me why I left Russia, and I told them I was fed up with anti-Semitism, you'd think I had expressed the worst blasphemy.

MARSHALOV. At least you can hold your head up as a Jew, not like in Russia where you'd have to deny being a Jew in order to play with the Moscow Art Theater.

SOPHIE. Do they know in Hollywood that you are Jewish?

MARSHALOV. It never even came up. That's so wonderful about theater and films in America. Did you know that the head boss at MGM is Jewish? Do you know that MGM are the initials of Goldwyn and Mayer, two Jews?

SOPHIE. What will happen when you have to take sides in politics? It's all not paradise . . . No place to hide.

MARSHALOV. My God, Sophie—don't you see how you're letting your whole life fly away while you dream of that . . . that . . . no, I won't say anything against him. He's a good actor, a great actor, but he's a half a world away from you, the Atlantic Ocean and the continent of Europe. If he loved you, he'd come here for you. I told you simply what's in my heart. I should be proud and not beg you to weigh my love with a dream far away in Soviet Russia. Sophie, I love you and want you to marry me and come with me to Hollywood . . .

SOPHIE. Oh Boris, I do love you, but . . .

MARSHALOV. Not enough to marry me?

SOPHIE. No. I've been in enough plays to have a curtain speech, but I feel so deeply that I can't say anything.

MARSHALOV. *(Changing his intensity to lightness.)* Then we'll reenact the farewells in an Italian opera—Adio! Adio!

SOPHIE. *(They both mockingly and laughingly sing.)* Adio! Ah Boris, I do love you.

MARSHALOV. But always that "but." *(An awkward pause.)* What will you do? You have a great talent and you must not waste it in night club appearances.

SOPHIE. It's a living. There's a Yiddish radio station that promised me an audition.

MARSHALOV. Like a gypsy. If only our Yiddish theater had its own home, a roof over its head, an ensemble in a real repertory . . .

SOPHIE. That's why, when I get enough money together, I'm going to Palestine. Maybe even in a Kibbutz.

MARSHALOV. They're starving there. No water, hard work, surrounded by Arab enemies . . .

SOPHIE. Where haven't you found the Arab mind? At least there the Jews are building a home . . .

MARSHALOV. I never knew you were a Zionist.

SOPHIE. I don't know if I am. But among Jews I won't be a stranger in Galuth.

MARSHALOV. You're not among stran-gers here. There are more Jews here in New York than anywhere else. And they've built a good life here.

SOPHIE. I'm not ready to go work in a shop or marry a successful man. I am an actress, and I want to, I must act.

MARSHALOV. Brave, brave girl. I love you. *(He is about to embrace her, but instead he bows and kisses her hand.)* I'll be at the MGM studios in Hollywood. You can reach me there. (MARSHALOV *exits with as much dignity as a rejected lover can command.)*

SCENE 3

Moscow, August 1939. Backstage at the Kamerny Theatre. Same setting as Act II, Scene 1.

JACOB *is setting the the stage props and furniture for a rehearsal.* LEV SHEININ *enters.*

LEV SHEININ. Hello, comrade.

JACOB. Hello. Can I help you?

LEV SHEININ. If you are Mikhoels, yes. If not, no.

JACOB. Sorry, he's not here. I'm one of the actors.

LEV SHEININ. *(With ill-disguised contempt.)* Hmm, an actor. I'll wait for the maestro.

JACOB. You don't like actors?

LEV SHEININ. Well, let me put it this way: actors are five kopeks a dozen. And very often, a baker's dozen.

JACOB. You'll have to wait outside. We don't allow loitering in the theater.

LEV SHEININ. I'm not a loiterer. I'm a Special Investigator for the KGB. And whether you like it or not, I'll wait right here for your great Mikhoels. (JACOB, *after contemptuously looking at* LEV SHEININ, *goes about his work.)* Soooo, you're an actor. (JACOB *ignores him.)* Are you a member of the Party?

JACOB. That's none of your business.

LEV SHEININ. You'll be surprised how I can make it my business. I must say you look very familiar to me.

JACOB. I look familiar to half of Moscow. As an actor, I've appeared on the stage. So you saw me on stage—so what!

LEV SHEININ. No. I've seen you before. Yes, I remember. You were in Lemberg, more than a dozen years ago, maybe more than fifteen years ago. You were with the troupe of Yiddish actors when the Polish hooligans made a pogrom . . . they killed dozens of Jews, actors too. (JACOB *remains silent.)* You should become a member of the Party, it can only do you good.

JACOB. I'm an artist and not a politician.

LEV SHEININ. Do you think you can hide because you're an actor? You're such a good actor, you must know what Shakespeare said.

JACOB. No.

LEV SHEININ. In *Julius Ceasar,* when the conspirators attack Cinna, believing he's his namesake the politician, he pleads with them: "But I'm Cinna the poet." Did it help him that he was a poet? Will it help you that you're an actor? No. They stabbed him to death.

JACOB. I see. You're warning me.

LEV SHEININ. Whatever you think. but back there in Lemberg, the progromists killed actors too.

JACOB. Obviously, I survived.

LEV SHEININ. You were in Marshalov's troupe?

JACOB. What if I was?

LEV SHEININ. Marshalov betrayed the Revolution. He ran away to the capitalistic United States. So how is it that you are still here and you're not a member of the Party?

JACOB. I didn't say I am or am not a member.

LEV SHEININ. We know more about you than you think.

JACOB. So—enjoy. *(A busy and dynamic* MIKHOELS *enters.)*

MIKHOELS. Jacob, are you set up and ready for . . . *(He sees* SHEININ.) Oh, hello. Can I help you?

LEV SHEININ. You certainly can. I submitted my play to you. I'm Lev Sheinin. I hope you read it.

MIKHOELS. Oh, yes, I remember.

LEV SHEININ. Did you read it?

MIKHOELS. Well . . .

LEV SHENIN. I can come back after you read it. Just tell me when.

MIKHOELS. The truth is, I thoroughly read the first two acts, and I had no appetite for the rest. But I did skim through the last act.

LEV SHEININ. So you read it. So tell me . . .

MIKHOELS. Whether I liked it or not is academic and no help to you. You see, and I must have told this to you when you first submitted the play, our repertoire is set, but firmly and solidly, for the next two years.

LEV SHEININ. So what is a playwright supposed to do? Starve till your theater is ready for him?

MIKHOELS. Why don't you submit your play to the Cultural Minister? Only officialdom can make us change our schedule.

LEV SHEININ. Officialdom! I am part of officialdom.

MIKHOELS. I know.

LEV SHEININ. But what you don't know is that every aparatchik is jealous of his authority. I'm as important, maybe more so, as the Cultural Minister. But . . . I can say more, but I dare not.

MIKHOELS. As an official, you must know that the Cultural Minister approved our schedule and only he can allow us to change it.

LEV SHEININ. *(Sarcastically.)* Tell me, you stickler by the rules, how many Yiddish plays do you get a year? Who in his right mind is writing plays in and about Yids?

MIKHOELS. Plenty—and great ones. If you are so interested in the Yiddish theater you know about the Soviet Jewish writers for our theater, like Bergelson, Kulback, Resnick . . .

LEV SHEININ. Be careful. You know what happened to Kulbak and Resnick . . .

MIKHOELS. So we do our great Yiddish classics, by Goldfadden, by Asch, by Sholem Aleichem.

LEV SHEININ. Exactly. And you are allowed to do them because you know how to pull the wool over the eyes of the Cultural Minister. You pretend to make these writers of ghetto plays, of discredited bourgeoise theater as part of our revolutionary struggle. But you're fooling no one. Where are the new Soviet Jews helping to build our glorious new nation? Your dirty old Jews in the decadent excrescence of their debased society . . .

MIKHOELS. Hold it! We do what we can and what we must. We are actors and do the best we can for our theater, for our Jewish heritage, and above all for our Soviet nation, our proletarian society. Peretz Markish has given us a truly patriotic play in his *Ovadis Family* and Halkin's play is beautiful. How about Isaac Babel and Osip Mandelshtam? Our Yiddish theater marches arm in arm with our Russian brothers . . .

LEV SHEININ. Fancy talk, that's all it is. *(Actors have been drifting in.)* Be careful, Mikhoels. There will come a time when you will need me as a friend.

MIKHOELS. I have never, nor will I, favor friends if such favoring conflicts with artistic truths.

LEV SHEININ. A very pretty speech, but that of a prig.

MIKHOELS. This is all pointless. I can't discuss this any more. We're about to start rehearsals.

ZUSKIN. *(He rushes in, wild with excitement.)* Mikhoels, everybody, did you hear what happened—it's unbelievable . . .

MIKHOELS. So tell us already!

ZUSKIN. Stalin and Hitler have just signed a pact of friendship and cooperation.

MIKHOELS. Impossible! Not Stalin . . . !

LEV SHEININ. Be careful what you say about Stalin. And remember, you'll need me as a friend. You know where to find me.

ZUSKIN. That isn't all. Hitler has invaded Poland, and . . .

LEV SHEININ. *(Arresting his departure.)* Ho, ho. So what do we Jews do now?

JACOB. Fly.

LEV SHEININ. Where to?

MIKHOELS. Stalin knows what he's doing. Trust him.

LEV SHEININ. You needn't say that to play safe with me. I'm a Jew, too, you know.

JACOB. If only we could run away to Palestine . . .

LEV SHEININ. I thought you said you didn't mess with politics. Soooo, you're a Zionist! I'll remember that.

ZUSKIN. Palestine? You'd be as safe there with the Arabs as we Jews were with the Czar's Cossacks.

MIKHOELS. The whole world is an Arab. We're safe here. I believe in Stalin. I trust him.

LEV SHEININ. You have no choice. (LEV SHEININ *exits.*)

ZUSKIN. *(Aside to* MIKHOELS.*)* You didn't have to put it on so thick to that rat.

MIKHOELS. Believe it or not, I meant it. Stalin won't dare to betray the heart of the Revolution. Enough politics now. We'll be called upon to work for our Soviet land. Let us rehearse . . . *(ad lib rehearsal action.)*

SCENE 4

Early 1943, Frunze in the Soviet Kirghiz Republic. A barren room converted into a pitifully small theater. Actors are seated about. MIKHOELS *is reading from a manuscript.*

MIKHOELS. Peretz Markish wrote this play—oh, yes, its title is *An Eye for an Eye*—specially for us to show the world how we Jews are fighting our country's enemies side by side with all the people of our sacred land.

AN ACTOR. Soooo, who will see it? From this isolated hole in the world, how will the world know what we're trying to tell them?

MIKHOELS. When we triumph, when we destroy the Nazis monster we will play in Yiddish theaters all over the world, show everyone like Goldfadden did in his *Bar Khochba* what our Jewish comrades . . .

AN ACTOR. You're laying little birds in your bosom. In what theaters? Where have you been since 1938? Our Yiddish theaters have been closed—they're kaput.

MIKHOELS. We must not despair. This is our war—and don't forget it! And our theater must show the determination of all—and I mean ALL—Soviet citizens to fight on to victory, to develop the best sides of a Soviet man's character, his optimistic devotion to his country, unafraid of any obstacle. Our theater will show the world that the Communist Party and our Marxian principles are forever. When this war is over, Yiddish theater will open and flourish again in Moscow, in Leningrad, in Odessa, in Kiev, and Minsk—and travel freely all over our glorious Soviet Russia.

AN ACTOR. From your lips to God's ears.

MIKHOELS. We have our work cut out for us here and now. We must rehearse, rehearse, and rehearse, and perfect our repertoire, bring our plays to our brave soldiers in the battlefields, to the workers in the factories, yes, to all the people in order to support and reinforce their morale, to uplift them in these brave times, and we do all this in our mother tongue— in Yiddish. We are the torchbearers who keep alight and alive our Yiddish language and its Yiddish-kayt. The party of Lenin is our salvation. We are a very important part of his revolution, a culture within a culture and an integral part of it. No where else in the world may we as Jews maintain our individual dignity.

JACOB. We can't fight only with words, with acting, with . . .

MIKHOELS. That is our job. Our assignment is to sustain the Army's morale, to encourage it, to feed . . .

JACOB. We should be out there with the army . . .

MIKHOELS. Here, with us, you are part of that army. Soldiers also repair tanks, soldiers fix airplanes, soldiers help their wounded brethren, they even bury the dead. And we do what we can, what we are told to do.

JACOB. You mean we are not to question our assigned roles? To accept on blind faith . . . ?

MIKHOELS. In Stalin we have a concentration of will—not only of centralized power, but also a definite living wisdom. From the mountain heights of this gray wisdom, according to his perception, all the ideals of good and the power of evil appear insignificant. Like my realization of the role of King Lear, I find in Stalin an amazing parallel in his challenge to the whole world.

JACOB. But I want to fight the enemies of *our* people. I want to be out there with the soldiers, fighting the Nazis. (*They are interrupted by the entrance of* LEV SHEININ.)

LEV SHEININ. Comrade Mikhoels, honored artist of the Union of Soviet Socialist Republics, wearer of The Order of Lenin, I bring you greetings from our comrade and leader, Josef Stalin.

MIKHOELS. This isn't another one of your grisly jokes, is it?

LEV SHEININ. Oh no—that will come in time. We should all be healthy and survive this war. No. Comrade Stalin has an important mission for you. (MIKHOELS *remains silent and suspicious.*) Here, I'll show you. First I'll read it to you: "Greetings to the Honorable People's Artist of the Union of Soviet Socialist Republics, Shloyme Mikhols. Our beloved land is engaged in a death struggle with monstrous evil, with the Nazi-Fascist beast that invaded our holy land. Although we will destroy our enemy, we must employ the goodwill and help of the world. In this enterprise, all the people of our beloved Soviet must and will help. The Jewish Anti-Fascist League is loyally sacrificing everything it can for our cause. They ask me, and I instruct you, together with your distinguished colleague

Itzhok Feffer, to visit England, Mexico, and the U.S.A where you will rally all the support you can for our holy cause. You may take with you not more than two of your company. Blessings on you and may you help bring us a speedy victory. Signed, Josef Stalin." There you have it.

MIKHOELS. When shall I leave?

LEV SHEININ. I've arranged for tomorrow morning.

MIKHOELS. I'll be ready.

LEV SHEININ. Who are the two you will take?

MIKHOELS. Well . . . how about you, Jacob?

LEV SHEININ. Only Party members may accompany you. We don't want any defections like your predecessor Granovsky.

JACOB. I don't want to go anyway. I'm volunteering to fight at the front, where I belong.

LEV SHEININ. Just as well. (*Then to* MIKHOELS.) Work it out, but remember: no more than two and they must be Party members. (LEV SHEININ *exits.*)

ZUSKIN. Like the devil—he always shows up when we don't need him.

MIKHOELS. Never mind all that. I don't know how long I'll be gone. Zuskin, you'll be the régisseur while I'm away. As for you, Jacob, I'll never understand you. Your love, your Sophie is in America. This is your chance to see her. So why don't you join the Party and come to America with me.

JACOB. I joined a party when I was circumcised. After the war there will be a Jewish state in the Holy Land. That's where I will go, and God willing, that's where Sophie will join me.

ZUSKIN. *(Sarcastically.)* Soooo, next year in Jerusalem.

JACOB. Yes, why not? When your Stalin signed a pact with Hitler, did you believe it would come to war between the two of them . . . ?

ZUSKIN. Go figure out the goyim.

MIKHOELS. Aha, so what happened to our cosmopolitan philosophe?

ZUSKIN. *(Truculently.)* There are always exceptions.

JACOB. And I'm one of them. Yes—next year in Jerusalem.

ZUSKIN. *(To* MIKHOELS*)* Give my regards to Broadway—at least to Second Avenue.

SCENE 5

New York, 1943. MIKHOELS *is appearing before a giant meeting of New York's Jewish Anti-Fascist League. He stands alone before a lectern.*

MIKHOELS. And in 1939 we produced Peretz Markish's play, *The Feast.* It portrayed the drama of the civil war in the Ukraine—a struggle against bandits where the Ukrainians and the Russians fight the bandits and their foreign allies. Under the banner of the Revolution, all the vital and healthy elements of the people armed themselves—among them the brave Jewish people. Hand in hand with the great Ukrainian and Russian people, the Jews fought to wipe away the shame and sorrow from our shtetls— scenes of unheard persecution and pogroms. Not only the young, not only the sons, but fathers heard this call to a new life and followed their sons to defend the dignity and freedom of our people. Peretz Markish created this most inspired, elevated song: "The people are immortals." His powerful, romantic perception of the heroic epic of our people is what our Russian State Yiddish Theater has been trying to present. Under our socialist actuality, we have been real-izing it. And when we defeat the anti-Semitic monsters, the murderous German Nazis, the wonderful Russian-Soviet land will once again be a haven for all peace-loving people who want to build a better world for all races and religions. It will be the promised land for the Jews. The Soviets have accomplished more than any other land in their brief time, in science, in culture, in social betterment, in inspiring the struggle against colonialism. And our Jews will flourish after the war as no other time in human history—yes, in Soviet Russia. Yiddishkayt will have a rebirth with our Yiddish theater in the avant garde. And so, as Jews, we must, for our own salvation, support this struggle by the heroic Soviet people against the Nazis . . . *(Applause from the audience. Lights dim briefly to show a passage of time.* MIKHOELS *has concluded his address; he is shaking hands with a few people who have come up to the buehne to meet him. The last to approach him is* SOPHIE*)*

SOPHIE. I've been hoping to meet you, Shloyme Mikhoels.

MIKHOELS. I'm sure I'm happy to meet you. But who are you?

SOPHIE. I am Sophie Finkel, a Jewish actress.

MIKHOELS. But of course. I've been hoping to meet you. I've heard so much about you, especially . . .

SOPHIE. *(Eagerly.)* Yes . . . yes . . . from whom?

MIKHOELS. You know that our Yiddish theater, although it is spread all over the world, is really like a little shtetl. What happens in the Yiddish theater in Buenos Aires, Johannesburg, or New York, we know right away in Moscow.

SOPHIE. *(Let down.)* Oh . . .

MIKHOELS. But I specially heard about you from Jacob Gold.

SOPHIE. *(Eagerly.)* Yes. Tell me, how is he?

MIKHOELS. The last I heard when I left on this tour, he had volunteered to fight with the soldiers against the Nazis.

SOPHIE. We have been corresponding, but I haven't heard from him in a few months.

MIKHOELS. Don't worry about our Jacob. He'll survive and come out a better man.

SOPHIE. He's as better as any man could be. And a great actor . . .

MIKHOELS. You needn't tell me. In my company he's one of the most talented. I wish you had come to Russia and been a member of our company.

SOPHIE. I only wanted to ask you about Jacob. You must be very busy and I feel guilty taking you away from your . . .

MIKHOELS. Oh, no. This talk is a great help to me. I've been working every minute of the day and night for our glorious war effort. Stalin himself gave me this mission. I must succeed.

You help me by keeping me aware of our normal life.

SOPHIE. You will succeed, I know you will.

MIKHOELS. When this horrible war is over, you must come to Moscow and join our company.

SOPHIE. No. When the war is over, I'm going to Palestine.

MIKHOELS. Ho ho, a Zionist?

SOPHIE. Call me what you wish, but I know that is where I belong. I will work on a Kibbutz, I will teach children, and maybe, God willing, I'll be an actress there, too.

MIKHOELS. Whether you admit it or not, you are a Zionist.

SOPHIE. So what if I am?

MIKHOELS. We are artists and can only fulfill ourselves in a truly socialist society.

SOPHIE. I am not interested in politics. I only want to act and lead a decent life.

MIKHOELS. Actors or any kind of artist cannot avoid politics. Even when they remain silent in a political whirlwind around them, their silence is a political statement. Actors are people, and people cannot, must not run away from living. Even your Jacob knows that his artistic fulfillment came in our socialist land. (SOPHIE *remains silent.*) Jacob, too, refused to join the Communist Party. Is he a Zionist, do you think?

SOPHIE. We never discussed it. But I hope, when the war is over, he'll join me in the land of the Jewish people.

MIKHOELS. Who knows what will happen after the war. But I have faith in Stalin. All rights and opportunities to recreate their national cultural life, like all other nationalities, are guaranteed by the Soviet Constitution. After the war, oh, Sophie, there will be a glorious rebirth of Yiddishkayt as no where else: Jewish schools will be opened, Yiddish language and Jewish history will be taught in Russia as never before—even in the regular Russian schools. Jewish newspapers and magazines will be published as nowhere else in the world. As Gorky once wrote, each people will be like an individual river flowing and joining the others as they surge toward one, great, harmonious sea.

SOPHIE. And you think the leopard will change its spots?

MIKHOELS. Let's not talk of this. I want one evening to myself. Please join me for dinner, and we'll talk of theater, of mutual friends, and above all, of Yiddishkayt. *(They walk off as the curtain falls.)*

SCENE 6

A few months after the end of World War II; in a Displaced Persons Camp along the border of Austria and Poland.

A troupe of Yiddish actors, under the leadership of HERMAN YABLAKOFF *have been bringing some respite from the gruelingly hard life to the Displaced Jews. The setting is a sparse, improvised hall. The audience may be suggested by a few Jewish D.P.s or the actual audience to the theater.*

HERMAN YABLAKOFF. Our troupe of Yiddish actors are proud to bring you some of our most distinguished schaushpielers from New York. You will see our lovely talented Sophie Finkel first. She is the darling of Second Avenue, a great prima donna. What will she sing? Just wait! Not only will you recognize it, but you'll want to join in with her. But please wait for the second chorus. Oh, yes, I want you all to give a loud hand to the Joint Distribution Committee for its wonderful work and making our appearance possible. *(He leads the ap-plause.)* And now I give you the beautiful, great Yiddish star, Sophie Finkel. *(Applause as he leads on* SOPHIE. YABLAKOFF *bows to her and kisses her hand, then he quickly exits. To the accompaniment of a piano,* SOPHIE *sings Goldfadden's "Raisins and Almonds." When she starts to repeat the verse, inevitably the audience joins in. When it is over, she enacts a dramatic monlogue. At the conclusion of her number, after the applause subsides,* JACOB, *dressed in catch-as catch-can clothing, rushes out from the wings.)*

JACOB. Sophie!

SOPHIE. At last, yes, it's you! Oh Jacob . . . *(They embrace.* JACOB *turns to the audience.)*

JACOB. All of you should be so blessed as I am. Here I am, a refugee like all of you. I didn't despair. Out of the horrors of this *hoorbin,* out of all this devastation of the Holocaust, I am reunited to the love of my life. Sophie Finkel and I, years and years ago, were actors together in Marshalov's troupe and we toured together in Russia, in Romania, in Poland. When her husband was murdered by Polish hooligans in a pogrom, we were separated. Through all these years I've been faithful to my love for her. Now, out of the ashes of this frightful fire of war, we meet again. I know we will never again be separated—if she agrees.

SOPHIE. Yes, yes, oh, yes! And we're going to make our home in Eretz Yisroel. (SOPHIE *and* JACOB, *hand in hand, beam as they walk off and the curtain falls.*)

SCENE 7

Before the curtain rises, there is the sound of distant guns. Curtain rises on a meagre apartment in the new State of Israel, January 1949. Three ISRAELI SOLDIERS *are lolling around. One is an officer; the others are privates. The sound of the guns are soon silent.*

1ST SOLDIER. Sounds like it's almost over.

OFFICER. Maybe. We won't know till we get official word. And I warn all of you, everybody: watch out! The enemies of Israel cannot be trusted. You never know what they'll do next.

2ND SOLDIER. But Ben Gurion and his cabinet are negotiating peace terms. (*Sound of sporadic gun fire.*)

OFFICER. Where are you? Are you deaf? What is that noise you just heard?

2ND SOLDIER. Guns—fighting.

OFFICER. Exactly. Let Ben Gurion negotiate, but we keep doing what we have to till it's officially over. And even then, I wouldn't trust the enemy.

1ST SOLDIER. So what do we do?

OFFICER. (*Exaggerated patience, speaks deliberately as though to a child.*) We remain on guard and ready for anything. When we get official word and official orders, then we'll know.

2ND SOLDIER. Can we play the radio? We should know what's going on.

OFFICER. Why not? I don't think Jacob and Sophie will object. (2ND SOLDIER *turns on a portable radio. The radio splutters static with interpolations of announcements of news items.* OFFICER, *annoyed, barks at* 2ND SOLDIER.) Tune that down—use the ear phones. (2ND SOLDIER *puts on earphones; radio is silent.* JACOB *and* SOPHIE *enter. They are dressed in army fatigues.*)

JACOB. Soooo, that's how it's going to be. My wife and I come home from a hard day's work fighting the enemy and we find our apartment has become an army barracks.

1ST SOLDIER. Don't complain. At least you have a home. You're not living in a truck or buried in a hole on the road to Jerusalem. Maybe if I became an actor, I could also rate an apartment.

JACOB. (*To* SOPHIE.) From one war to another. From one crisis to another. All right, we're used to it.

OFFICER. You invited us.

JACOB. To visit, not to move in.

SOPHIE. I'll make some tea.

2ND SOLDIER. Now you're talking.

1ST SOLDIER. Say, don't you have any schnapps? Where's your hospitality. Let's celebrate.

JACOB. What are we celebrating?

1ST SOLDIER. Do we need a reason?

OFFICER. I'll give you a reason. We used to say, "Next year in Jerusalem." I'll toast with, "Tomorrow in Jerusalem."

JACOB. (*Busy bringing out schnapps and glasses.* SOPHIE *prepares tea.*) I'll open my last and only bottle—we can't refuse that toast. (2ND SOLDIER *is getting excited as he listens to radio via his earphones.*) What's going on? You got shpilkes?

2ND SOLDIER. Hold it everybody. The hourly news bulletin. Here it comes . . .

OFFICER. Take off your earphones and let us all hear it. (2ND SOLDIER *takes off earphones and adjusts the radio so all hear the broadcast.*)

ANNOUNCER. It appears to be about to happen. A statement will be issued in five minutes by Ben Gurion. Stand by. (*Although* SOPHIE *has been avidly listening, she continues with her chore of serving tea while* JACOB *dispenses the whiskey.* SOPHIE *and* JACOB *make noise with the glasses and cups. They are shushed by the* OFFICER.)

OFFICER. Sh, sh. Cut out the noise. We want to hear.

SOPHIE. That's a Jew for you: No matter how many problems he has, he could be dying, but he has to know what's going on in the world.

JACOB. So, all right already. Let's hear. (*All are silent as the radio announcer speaks.*)

ANNOUNCER. We will now have a brief interlude of music. Please stand by for an important announcement from government headquarters in Tel Aviv. (*Music plays,* SOPHIE *serves tea while* JACOB *pours whiskey. Music stops.*) Word in from headquarters. The first cease fire is about to be signed with one of the Arab nations. It is unclear which one, but it is official and definite that the anti-Israel Arab front has been broken. On to victory and peace!

OFFICER. (*Raising his glass of whiskey, as do the others.*) To victory and peace! Long live Israel! *The others drink, cheer, embrace, laugh, and cry. The radio plays music that is interrupted by news bulletins.*)

ANNOUNCER. We've just received word from Washington that President Truman congratulates the State of Israel in bringing peace to the much troubled Mid-East. Word from Paris and London echo the same sentiment. Here, in Tel Aviv, there is much joy and celebration. Ben Gurion will address the nation precisely two hours from now. We have been trying to get through to other world capitals. Silence from the Arab states. The same holds true for word from Moscow. However, we have just received a special bulletin from the Soviet capital: the world renowned actor and director of the Soviet State Yiddish Theater was killed in an auto accident in Minsk this morning. His bloody body was found in the snow at dawn. There is considerable mystery surrounding his death. It appears he journeyed to Minsk at the request of Stalin. No one has been allowed to view his body . . .

JACOB. (*Throughout the foregoing announcement he has been gasping.*) "No . . . no . . . no . . .

SOPHIE. (*To* 2ND SOLDIER.) Turn it off! Please, we can't take any more! (2ND SOLDIER *turns off radio.* SOPHIE *and*

JACOB *are alone.* SOPHIE *turns to* JACOB.) I can't believe it. He was so alive, so filled with hope, belief, loyalty . . .

JACOB. Loyalty to whom? To a politician? To Stalin? Maybe if I became a Party member and remained in Russia, they would not blame him for the defections of non-Party members like myself.

SOPHIE. You can't, you mustn't blame yourself. Look at all the great Jewish immortals whom Stalin murdered— (SOPHIE *lifts her glass as though to toast.*) First, Mikhoels . . .

JACOB. *(Lifting his glass. They both hold their glasses aloft as they toast each name.)* Shloyme Mikhoels. *(A voice from the audience: "To Shloyme Mikhoels".)* Bergelson. *(As* JACOB *and* SOPHIE *raise their glasses, a voice in the Audience: "To Bergelson." As* JACOB *and* SOPHIE *toast the memory of each of the names of the martyrs, a voice in the audience echoes the toast until—it is hoped—the* AUDIENCE *in its entirety will take up the refrain.)* To Markish. To Feffer. To Kulbak. To Resnick. Erlich. Alter. Litvakoff. Dimenshteyn. Frumkin. Kharik. Hofshteyn. Kvitko. Lozovsky. Nusinov. Persov. Spival. Zuskin. Tsimberg. Reisin. Axelrod. *(After the last name is toasted,* SOPHIE *and* JACOB *proclaim their last toast.)*

JACOB and SOPHIE. Long live Israel!

THE END

A SHTETL IN THE BRONX

Today we are living in an age of amnesia; everything will probably be forgotten in a decade or so. The gentrification of our cities erases many historic street cultures, and folk traditions survive only with difficulty. Thus, we have to take refuge in recording them.

David Lifson provides the "refuge" for such Jewish traditions, rescuing them through both artistic and academic means. His *The Yiddish Theatre in America* engendered further studies by a younger generation, yet it remains the authoritative English-language survey of the history of the Yiddish theater. His *Epic and Folk Plays of the Yiddish Theatre* and his other English adaptations and translations from Yiddish literature, including Sholem Aleichem's work, are outstanding contributions, ones that artistically preserve a folk tradition threatened with oblivion.

But in an age of forgetfulness, one cannot protect a tradition by mere preservation of literary texts and retrospection. Because cultural losses occur continually and pervasively, one can only rely on creative memory and flexible imagination to understand the same spirit in different social and ethnic traditions. To this end David Lifson has also contributed a good number of original, creative works, among them his plays—*Familiar Pattern, Mummers and Men, Le Poseur, How to Rob a Bank*—and his novel, *Headless Victory*. The worlds of these works are not confined to the Jewish milieu, and this breadth of view is the result not only of Lifson's versatility, but also of his penetrating observation of similar underlying values in various cultural guises.

His newest play, *A Shtetl in the Bronx,* celebrating Simchat Torah, reveals an epic ear and eye for the old Jewish resources. Through this play, both Jewish and non-Jewish readers can participate in a recovery of folk traditions that draws upon the very essence of their origins. The action of the play revolves around the central image of the "comradeship at Yoshe's." Yoshe offers the other characters a large, free space, which serves as a family kitchen, dining room, and a gathering place for the *landsleit*. Its habitués travel back to *der heim* when they assemble at Yoshe's,

189

and they figuratively re-create the shtetl where every human drama had occurred for them. Thus, Yoshe's house and the world of this play are a microcosm of the shtetl.

The shtetl is specific to Jewish life and cannot be separated from Yiddishkayt; it constitutes a unique model of a folk communication space. However, the concept of the shtetl is universalized whenever one person communicates with another in comradeship—*bruddershaft*. When the institution of the shtetl disintegrated, the communication between human beings lost something definitive and special. The loss of the shtetl has deprived us of mutual understanding.

However, *A Shtetl in the Bronx* proposes that the experience of the shtetl can be revived, and moreover, that it can be reestablished not only in terms of Jewish culture, but also in an expanded form that embraces other traditions. Yoshe left the shtetl in Russia, but he re-created it in his own way: "He knocked down the walls of the three rooms and made the large room."

Tetsuo Kogawa

Tetsuo Kogawa is a journalist, an established author, a professor of philosophy at Waco University in Tokyo, and a Yiddishist.

A SHTETL IN THE BRONX

by *David S. Lifson*

CHARACTERS

NARRATOR (Willie, grown up)
MOTHER
WILLIE
MARTIN
FATHER
MOISHE
VELVEL
ABE
NATHAN
CHARLIE
WOMEN
CHILDREN

THE SCENE

The play opens with the NARRATOR standing in front of the set which is a converted three-room flat behind a paint store in the Melrose section of the Bronx soon after World War I.

The walls of the flat's rooms have been removed, leaving one large room. What was a dish cupboard is now covered with a curtain of deep maroon velvet topped by a valence of the same cloth

191

on which is embroidered two golden lions of Judah; this is the Ark for the Torah's Holy Scrolls. This section separated by a curtain. In the center of the room is a large, round oak table on which the Torah is rolled open. The table is covered with a white table cloth. On the drainboard alongside the sink are four long-necked whiskey bottles flanked by many shot glasses. Hard by it is a table on which are arranged platters of pickled herring, schmaltz herring, marinated fish, dilled pickles, and tomatoes, honey cake, sponge cake, and black bread. A jug of sacramental wine stands near the cakes. It is the morning of the first day of Simchat Torah.

NARRATOR. I was a little boy, maybe eight or nine. My brother and I slept late because there was no school on the Jewish holiday. We loved the Jewish holidays: except for Yom Kippur, they all lasted two days. We observed them, not because we were devoutly religious, but we were free from school. Alas, we were not allowed to sleep. My mother charged in from the store to awaken us.

MOTHER. (Mother *enters while the* NARRATOR *exits stage right.*) You still sleeping! Get up already. (*Childish groan from off left.*) Nu! I have to go to the store so Poppa can come to dress. You have to go with him to shule. Get up! (*No sign of the boys.*) To my troubles there's no end. Quick into the toilet. I'll get yet a goiter from you. (WILLIE, *aged seven, and* MARTIN, *aged nine, enter wearing only their old-fashioned underwear—and sleepily walk off toward other side of stage, presumably to the*

toilet.) Hurry up. I'll fix your cocoa and I'll butter some rolls. Be quick. Poppa will be here right away. (*Lights dim and stage is clear.* NARRATOR *reeneters.*)

NARRATOR. Yes, we slept in our underwear. Who ever knew about pyjamas? When the boys had finished their ablutions, when they had finished their breakfast of buttered rolls and cocoa—we never knew of orange juice, but we did occasionally have farina or mamaleega—that's corn meal mush, and deeelicious with real, heavy sweet cream. We'd get it from Mr. Schweid's corner grocery. We'd carefully watch him ladle it out, a half a measure for a nickel. Oh, I can tell you about other exotic delicacies, but it's Simchat Torah morning and we must get to shule at Yoshe's. (*His* FATHER *enters, dressed in a dark blue suit with white piping on the vest. He is freshly shaved, his hair parted in the center, and he smoothes and curls his moustache, combed in the style of the Czar.*) That's my father. Always on the holidays he was a revelation to me: no longer the workhorse in a grimy pair of overalls. Look at him, he was the most handsome man I ever saw. (*The two* BOYS *enter. The* FATHER *hands one his talith pouch and the other a sidar—prayer book. They exit off left.*) They're off to Yoshe's, by way of the Third Avenue El. I'll tell you about Yoshe. Like our father, he was one of the *landslayt* who came from the same little shtetl in Russia. He had a hardware store in the lower part of the Bronx, a section that was mostly Italian. It was called the Hub. The store was in a tenement that Yoshe owned. As his business flourished, he moved his family upstairs into a five-room flat from the meagre three rooms behind the store. He knocked down the walls of the three rooms and made one large room which served as a family kitchen, dining room, and hangout for the frequent visits of his *landslayt*. For them this place was a little bit of *der heim*, the shtetl in the old country. And they came from all over, from Williamsburg and Brownsville in Brooklyn, from the cold-water-toilet-in-the-hall tenements of the lower East Side, from the affluent west side and Harlem, even from Paterson in New Jersey. They came to observe the holiday and yet once again to share their comradeship at Yoshe's. They were all members of the same *verein*. A handful of them had organized it, and it was more than the usual and numerous burial societies, for it held them together in this new land among strangers. When a landsman needed money for rent, when he had no job and no food in the house, when one in his family was deathly sick and he was in frightened despair, when he needed advice about a new business venture, when he was baffled and frustrated by the intense tempo and demands of the new way of life and simply needed a few moments of brotherhood—*brudderschaft*—encouragement, or only refuge from the unceasing struggle to survive, it was to Yoshe he came. When a landsman had trouble with his landlord, Yoshe went to court and pleaded for him. When a desperate father called in the middle of the night, where to turn when his consumptive son was hem-orrhaging his life away, Yoshe would go to him, sit the night through with him, give a comfort out of his own bloodstream. *(The lights go on full on the room.)* There they are, but not all yet. The others will come, and their womenfolk and children will arrive later. That old man with the albino-like white beard and hair is Moishe. He is the oldest and prays and shuckles there at the window that faces East. At the table reading the Torah is Velvel; next to him is Abe; then there is Nathan who is sneaking a shot of whiskey; and standing apart is Charlie, the rich one. One is a butcher, another a carpenter, that one is a house painter, and so on. Ah, but here comes my father and the boys. Others will soon come, too. But I don't see Yoshe. *(The* FATHER *and* WILLIE *and* MARTIN *come in.)*

FATHER. Sholem aleichem. *(Ad lib hello all around.)* Where's Yoshe?

VELVEL. He's at the hospital with Chaim . . .

FATHER. *(Interrupting.)* Oy vay! What happened? So talk already . . .

VELVEL. So give me a chance. Last night, Chaim's younger son, you know Sammy, was playing on the fire escape . . .

FATHER. Gevald! Don't tell me . . .

VELVEL. Yes. He fell off, down four flights. We're waiting to hear.

NATHAN. America gonnif! In our shtetl, who heard from fire escapes.

FATHER. *(Turning to* CHARLIE.*)* You'll pray maybe for your nephew? *(*CHARLIE *tries to bury his nose in the prayer book.)* Don't you think it's time you behaved like a mentsch? God will forgive you if you don't pray to him this Simchat Torah. Go to the hospital. Make up with your brother. He needs you—now! (CHARLIE *spreads his arms helplessly as though he is at a loss what to do. He walks over to the table, pours himself a shot of whiskey and quickly drinks.*) So that's your answer. (*The* FATHER *busies himself in arranging his talith across his shoulder. Like the others, he does not don a yarmulke but wears his hat. During the ensuing dialogue, he approaches the table and reads from the Torah as do the others intermittently and in turn. The* BOYS *approach* MOISHE.)

MARTIN. Reb Moishe, do you have a shmeck tabac? (MOISHE *interrupts his prayers, smiles at the boys, wiggles a reproachful finger at them and conspiratorially places his finger to his lips to indicate silence. He finishes the passage of his prayer, then he draws the boys to a corner where they will not be observed. He fetches out of his tail pocket of his Prince Albert coat a small snuff box. The* BOYS *each take a pinch under* MOISHE's *guidance and insert it in their nostrils. They stand quietly a moment in anticipation.* MOISHE, *pleased with himself, returns to his shuckling and praying. Soon, one at a time and then in unison, the boys gleefully start to sneeze.*)

NARRATOR. (*Two more landslayt come in. Ad lib greetings. Like the others, they don their talithes.*) A problem: the tenth man is missing to form the minion for the celebration of Simchat Torah. They'll simply have to wait.

VELVEL. Where is it written that your two boys can't be figured in a minion?

FATHER. Simply because they have not been Bar Mitzvahed. Don't give them ideas before their time.

MARTIN. (*He has overheard.*) Why must I wait? I'm a man.

FATHER. You certainly are. Come, I have something for you and Willie. (FATHER *approaches one of the cupboards and takes out ritual paper flags and small candles. He hands one apiece to each of the boys and helps them attach the candles to each flag; then he lights them. The* BOYS, *holding the flags aloft, march around the table.*)

CHARLIE. (*Approaches* VELVEL.) What hospital is my nephew? Maybe I can telephone there.

VELVEL. Lebanon Hospital. Better you should go there . . . (CHARLIE *exits to the store. Two more landslayt enter. Ad lib hellos, don their talithes.*) Aha, now we have a minion. There's Moishe and me and Charlie and . . . (*The others hush him.*)

MOISHE. It is forbidden to count the living.

VELVEL. All these rules! No wonder the rabbis spend a lifetime studying. Anyhow, we now have a minion.

NATHAN. So let's first make a blessing with a little schnapps. (*While the* MEN *crowd the table and imbibe, the* NARRATOR *steps forth.*)

NARRATOR. The landslayt take turns in reading from the holy Torah, each chants his proper portion. Then they circle the table, with a frequent visit to the drainboard to the East Side staple of schnapps, the Itzhok Goldberg long-necked bottles that was the Chivas Regal, the Johnnie Walker, the Jack Daniels of those golden days. And look, there is my father ready for his moment at the Torah. Like the others, perhaps with an ecstasy heightened by the schnapps, his rich, lyric tenor sings of his faith, he's no longer the lowly work-horse in oily, grimy overalls in the store. He is a leader, the voice of a man freed from the smells of the ghetto, with a tenuous rescue from the tormenting fears for the survival of his children, with redemption for the woebegotten, with removal from chaos, from confusion, with salvation from all evil. Like a disembodied spirit, he sings of joy in unfailing hope, of spiritual peace, of pious exultation, of cosmic order rooted in eternal truths from on high. In communion with his God, he is a voice for his sons, for his beloved ones to his beloved God.

ABE. (*To* FATHER.) So, where is the missus?

FATHER. She'll come later. She had to tend the store this morning.

ABE. On yontiff? Shame.

FATHER. My dear Abe, since when are you such a saint? It's hard enough making a living without you kibbitzing about my piety. We do what we can.

ABE. But, on yontiff . . .

FATHER. We keep the store closed on Rosh Hashonna, on Yom Kippur, on the first two days of Pesach. My customers are goyim, the janitors and superintendents in our neighborhood. Thanks to them, we stay alive.

ABE. But on yontiff . . .

FATHER. Stop already with your "but on yontiff." I'm as good a Jew as you are. We keep a kosher house, my sons go to cheder, and we do good deeds in charity. So you're so pious, so tell me, do you put on your phylacteries every morning . . . ?

ABE. I got to get to the shop early. My boss . . .

FATHER. Don't say another word. We do what we can. God doesn't expect more. (CHARLIE *returns from the store. He is greeted by an anxious* VELVEL.)

VELVEL. Nu, so talk. What's the news? (*The others stop what each is doing and eagerly listen.*)

CHARLIE. They don't know yet. They're operating. He's been under the knife for three hours. (*He stifles his weeping.*)

ABE. At least he's alive. It's gonna be all right. We can really celebrate Simchat Torah for real.

FATHER. When will we know?

CHARLIE. I spoke with Yoshe. He said he'll phone when they bring the boy down from the operating room. (WILLIE *and* MARTIN *run out the door to the store. Their* FATHER *yells after them.*)

FATHER. Watch out for the Benzine and Kerosene. Don't light the candles, Remember!

NARRATOR. By now you should know that I am that Willie. Before the service is over today, my father and I will say Kadish for Martin. He volunteered to fight the Nazis. He died in Guadalcanal. How I idolized him.

FATHER. We should now begin. (FATHER *draws aside curtain of the sanctuary, and with a prayer, opens the maroon drapes, then the doors of the Ark. He chants the* Hakophas. *With the others behind him, he sings the* Hashonnas. *He leads the* MEN *in a joyful march around the table. All the men sing and dance around the table.* WILLIE *and* MARTIN *return and join the singing and dancing. During these festivities, a woman with a child, and . . . then another with two children—each woman a wife of one of the men—enter. The* CHILDREN *join* WILLIE *and* MARTIN *who obtain flags and candles for each of the newcomer children. When the* MEN *sing and dance, the children join. At appropriate times the women will drink some sacramental wine—one will dunk her piece of sponge cake in it. The Simchat Torah ceremony continues.* FATHER *reads aloud the Hebrew portion for the day while the other men silently move their lips in echo and shuckle as they do so. At the conclusion of the portion,* FA-THER *says Amen (pronounced: Oh-mayne); the others all repeat the Amen.* ABE *edges alongside* FATHER *in preparation to read a portion.* FA-THER, *with a fringe from his talith, points out the starting point in the Torah.* ABE *reads the prayer aloud. While so doing, the* NARRATOR *speaks.*)

NARRATOR. In accordance with the ritual, Abe is reading a portion of the prayer. He ends with the Kadish, a prayer for the dead. The others will soon do the same with a prayer or a blessing for a wife or young son or daughter, all of them still back home—in *der heim* in their shtetl in Russia. Or they may pray for a brother lost in the Czar's army before the Revolution, where he was snatched, impressed unwillingly for twenty-five years' service as a Nic-

helayevska Soldat, or for a child who died while waiting to be sent for by the father in the new land, or for a mother or father dead or dying. Tears stream down their faces as they sing, as they pray, as they dance. The weeping is quiet, but not hidden, for each shares the other's grief, the other's anguish—and infrequently the other's triumph. As each intones his prayer and blessing, he sings and there is pathos, he sings and there is the joy of peace, he sings and there is the bitter deprivation of the Diaspora, he sings in longing for those left behind so far away.

FATHER. (*After conclusion of this part of the celebration, . . . calls to the* CHILDREN.) Which one of you will lead us with the Torah? (*He looks about.*) Where's Martin and Willie?

ANOTHER BOY. They're playing in the store.

VELVEL. I'll go get them. (*He hurries out to the store. He soon returns with the two* BOYS.) What do you think these two rascals were up to? They were climbing all over the desk. They knocked over some paint cans and made a tell out of the desk. I had to put the phone in place again. It was buzzing like crazy.

ABE. (*To* CHARLIE.) No wonder we couldn't hear the phone if Yoshe was trying to get us from the hospital.

CHARLIE. Gevald. What should I do?

VELVEL. What we told you. You should have gone to the hospital. Your brother needs you. (*A phone is heard ringing out from the direction of the store.* CHARLIE *rushes out to answer it.* NATHAN *leads the others to the drain board where they freely drink the schnapps, eat of the delicacies on the table, and fraternize. Some of them edge to the door, where* CHARLIE *has exited, in anticipation of his return.*)

ABE. What's taking him so long? I'll go in and find out.

VELVEL. If it's bad news, he'll want to be alone.

ABE. If it's bad news he'll need someone.

FATHER. Remember, if it's bad news, no one should reproach Charles . . .

NATHAN. Why not! He's so rich. He lives in a private house in Paterson. What would it harm him if he had helped his brother Chaim with a decent job and a place to live! Did Chaim have to live in a stinking slum walk-up while his brother is so rich! Did . . .

FATHER. Don't put salt on everybody's wounds. Many families have fights. They haven't spoken in over seven years.

NATHAN. Why not? Maybe they couldn't figure out how to divide their grandfather's legacy. Pooh! They came to this country no better than beggars. If it weren't for Yoshe, Chaim wouldn't even have a roof over his head. You call Charlie a brother? Pooh!

ABE. Sha. Shah! Here he comes. (CHARLIE *enters. He is silently weeping into his handkerchief. The others either drop their hands in despair or wring their hands in woe.*)

FATHER. We're waiting. What's the news?

CHARLIE. He'll live. (*Everyone expresses joy, some with Mazel-tovs.*)

VELVEL. So why are you crying?

ABE. Jews need a reason to cry?

CHARLIE. Because he'll live. He'll grow up to be a big . . . (CHARLIE *weeps more violently.*) . . . grow up to be a good, a pious Jew.

OTHERS. Amen! (*Pronounced: Oh-mayne*)

FATHER. Yoshe and Chaim aren't here. We'll continue the services till they come.

CHARLES. I . . . I . . .

FATHER. What is it?

CHARLIE. Nothing. I want to pray. (*He approaches the open scroll of the Torah. The* FATHER *lifts it with each lower hand in each of his hands. He turns the scrolls in upright position and then replaces the Torah on the table. He points out the proper place with the edge of his talith to* CHARLIE, *who briefly prays, falters, then lifts his head.*) They're amputated his right leg. (*He weeps. There is consternation among the others.*)

MOISHE. (*Lifts his voice in prayer.*) Blessed be the Lord, God, King of the Universe. We thank Thee for Thy wisdom in sparing us this child Sammy.

CHARLIE. Sammy will be like a son to me. I will set aside a fund for him. He will not want for a thing. Blessed be the Lord . . .

FATHER. It is Simchat Torah. Which of you boys will lead us? (MARTIN *succeeds in edging the other boys away. He leads the others, with the Torah clutched to his bosom, and they all sing and dance the* Hashonnas *and the wordless sequel to it.*)

NARRATOR. When the leaves have turned bright colors, when the wind out of the West becomes crisp in the mornings, when the dusk comes earlier, and the evenings grow chill, I recall . . . Chaim is gone, my father is gone, Martin never returned from the Pacific, and where the Hassidm sang, danced, prayed, and wept, there are now bulldozed, empty lots being prepared for a superhighway. *(Lights dim. Curtain falls.)*

THE END

EMERITUS

by David S. Lifson

CHARACTERS

MAURITZIUS BECKER, an actor; now artiste emeritus
ILEANA, a young, beautiful actress-student
GEORGE, an American Fulbright-Hays Scholar; he is not quite thirty years of age.

The play takes place in the living room of MAURITZIUS BECKER, *in an old-fashioned apartment building in the center of an Eastern European capital.*

Time: the present.

The curtain rises on the living-room, also the study. It is mid-afternoon of an autumn day. He is in his mid-sixties and is dressed in a velvet smoking jacket of deep maroon, with an open shirt collar, a colored silk kerchief around his neck. His flowing gray hair crowns his head in a leonine fashion. He is a dynamic man.

ILEANA *is a beautiful girl, about nineteen, who can be both disarmingly naive or sharply astute. She is simply but charmingly dressed. The neatness, the*

authentic period of the room barely saves it from its deteriorating seediness. The furniture is over-stuffed ante-World War II vintage with the suggestion of art deco. On the walls are pictures of theater scenes, theater posters, portraits signed by actors, and a few of MAURITZIUS *himself in various roles, and a few signed scrolls that are as imposing as a medical doctor's framed diplomas.*

MAURITZIUS *and* ILEANA *are rehearsing a scene from* Richard III; *each holds a script in hand. From time to time, he will nervously light a fresh cig-*

199

arette. He will rarely refer to his script, while she will seem dependent upon hers. He is a veteran actor, for all his being the poseur, and instructs her with well-founded authority while he animatedly walks about the room.

ILEANA. *(Reading.)*

"Set down, set down your honourable
   load
If honour may be shrouded in a hearse,
Whilst I a while obsequiously lament
The untimely fall of virtuous
   Lancaster . . .

MAURITZIUS. *(Interrupting.)* Why are you screaming!

ILEANA. I'm not screaming. She's a queen, she gives orders . . .

MAURITZIUS. She may be a queen, but you are an actress. And one fundamental rule you must learn: don't throw your thunderbolt at the beginning of a long speech or scene. You have to build. If you give your all at the start, you've nowhere to go but down. It isn't like a Beethoven symphony with a theme crashing in at the beginning and then the entire orchestra can play around with the variations. You have one voice, one being to sustain yourself. Now try again. Remember, you are weary of the immediate funeral cortege, weary of the burden of queenship, weary of adverse fortune . . . try it again.

ILEANA. From the top of the scene?

MAURITZIUS. No. They've set down the coffin. Now continue.

ILEANA.

"Poor key-cold figure of a holy king!
Pale ashes of the house of Lancaster!
Thou bloodless remnant of that royal
   blood!

Be it lawful that I invoke thy ghost
To hear the lamentations of poor Anne,
Wife to thy Edward, to thy slaught'red
   son . . .''

(MAURITZIUS *is lighting a cigarette and is about to place extinguished match in an ashtray.)*

MAURITZIUS. For God's sakes, you cleaned the ashtray!

ILEANA. I always tidy up your rooms. You asked me to be specially exact today.

MAURITZIUS. But I told you I wanted to impress him with my desperate condition, That I'm frantically smoking away my lungs, that I've an acute case of emphysemia, that . . .

ILEANA. At the rate you're going, you'll fill that ashtray with butts till it overflows in five minutes.

MAURITZIUS. Don't be so fresh with me. *(He retrieves from waste basket a handful of butts and places them into ashtray.)* Continue.

ILEANA. From where?

MAURITZIUS. From where we were interrupted. No. Give me the cue for my entrance.

ILEANA. But did I give you what you asked for?

MAURITZIUS. It will do. That opening leads to your cursing Richard. I want you to know the object of your venom, justified though it may be. Then, after our guest leaves . . . what time is it?

ILEANA. Two o'clock.

MAURITZIUS. He's due any moment. After he leaves, we'll go through the entire scene. Now, let us begin:

"Stay, you that bear the corse, and set it down.''

ILEANA

"What black magician conjures up this
    fiend
To stop devoted charitable deeds?"

MAURITZIUS

"Villains, set down the corse; or, by
    Saint Paul,
I'll make a corse of him that disobeys."
And so on and so on speech by the
    flunkey.
"Umanner'd dog! stand thou when I
    command.
Advance thy halberd higher than my
    breast,
Or, by Saint Paul, I'll strike thee to my
    foot,
And spurn upon thee, beggar, for thy
    boldness."

ILEANA

"What, do you tremble, Are you all
    afraid?
Alas, I blame you not, for you are
    mortal,
And mortal eyes cannot endure the
    devil.
Avaunt, thou dreadful minister of hell!
Thou hadst but power over his mortal
    body,
His soul thou canst not have;
    Therefore, be gone."

MAURITZIUS

"Sweet saint, for charity, be not so
    curst."

ILEANA

"Foul devil, for God's sake, hence, and
    trouble us not;
For thou hast made the happy earth
    thy hell,
Fill'd it with cursing cries . . ."

(*Out of* ANNE's *character.*) I'm con-
    fused.

MAURITZIUS. Why do you suppose I
    chose this scene for you? You go
    through a complete gamut of emo-
    tions and end with an amazing meta-
    morphosis.
ILEANA. But I must know why? Is she
    sincere in her grief? Is she always
    playing a role?
MAURITZIUS. That . . . and everything
    else that makes up the amazing com-
    plexity of the feminine psyche.
ILEANA. I can't believe it is you, actu-
    ally you, saying these things. "Femi-
    nine psyche" indeed! It is a struggle
    for power among this decadent ex-
    crescence of antiquated notions of
    social structures. It is . . .
MAURITZIUS. You may be right. Let us
    try to understand her role in terms of
    her upbringing, her bourgeois frame
    of reference. Shakespeare may have
    been a prescient Marxist—perhaps.
    That is what our director of cultural
    activities tells us. But we may be cer-
    tain that he saw his women, all of
    them in all his plays, as pragmatists.
    Let us take his most abject victim of
    exploitation, with her molding of
    character by a male dominant society.
    If Shakespeare had one philosophy, it
    was the one of pragmatism.
ILEANA. I think I see it. She's looking
    out for her own skin.
MAURITZIUS. Exactly. And that's how
    Shakespeare saw it. We have evi-
    dence in his other plays. You can see
    it in his *Troilus and Cressida*. Some
    may say he was cynically showing his
    contempt for the fickleness, the op-
    portunism of women. Thus far, you as
    Anne, are justifiably outraged.
    Richard has been the most vile of
    villains. But you, Anne, will not give
    up your entrenched position without

a struggle. That's out and out Marx. Your struggle will take the form of accommodation to the most outrageous of villains.

ILEANA. Mightn't her change come out of her elementary fear of him, her clinging to survival?

MAURITZIUS. That's too obvious, too simple, not dramatically viable. I want you to read it first as though you are the witless victim of history, then try it again as a woman, sensually fascinated by Richard's malevolence. Now, as long as we stopped for this analysis, let's make sure of our cues when the American arrives. I can't understand why he's late.

ILEANA. He's not late. It's not quite the hour. If you hadn't sold your wristwatch, you'd know what time it is.

MAURITZIUS. I had to choose between time and food.

ILEANA. I have enough for both . . .

MAURITZIUS. There is one thing, one thing only I want from you—your devotion, your love . . . *(They are quickly in each other's arms.)* Ah, liebchen. I could not continue without you.

ILEANA. I love you.

MAURITZIUS. *(After a lingering kiss.)* I could not . . . I need you . . . (MAURITIZIUS *disentangles himself from their embrace.)* He'll be here any moment. Now remember, he'll find us in the midst of our rehearsal. We'll ask him to sit and wait—not too long. Then, I'll say I'm out of cigarettes. You'll offer to go for them. I'll protest about sending you on an errand. These Americans are devoted to some kind of chivalry where you don't send females on errands. I'll insist upon going myself. I'll hint about the black market . . .

ILEANA. But suppose . . .

MAURITZIUS. Don't interrupt. Simply follow directions. I'll leave for the cigarettes and leave the two of you alone, together.

ILEANA. And then?

MAURITZIUS. Good God, girl, don't you know what to do! Here is a rich American and . . .

ILEANA. How do you know he's rich?

MAURITZIUS. They all are and . . .

ILEANA. But he's only a student.

MAURITZIUS. *(Impatiently.)* I've met him at the theater. He takes taxis all over town. His clothes are of the finest cashmere. He eats at the finest hotel restaurants. I've seen him . . .

ILEANA. All right, so he's a rich American.

MAURITZIUS. He doesn't have to be too rich. Between me and ruin stands only a miserable one hundred American dollars. On the black market I can get 2500 lei for the hundred. That's more than my miserable monthly pension—I used to earn ten times that for one night's guest appearance!

ILEANA. When I am appointed to a theater and am working, I'll be making enough for both of us. Whatever success I'll have—and I will be successful—I'll owe it all to you. I'll pay you back more than . . .

MAURITZIUS. If I live that long.

ILEANA. You will. You're in your prime.

MAURITZIUS. *(Embracing her.)* You sustain me. I don't know where I'd be, what would become of me without your devotion, your loyalty . . .

ILEANA. You are my inspiration, my life, my art.

MAURITZIUS. And you are mine. You have an extraordinary talent—and I shall bring it forth. You should play on the great stages of the world, in Paris, in London, in . . . I'll direct you in the great classic roles, in Phaedra, in Mrs. Alving, in Hedda, in . . .

ILEANA. I'll only play those roles if you'll direct me.

MAURITZIUS. Alas, my love, I am an artiste emeritus. Only for a gala, for a special event, for a hoary, dusty revival do they call me back to direct a play. I'm now on the scrap heap . . .

ILEANA. Don't say that! You are the living symbol of all that is great in our country's theater. They come from all over the world to see you, to interview you, to write about you.

MAURITZIUS. Not lately. This American is the first in almost a year.

ILEANA. They've heard of you. He's come all this way just to interview you, Mauritzius Becker.

MAURITZIUS. What is this . . . this Fulbright something fellow . . . ?

ILEANA. The American government and ours exchange important scholars to do research, to lecture, and to publish their work in their fields. The man, the scholar who is visiting you today, specially arranged through our cultural bureau to interview you, is here because you are the living spirit our nation's cultural awakening since the Fascist war.

MAURITZIUS. *(Cynically applauding her.)* That is why I am kept barely alive on a miserly pension! You as a student get twice what I do.

ILEANA. I have to help my family, too. And I can barely spare the little money I pay you for coaching me.

MAURITIZIUS. If I weren't so enthusiastic about your great, divine talent, and the excitement of your loveliness, your incredible beauty—I

wouldn't take you on as my pupil for ten times what you pay me.

ILEANA. If I ever become famous, I'll owe it all to you. Maybe I'll go on tour to France, to England, to America. Maybe I'll be asked to star in a cinema in Hollywood . . .

MAURITZIUS. Bah! The cinema? Phooey! That's for puppets, not for artistes! Soooo, you'll leave me for the glamor of Hollywood?

ILEANA. *(Cuddling in his arms.)* I'll never leave you. *(They warmly, lovingly embrace. He interrupts the very sensuous situation.)*

MAURITZIUS. You are exquisitely lovely. The American won't be able to resist you, if we work it right.

ILEANA. Just tell me what to do. I don't have the experience. I'll do anything you tell me—for you.

MAURITZIUS. *(Holding her tightly and gazing lingeringly at her.)* We must not lose sight of our objective. He's rich and we . . . remember, we learn with our ABCs that Americans are rich—and if he's not personally rich, he has a stipend from both his government and ours that is many times what you and I together get to keep our souls alive. Now, for our plan. I will have some small talk with him— oh, about life in our country, how it was before the war, always about the absence of simple things—bread and milk—and cigarettes. Soon, after we've talked for a while, I will discover I am out of cigarettes. I will say I must run out to get some more of my special brand. I leave—leave him alone with you.

ILEANA. Suppose he has some American cigarettes and offers you some?

MAURITZIUS. As tempting as that may be—ah, those American cigarettes!

Not like our native cow dung—I will tell him I must have only my own special Turkish blend. I'll go out and leave him alone, with you. *(Pause).* That will be your cue. What do you do when I leave?

ILEANA. What do I do?

MAURITZIUS. My God! Can't you actors improvise, ad lib? Must you always have a script!

ILEANA. I will try to become friendly, ask him about his life in the U.S.A.

MAURITZIUS. Suppose he decides to tell you! I'll be going out only for cigarettes, not on a year's vacation!

ILEANA. I'll quickly turn the conversation around to you, about your great talent, your monumental achievements in our country's theater, in . . .

MAURITZIUS. In the world's theater!

ILEANA. *(Bowing in acknowledgment)* In the world's march of drama . . .

MAURITZIUS. Good. And then?

ILEANA. Then I sigh, I moan, I weep for "how the mighty have fallen." How you subsist on a miserly pension. How perhaps a mere fifty American dollars stand between you and penury if not starvation—

MAURITZIUS. Good, good! But maybe you should make that seventy-five dollars. You could always come down to fifty, but it would be awkward to go up.

ILEANA. Why not.

MAURITZIUS. Good. Of course you will improvise as your tête à tête progresses.

ILEANA. What if he becomes aggressively amorous?

MAURITIUS. Improvise. Hold him off with the hint of a future meeting, just the two of you, a rendezvous.

ILEANA. I've never had a "rendezvous," no less arrange for one.

MAURITZIUS. Nor will you with him or anyone else if I have anything to do with it. Remember, you are mine!

ILEANA. *(Embracing him.)* And you are mine, forever. How could I ever forget it!

MAURITZIUS. Forever. *(They kiss.)* He may be here any moment now. Let me look at you. *(He examines her face, wipes off a lipstick smudge, pushes back a stray lock of her hair, adjusts her dress.)* You look ravishing. Virginal . . . other worldly . . . saintly . . .

ILEANA. Come, don't overdo it. You know better.

MAURITZIUS. Ah, yes, leibchen. Now for the scenario. When we hear him approaching outside the door, we will be rehearsing. When he enters, he will discover us with script in hand, in the midst of the scene from *Richard III*. Actually, we should be rehearsing. After he is here for a while, I'll ask you to serve us brandy. Oh, yes, I neglected to do it . . . it's too late now. Please remember carefully: you'll pour that fresh bottle of our domestic brandy into the empty bottle of French brandy. When you serve it, he will ask you to drink with us. You will refuse.

ILEANA. But I like brandy.

MAURITZIUS. Ach! You are a virginal, simple, sweet, unspoiled girl. The American dream . . .

ILEANA. *(Mussing his hair, playfully.)* I was only teasing. *(The sound of a distant door.)* Quickly. The scene. *(They start once again to rehearse the scene from* Richard III. *Their voices are slightly louder than heretofore.*

Soon, in the midst of the scene, the doorbell buzzes. MAURITZIUS *signals* ILEANA *to open the door and greet the newcomer, while* MAURITZIUS *assumes a dramatic pose of being in deep thought.* ILEANA *opens the door to admit* GEORGE GREEN. *He is dressed casually but well in a tweedy outfit that is almost the stereotype of the scholarly figure. He is obviously awed by* ILEANA's *beauty)*

MAURITZIUS. Come in, come in. Soooo, you are the American Mr. Green, or is it Professor Green?

GEORGE. I suppose it is, but I hope we won't stand on ceremony or some silly protocol, and that sort of thing. I suppose in your country we are all the same—the classless society.

MAURITZIUS. (*Exchanging laughter with* ILEANA.) Oh, no, snobbery is not a privilege of the capitalistic society only. Seriously, however, I would subscribe to the Aristotelean precept of aesthetic distance, like a painting should have a frame to separate it from a more mundane setting.

GEORGE. Or private toilets for the members of the college faculty.

MAURITZIUS. Come in, come in. You know, I think I'm going to like you. (GEORGE *enters into the room.*) Let me introduce you to my most talented student, Contenescu Ileana. Ileana, this is Professor Green George.

GEORGE. George. George is my first or given name. I should be accustomed to your system of identifying a person by his or her family name first.

MAURITZIUS. I shall address you as Professor George . . .

GEORGE. Simply George will do.

MAURITZIUS. And you will address me as Mauritzius. Now, Ileana is one of my students, my most talented student I may add. And, Ileana, Profes— I mean George, George is here to interview me about our country's dramatic heritage.

ILEANA. Oh, I will be in the way. I'll go.

GEORGE. I hope you won't go. I mean you won't be in my way, unless Mauritzius objects to your staying.

MAURITZIUS. By all means stay, my dear girl. You are all that our theatrical heritage and art are all about. George, remember this moment, this day when Mauritzius Becker presented you to the most talented actress who ever trod the boards. When she is acclaimed, and I will stake my life and reputation on it, as the brightest star in the world's galaxy of stars, remember that I discovered her, I trained her, and I enriched the world's theater by bringing forth her genius.

ILEANA. You embarrass me by this extravagance. But I must confess I hope you are right.

MAURITZIUS. Good. A great artist should not have false modesty.

GEORGE. Then why is it that you have been so hard to pin down for an interview? In all my research in the archives, your name stands out as the most prominent director and actor in your country's theater. I've tried repeatedly to arrange a meeting with you. You've no idea how difficult it's been.

MAURITZIUS. I will be honest with you. That's the only credo I know—honesty. The truth is I cannot, must not meet with nor have any traffic with a foreigner until and unless I receive permission from the director of our cultural bureau. Actually, I've no right to let you know that, and if you repeat it ever, I shall deny I said it. Yet, I must trust you, your sense of honor, for if you are ever tempted to repeat it, remember that you will place me, my freedom, perhaps my life in serious jeopardy.

GEORGE. Is that why you would not meet me at the American Embassy or the American Cultural Center?

MAURITZIUS. (*Staring significantly at* GEORGE.) I neither received your invitation nor will I answer your question. Your questions must be confined to my country's drama and theater. (GEORGE *is embarrassed.*) Come, come. This is a bad start. Sit down and make yourself comfortable. Now, before we start, a cognac?

GEORGE. If you are having any.

MAURITZIUS. Of course. Ileana, bring out the cognac for our guest. (ILEANA *exits.*) I hope you are enjoying your visit to our poor country.

GEORGE. A country so rich in warm human beings is not poor.

MAURITZIUS. Let us understand each other. I will be forthright with you, but—how do you Americans say it— it must be a two-way street. Don't give me any diplomatic platitudes, and do not patronize me.

GEORGE. Oh, I'm sorry. I meant no harm. I'm serious. All the people I've met have been wonderful to me. They go out of their way to help me. More than our damned American Embassy who don't give a damn about us even though we're supposed to be its wards. But I'm not here to bitch about our ruptured State Department's indifference and incompetence. Now I'll get down to business. (*He opens a notebook and is poised with a pencil.*) I can't help but won-

der, and believe me, I am sincere, you appear to be vigorous, active, dynamic. So how is it that you are retired—Artiste Emeritus?

MAURITZIUS. Alas, that is our system. I have served my country and my art. Now I must make way for the next generation. They will carry the torch.

GEORGE. But your great talent, your . . .

MAURITZIUS. I am not on the scrap heap yet. They have not forgotten me. From time to time I am called upon to direct one of the great classics that I have made famous. Or I may be called upon to participate in a memorial dramatic concert when I re-enact one of the roles identified with my career.

GEORGE. In America, in England, and other countries, we have actors and directors who are octogenerians, still active and popular on stage, in film, and on TV.

MAURITZIUS. Perhaps one day Ileana will become a great star in your country too. She has an extraordinary talent. But the poor child starves herself for her art. She can barely pay me the little money she does for my coaching her. But what can I do? The little money we're allowed barely keeps us alive. My one dream is for her to meet my famous cousin in America. He would recognize her talent and make her the great, international star. Perhaps you know him, Hugo Feininger.

GEORGE. Of course I know of him. Famous director and producer, among the best, right on top. But I never met him. He's your cousin?

MAURITZIUS. Yes. I'll never forget when we were in Vienna together. I'm originally Austrian, you know. Well, it was just before Anschluss. Dolfuss had been murdered. Hugo came to me one night. He begged me to leave for America with him. Oh, how he begged me. He was only a clerk then, but he idolized me. I was perhaps the leading actor on the Viennese stage, with my career just beginning to come into its own. I was about to open in the leading role in the most popular musical—*The White Horse.* He pleaded with me. I was foolish— an actor and a role or a stranger in a new world. He went, I stayed. Now he's a great Hollywood director, a millionaire, and I'm a pensioneer waiting for the last curtain call.

GEORGE. At least you have security, a home, not in need . . .

MAURITZIUS. *(He agitatedly walks about.)* Not in need! Ah, my friend, how can you know where another's shoe pinches. My pension, it amounts to seventy-five of your American dollars a month. This little apartment, true it is only fifteen dollars a month under our great socialist system. But I cannot travel in the overcrowded buses, I must use a taxi. Do you see these cigarettes? The finest Turkish. I won't smoke the cow's dung they sell as our domestic kind. And these cost over one dollar a pack.

GEORGE. Would you like American cigarettes? Our Embassy is conduit for duty and tax free cigarettes, maybe ten cents a pack.

MAURITZIUS. No, but thank you. I'm too old to change brands. If cigarettes will kill me, let it be a luxurious weapon. (ILEANA *enters; she carries a tray on which is a bottle of Courvoisier brandy and two small glasses.)* Here we are, a drink. Yes, and another thing: we have a good local brandy, but I can only drink this French cognac. Don't you think that Mauritzius Becker has earned the right to indulge himself? This brandy is hard to get, but I manage—at a price. (ILEANA *pours and offers a drink to each man.)*

GEORGE. Aren't you joining us, Miss Ileana?

ILEANA. I do not drink. Anyway, soon I must go to the theater institute.

MAURITZIUS. *(Salutes* GEORGE *with his drink and then sips.* GEORGE *does likewise.)* It's hard to get, but I manage—at a price. It's not sold in any of the stores. We may be building a socialist society, but I will not change my life style. *(He laughs.)* I'm still a spoiled, decadent bourgeoise.

GEORGE. It's very expensive, even in America.

MAURITZIUS. So it is. So what. One of these days I'll get up enough nerve to write to my millionaire cousin Hugo in America. I won't ask for much, just enough to get me out of the clutches of the loan sharks.

GEORGE. *(Incredulous.)* Wha-a-a-t? Loan sharks? In a communist country?

MAURITZIUS. Don't be naive. The acquisitive nature of the human being is universal. There are vultures who prey on the weaknesses of people all over the world.

GEORGE. I can't believe it. I've been here three months. I've met visitors in the main hotels, I walk your boulevards, I go to your wine cellars, and I've never met a prostitute, not one . . . *(He turns to* ILEANA.) Oh, excuse me.

MAURITZIUS. Ileana is not a child. She knows the facts of life. It seems to me you don't know where to go. There are certain bars where they are available. The officials know it and take their percentage. Just as much as they know the money changers in the black market. Yes, one day I will come into maybe one hundred dollars and start to breathe again, I'll free myself from the loan sharks and their ten per cent a week interest. *(He fumbles in his pocket for a packet of cigarettes.)* Ach, I'm all out of cigarettes. Please excuse me, George. I'll run out and get some. I'll be back before you know I'm gone.

ILEANA. Can't I get them for you?

MAURITZIUS. You're too young to get involved with the black market. And, they won't even talk to you. Keep George entertained. (MAURITZIUS *hurries out.* ILEANA *and* GEORGE *smile tentatively at each other.)*

GEORGE. What were you rehearsing when I came in?

ILEANA. A scene from *Richard III.*

GEORGE. Where did you learn such good English?

ILEANA. At school. And we frequently speak it at home. My father is an engineer and . . .

GEORGE. It seems all the men I meet in your country are either connected with the theater or they're engineers.

ILEANA. They are important. We have to catch up with the industrial West. My father works with components from England and America. The manuals are mostly in English.

GEORGE. And your mother?

ILEANA. She's a teacher in the English school where the children from the embassies go. It's really run by the Anglican church.

GEORGE. I've been admiring your dress. If I didn't know where I am, I'd say you could easily be a model on Fifth Avenue in New York.

ILEANA. *(Rises and pirouettes.)* I'm glad you like it. I made it myself.

GEORGE. Marvelous! Where'd you get the style?

ILEANA. All the women in our country make their own clothes. You'll never guess where we get the patterns and styles.

GEORGE. The cinema.

ILEANA. We see mostly Westerns or films from the communist countries. Oh, yes, we see Kojack on TV. But one can't get styles from them. We get them from one of your magazines, the most popular magazine from the West in our country: *Vogue.*

GEORGE. That's fantastic. *(Pause.)* Are you sure you won't have some brandy?

ILEANA. Mauritzius wouldn't approve.

GEORGE. Oh, just a sip. *(He offers her some in* MAURITZIUS' *glass.)*

ILEANA. *(She giggles and then takes a sip of brandy.)* Ugh! That's strong. I don't think I specially like it.

GEORGE. Brandy's an acquired taste.

ILEANA. Mauritzius has spent a lifetime acquiring it.

GEORGE. Tell me about yourself.

ILEANA. Not much to tell. I'm a student at the Institute for Theater and Cinema Arts, now for two years. I've two more years to go.

GEORGE. And then?

ILEANA. I will be selected to join a company either here in the capital or in one of the principal provincial cities.

GEORGE. *(Writing in his notebook.)* Are you sure that you'll be selected?

ILEANA. Of course. All students, after completing the four-year course, are selected by the regisseur—that is the director—of one of the companies and they become members of the troupe.

GEORGE. It's different in America. If someone wants to become an actor, he applies for a role when the play is being cast.

ILEANA. And if he doesn't get the role?

GEORGE. He or she simply keeps trying.

ILEANA. All their lives?

GEORGE. Yes. There are thousands of actors always out of work in America.

ILEANA. How awful! And how humiliating. No actor is ever out of work in our country. The government supports the theaters and the theaters support the actors. Each theater has five or ten plays constantly in its repertory. Each night it presents a different play from its repertory. So, plenty of roles for all actors.

GEORGE. Sounds like Utopia. And the pay?

ILEANA. At least, in American money, one hundred fifty dollars a month. That's good pay. Rent, with electricity, is fifteen dollars a month. Food is cheap. For example, bread is ten cents a loaf; rolls are ten cents a dozen. Some foods are hard to get, like some meat and fish, so we have to queue up at the stores. The actors' pay is enough.

GEORGE. But not enough for French brandy or Turkish cigarettes.

ILEANA. *(Ignoring this last remark.)* We can become stars, just like in western countries.

GEORGE. Do stars earn more money?

ILEANA. They don't need more.

GEORGE. In America, a star can make a million dollars a year.

ILEANA. I'd love to come to America.

GEORGE. Maybe you will one day.

ILEANA. Hardly likely. Unless one of our companies, and if I'm in one of the companies that goes, goes on tour. Like last year our National Theater was invited to the Edinburgh Festival.

GEORGE. *(Rises and walks about as if trying to escape from a straitjacket.)* You're pretty much confined, aren't you?

ILEANA. Alas, yes. I'd love to travel.

GEORGE. When you do, you must visit me in America.

ILEANA. That would be divine.

GEORGE. I'd like to see you again.

ILEANA. Why not. *(Pause.)*

GEORGE. You're extraordinarily beautiful.

ILEANA. Thank you. *(Pause.)* American girls are very beautiful.

GEORGE. So-so. I suppose there are beautiful girls in every country.

ILEANA. My classes at the Institute are finished every day at two o'clock.

GEORGE. I'd like to meet you after class. Would you help me in some of my research, giving me digests of some of the articles in the archives? I'll pay you for the work.

ILEANA. That won't be necessary.

GEORGE. Oh, no, I insist. Part of my stipend provides for such assistance. I'll tell you what, let's meet tomorrow at two o'clock, outside the Institute. We'll go to the Bibliotech and I'll show you what I'm doing. Then we can have an early dinner . . .

ILEANA. Tomorrow will be good. I don't have a session with Mauritzius tomorrow.

GEORGE. Oh, yes, about Mauritzius. What I've dug up in the archives shows that he was the great . . .

ILEANA. Greatest of the great. When I was ten years old, my parents took me to see him in *Resurrection*. I'll never forget it. Yes, great.

GEORGE. Not only in your country, but in all of Eastern and Middle Europe. After the war, he, almost alone by his powerful drive, revived your country's theater and made it into one of the most significant in the world.

ILEANA. Alas, and look at him now. He used to have a valet, a manservant or dresser, a magnificent automobile with a chauffeur. And now, he lives in such poverty while he clings to little symbols of his greatness, such as French brandy, Turkish cigarettes. If I had a chance to go to America and be a star, make a lot of money, I'd send him half of all I make there.

GEORGE. I can't believe that here, in a communist country, you have loan sharks.

ILEANA. Oh, yes, it's true. A black market in everything: nylon stockings, radios, foreign exchange of money, contraceptives . . .

GEORGE. Contraceptives!

ILEANA. Oh, yes. The government is trying to encourage our population to increase from thirty million to fifty million. So, no contraceptives allowed to be sold. *(Pause.)* Poor Mauritzius. To think that only a little thing like a hundred dollars stands between his peace of mind and possible violence from the loan sharks. *(She sighs.)* I'd do anything to help him. Not only is he a great artist, a genius, he's so good, such a kind soul.

GEORGE. *(Disturbed.)* Why doesn't he write to his rich cousin in America?

ILEANA. Pride. He's devoted his life to his art. Oh, he could have fled during the confusion at the end of the war. But he was determined to build a national theater. He has been honored more than anyone in our theater world. Just look at these awards and citations. *(She points to the framed scrolls on the walls. She dabs a handkerchief to her eyes.)*

GEORGE. *(He approaches her.)* Oh come, you mustn't weep. There must be a solution.

ILEANA. What? It's hopeless.

GEORGE. *(Puts his arms around her.)* Maybe I can help.

ILEANA. *(Clinging to him.)* Oh, if you only would.

GEORGE. Yes. I think I can.

ILEANA. *(Kisses him.)* You are sweet and kind.

GEORGE. *(Still holding her.)* You said he's in hock to the loan sharks for one hundred dollars?

ILEANA. Yes. That's a great deal of money.

GEORGE. I think I can manage it.

ILEANA. *(A passionate kiss.)* You are the most wonderful, generous, grandest person I ever met.

GEORGE. Not really.

ILEANA. He's so independent. I don't know if he'd accept it from practically a stranger.

GEORGE. *(While she clings to him.)* I think I have a solution. Let's do it this way: I'll give it to you, and after I leave you can give it to him. You can explain it to him any way you like. You can even tell him it's a loan—at no interest. Here you are. *(He takes out his wallet and counts out one hundred dollars which he hands to her.)*

ILEANA. I'll do all I can to convince him to accept it.

GEORGE. I'll rely on you. And tomorrow

when we meet, you'll tell me how he took it. I mean the idea of my giving it to him.

ILEANA. I will. You can depend on me.

GEORGE. *(Embracing her.)* You're wonderful. He must really be great for him to have such devotion from someone as beautiful and talented as you are.

ILEANA. It is you who have the generosity. You have such a good, big heart.

GEORGE. *(Kissing her.)* And now you have my heart. *(Noise from outer door.* ILEANA *and* GEORGE *break apart. She hastens to the door, opens it in anticipation of* MAURITZIUS' *entrance.* GEORGE *seats himself in an easy chair on the opposite side of the room from the door.)*

ILEANA. *(Whispers to* MAURITZIUS *as he enters.)* Perfect timing.

MAURITZIUS. *(Also whispers.)* Did you get the money?

ILEANA. *(Still whispering.)* Yes. I'll give it to you after he leaves. *(In a normal voice.)* You hurried out without finishing your drink.

MAURITZIUS. I'll finish it now. Meanwhile, please make some coffee for our guest. *(As* GEORGE *starts to protest.)* I want some, too. George, this is good, American instant coffee, not the mud you get all over Europe. *(ILEANA exits to kitchen.)* A little thing like coffee which you Americans take for granted. For us it's like diamonds—the American kind.

GEORGE. We get coffee, cocoa, whiskey, cigarettes at prices cheaper than they are back home. It's through a buying service in Denmark, and we get it through the Embassy. I'll bring you some.

MAURITZIUS. Only if you'll let me pay for it. It's not for myself, you know. That talented girl could use some of the good things of life.

GEORGE. We'll worry about the payment after I bring it.

MAURITZIUS. *(While he lights a cigarette with a flourish.)* Your mission here is to interview Mauritzius Becker, Artiste Emeritus, Actor and Regisseur. How do you say it in America—shoot.

GEORGE. I'd like you to tell me in your own way, in your own words about your life before you came here, how you managed to come here, and so on. I will interrupt if anything needs clarification or additional data.

MAURITZIUS. Where does one start?

GEORGE. How did you start to act? How did you know you could act?

MAURITZIUS. It was in a school play. Oh, some sort of patriotic pageant. In the gymnasia. I simply got the part, learned it, and walked on stage and did it. It came to me like any child learns to roller skate. You get on the skates and simply roll away.

GEORGE. Your career in Vienna is well documented. If you can recall any anecdotes, I'd appreciate your telling them to me. But first let's get to the historical sequence. What happened after Anschluss?

MAURITZIUS. I barely got out of Vienna, maybe two hours before the Wehrmacht marched in. There was celebration all over. The trains stopped running for that day. My first idea was to get to Switzerland. But the Nazis had roadblocks on all roads leading north and west.

GEORGE. Why did you have to flee? What were you afraid of?

MAURITZIUS. I had been married to an actress who happened to be a Jew.

Also, my grandfather on my mother's side was half Jewish. When the Jewish Vilna Troupe came to Vienna in the early 1930s, I was on a committee to welcome them. They made me an honorary member. During my last few months in Vienna, I began to feel a change. My so-called "dearest friends" in the theater began to avoid me. Ha-ha, it didn't help them. Most of them are kaput, gone. The Nazis saw to that. A familiar story, no?

GEORGE. How did you finally get away?

MAURITZIUS. I walked to the east.

GEORGE. Why?

MAURITZIUS. Obviously, I dared not stay. The only roads open were to the east. It took many weeks—they seemed like years. Each day I didn't know if I would be alive the next. Some people were good, some were brutal; just like all over the world. Ach, I could tell you stories that would sicken you.

GEORGE. Please do.

MAURITZIUS. Not now, our first meeting. Maybe I'll write my memoirs. How else can an actor leave his mark for posterity. Well, I finally passed through Transylvania, kept going east, and arrived here.

GEORGE. How did you live? How did you get money?

MAURITZIUS. I told you some of the people along the way were kind. Some actually knew of me. I had some money with me, and then I sold some family trinkets, even some clothing off my back. I remember once I was leaving a town, going through side streets and through back yards of nice houses. I saw a lovely silk chemise hanging on a line to dry. I stole it and in the next town gave it to a farmer's wife for a meal. When I arrived here, conditions weren't bad yet. The entire theater profession knew me or of me. I was welcomed enthusiastically. There was a German language troupe here. They took me on as a prompter. Then came the war. (*He finishes off his brandy and lights a cigarette.* ILEANA *enters with the coffee. She serves the two men, takes a cup for herself, and sits in the background.*) Yes, then came the war. The Germans came in. All the big-shots and the microscopic amoeba in every bureau of the government suddenly wanted to learn German. I became a private tutor and was able to survive. Then they purged the government schools, the businesses, and of course the theater. All persons even suspected of faint traces of Jewish blood were dismissed, ghettoized. Oh, yes, I could have said I had no Jewish blood and become a star in the theater. I must confess I was very much tempted, but not after that Black January. (*He puts down his coffee and rages about the room.*) There was a struggle between the Fascisti and the government. There were bloody battles on the streets. The government called on the Jews to support it. That was the cue for the Fascists to launch a vast and horrible pogrom. That was January 21, 1941. The number of Jews murdered that day will never be known. But we know that hundreds were hung by their lips on meat hooks in the abbatoirs with signs on them, "Kosher Meat." (*He turns to* ILEANA.) Where is the brandy? (MAURITZIUS *lights another cigarette while she exits and quickly returns with the brandy and two glasses*)

GEORGE. (*Busily writing.*) Not for me,

thank you.

MAURITZIUS. But we must get back to the theater, yes? The most brilliant scholars in the universities were thrown out of jobs because of suspected Jewish blood. The Jewish community organized its own schools and operated them in the synagogues and in the Jewish center. The irony is that the Jewish students, the children, were taught by the best brains of the country, by world-famous scholars, scientists, mathematicians, musicians, and so on. Well, at the Jewish center, the Fascist permitted Yiddish theater. Two kinds: dramatic and musical. The musicals were in cabaret style. You know, these two theaters became the most popular in the country. The Jewish actors simply had to act like they had to eat, to sleep, to live. Some of them performed dramatic concerts in the synagogues. But the Fascist bureaucrats would not permit any secular activity in the holy places. So the actors devised a subterfuge. They would announce a memorial service for the birthday or death of a notable Jewish writer. You know, like for Goldfadden or Peretz. One official censor was puzzled that the Jews in their synagogues celebrated Sholem Aleichem's birthday three different times during the year.

GEORGE. How did you perform?

MAURITZIUS. We read dramatic poetry, we presented scenes. Because my German was of the Austrian type of dialect, I fit into the Yiddish of this country. The congregation—and they filled the synagogues to overflowing—were not allowed to applaud. But at the end of a spirited poem or dramatic piece, they all raised their fists in unity.

GEORGE. How about the theaters in the Jewish center? Were the performances in Yiddish?

MAURITZIUS. Not exactly. The dramatic performances were in Yiddish from the classic repertoire. But the musical cabaret was in the language of this country. Ah, how inspiring that was! Everyone came. Of course, in the Yiddish plays, there wasn't the slightest hint of politics, only the standard plays, but very well done. Highly professional. I directed a few. Everything had to be approved by the authorities, the censors.

GEORGE. You said everyone came, everyone attended. Who?

MAURITZIUS. Everyone! *(He laughs.)* Standing room only. In the cabaret the audience was mostly non-Jewish. There were high-ranking army officers, even ministers of state. They were—how do you say it in English—*begeistertd*. They collaborated, but they all, to a man, hated the Nazis who overran the country. I'll never forget one song and what it meant to all of us. I stood, dressed like a scarecrow, in a field. All around on the field, on my outstretched arms, on my head and shoulders, were many, oh, so many black crows. I sang that one day, soon, a mighty wind will blow in from the east and sweep away this plague of black crows. Obviously the "black crows" were a metaphor for the abominable Nazis. What happened at the end of the song I have never experienced in the theater or elsewhere, and I don't expect to ever again. Every person in the audience rose to their feet, they cheered, they applauded, they laughed, they cried, they embraced and kissed each other.

We actors were soldiers also in the anti-Fascist battle. (*Pause.* MAURITZIUS *raises his brandy glass;* GEORGE *does likewise.*) To my fellow soldiers on the battlefield of the stage. (*Both men drink.*) George, when you come again, I will have looked through my files and found some programs and photographs of that time.

GEORGE. That would be wonderful. This is more exciting than I expected.

MAURITZIUS. Yes. Perhaps, now that you have met Mauritzius Becker and know who he is, or should I say who he was . . .

GEORGE. No! Oh, never in the past tense. Remember that saying, "All that is past is prelude . . ." Please believe me, I find you more exciting, more dynamic than all the power in an All-American football team. I'll use your phrase, I am *begeisterdt* by you.

MAURITZIUS. You are kind. Now I must get back to this lovely actress and guide her to greatness. So, when will you come again?

GEORGE. The day after tomorrow, same time if convenient for you.

MAURITZIUS. Good. (*Ad lib* GEORGE's *exit*)

GEORGE. Auf Wiedersehen. (*He leaves after exchanging significant looks with* ILEANA. MAURITZIUS *remains at the door with his ear cocked, hears the distant closing of the outside door, then turns to* ILEANA *who is busy collecting the coffee cups and brandy onto a tray.*)

MAURITZIUS. (*He eagerly dances back to* ILEANA.) Alzo—don't keep me in suspense, my liebchen. Did you get it?

ILEANA. (*Reaching into her bodice and extracting money.*) Yes.

MAURITZIUS. (*Embraces her while he takes the money.*) How much?

ILEANA. Forty dollars.

MAURITZIUS. It will bring more on the black market. At least it will help. It's a beginning.

ILEANA. Yes, it is a beginning. (*Curtain falls.*)

THE END